Advance Praise

Innovative and important, this book sheds new light on India's rich, fluid, and fraught landscape of gender and sexual nonconformity. Rather than adding to existing studies on *hijras* and queer subjects, it urges our attention to the emergence of trans women and the ways they fashion themselves at the intersections of regional, national, and global politics. Meticulous ethnography and lucid writing power this eye-opening story of how trans women respond to the imperatives of sexual respectability and caste and class mobility, while distancing themselves from *hijras*. A sobering account of modernity and economic liberalization's impact on *hijra* life-worlds, it also offers fresh insights into the possibilities of trans women challenging social hierarchies. This book is set to become a pivotal reference in fields ranging from trans, gender, and sexuality studies to South Asia studies and beyond.

Jyoti Puri, author of *Sexual States: Governance and the Struggle over Antisodomy Law in India* (2016)

Liz Mount's book provides an ethnographically compelling and sobering assessment of ongoing transformations in the lives and identities of gender nonconforming people in urban India. Drawing on interviews, ethnography, and textual analysis, Mount demonstrates how an increase in the forms of upward mobility available to trans and gender nonconforming people in the context of economic liberalization and NGOization also corresponds to new forms of hierarchization and exclusion that build upon entrenched ideals of middle-class respectability. Mount's book will appeal to all those who are interested in grappling with the complex, conflicted expansion of LGBTQ+ rights and freedoms in a 'new' India, where increased avenues of upward mobility have often been accompanied by the remaking of age-old inequalities.

Aniruddha Dutta, author of *Globalizing through the Vernacular: Kothis, Hijras and the Making of Queer and Trans Identities in India* (2024)

Mount's research on gender nonconforming (GNC) people, especially trans women, in Bengaluru takes us through NGO offices, queer pride marches, and photo exhibitions to offer an account of the growing divide between trans women and *hijras*. Through identity work and aspirations for upward mobility, the "new" trans women not only distinguish themselves from their "traditional" counterparts (*hijras*), but also uphold values of modesty and respectability often associated with middle-class women. Mount shows in rich detail how gender is central to constructing class differences in contemporary India.

Chaitanya Lakkimsetti, author of *Legalizing Sex: Sexual Minorities, AIDS, and Citizenship in India* (2020)

"New" Women

Recent global attention to transgender issues and new opportunities for trans people can appear as positive and progressive social change. *"New" Women* challenges this assumption through an ethnography of emerging trans women and traditional gender nonconforming *hijra*s in India. In many countries, people identify as either cisgender or non-cis identities like transgender and nonbinary. India is unique for its recognized, yet stigmatized, gender nonconforming *hijra*s. This book explores changes in *hijra* groups due to economic liberalization and LGBTQ+ advocacy, particularly the rise of the trans woman.

Liz Mount locates trans women within patriarchal and postcolonial histories that shape ideal womanhood in India. As trans women align themselves with middle-class, respectable (cisgender) womanhood, they distance themselves from *hijra*s, perpetuating their exclusion. Ultimately, this intersectional feminist analysis shows that new forms of gender identity can reinforce old inequalities and what appears as progressive change for some trans people can marginalize others.

Liz Mount is an Assistant Professor of Practice at Texas Tech University. *"New" Women* is her first book.

"New" Women

Trans Women, *Hijra*s, and the Remaking of Inequality in India

Liz Mount

CAMBRIDGE
UNIVERSITY PRESS

Shaftesbury Road, Cambridge CB2 8EA, United Kingdom

One Liberty Plaza, 20th Floor, New York, NY 10006, USA

477 Williamstown Road, Port Melbourne, VIC 3207, Australia

314–321, 3rd Floor, Plot 3, Splendor Forum, Jasola District Centre, New Delhi – 110025, India

103 Penang Road, #05–06/07, Visioncrest Commercial, Singapore 238467

Cambridge University Press is part of Cambridge University Press & Assessment, a department of the University of Cambridge.

We share the University's mission to contribute to society through the pursuit of education, learning and research at the highest international levels of excellence.

www.cambridge.org
Information on this title: www.cambridge.org/9781009343435

First published 2024

Printed in India by Thomson Press India Ltd.

A catalogue record for this publication is available from the British Library

ISBN 978-1-009-34343-5 Hardback

Cambridge University Press & Assessment has no responsibility for the persistence or accuracy of URLs for external or third-party internet websites referred to in this publication and does not guarantee that any content on such websites is, or will remain, accurate or appropriate.

To the memory of my grandmother,
Helen Deal Mount (1915–1991),
who taught me to read and to love learning.
And to Vihaan,
in whom her fondness for books lives on.

Contents

Introduction: "Modern Girls": Conceptualizing the
Trans Woman–*Hijra* Divide   1

1. "New" Women and Old Hierarchies: Gender, Class, and
Women's Opportunity   29

2. Sex Work versus Office Work: Gender Nonconforming
Identities and Employment   52

3. *Hijra* Families Today: Social Change and "Choice" for
"New" Women   75

4. "You Can Do Whatever": Shifting Authority in *Hijra*
Family Relationships   101

5. A Family Resemblance: Explaining Changes in
Hijra Relationships   127

Conclusion: "I am Not a *Hijra*": Opportunities, Inequalities,
and the Perils of Inclusion   150

Acknowledgments   169
Bibliography   171
Index   185

Introduction

"Modern Girls"

Conceptualizing the Trans Woman–Hijra Divide

This project started with a mistake—a mistake I made while trying to understand the lives of gender nonconforming (GNC) people[1] in South India. What initially began as an awkward social blunder evolved into the focal point of my investigation, ultimately shaping the narrative of this book. Let me explain.

One warm, sunny morning, I sat in a small front room of a sexual rights nongovernmental organization (NGO) in Bangalore, India. In addition to the sunlight peeking in through the front windows, the room was lit by a flickering fluorescent "tube light," creating a maze of shadows. The workday was just beginning, so the office was abuzz with activity. There were people coming in and out, happily greeting one another. It was one of my first days visiting this office, so I did not know many people working there yet. Indeed, many looked my way quizzically, probably wondering why someone like me was there before hurrying off to begin their work.

Sexual rights NGOs first emerged in India in the early 1990s as a response to the global concern over the HIV/AIDS pandemic. These NGOs attracted increased international funding for advocacy targeting groups considered "high risk" for HIV transmission, like feminine-presenting GNC people. Through their advocacy, sexual rights NGOs also inadvertently shaped how both traditional and emerging groups of GNC people are understood in India—by themselves and others around them. That understanding is the subject of this book.

In the midst of this activity at the NGO office, I sat chatting casually with a fluctuating group of between four and six people. Most were paid employees of the NGO, so they would sit and listen or contribute to the conversation for

10–15 minutes before going to do some work, then return later on. As people added this or that idea to the conversation only to leave a moment later, I felt as if they were slowly painting a portrait for me of the larger picture about GNC identity in India—one that I had only the barest outlines of at the time. Looking back on this experience, I realize that the fragmented nature of our conversation reflected the different fragments I have pulled together in this book to explain the emergence of newer groups of transgender women and how ideas about these trans women impact the traditional GNC groups they are often contrasted with.

Since it was my first time meeting this group, I asked broad questions about the organization and the work they did. Deepa, who was in her thirties and identified as a transgender healthcare worker, was dressed in fitted jeans and a V-neck shirt with a bright scarf thrown over her shoulder. She expressed palpable excitement about the organization's work as she enthusiastically moderated the discussion. I was particularly interested in hearing more from Priya, a 20-something, slender, feminine-presenting GNC person who had not yet said much. That day, Priya was elegantly draped in a bright indigo-colored sari as she sat across from me with her legs demurely crossed at the ankles. I was curious about her perspective on the NGO's work, partly because I assumed from her clothing that Priya was a *hijra*. *Hijra*s are feminine-presenting GNC people with a long history and public presence in South Asia.[2]

During my fieldwork up to that point, I had heard a little about the differences between the newly emerging category of transgender women and their traditional *hijra* counterparts. I had recently attended an "Introduction to Gender and Sexuality" discussion at a local college led by a trans woman NGO worker in her thirties named Akrithi. One of the first items Akrithi discussed was the different types of gender identities within "the community" of GNC people in India. During this discussion, Akrithi highlighted the differences between trans women and *hijra*s. Part of this difference was about clothing and hairstyle: "See, *hijra*s must wear *sari*s and have long hair," she explained to the students. In contrast, trans women, she pointed out, wear any type of "women's clothing," including tunic tops and loose-fitting pants known as *salwar kameez* or even Western clothes like jeans and T-shirts. Unlike *hijra*s, trans women also wear their hair in different ways—"Like me," Akrithi said, smiling and motioning to her short, stylish coif.

Since this is how the trans woman–*hijra* distinction was initially presented to me, I interpreted Priya's long hair and *sari* as signals that she was a *hijra*. I was eager to speak with *hijras* because I had heard that many of them did not appreciate the work of sexual rights NGOs. This is partly because NGO interventions have exposed aspects of *hijra* groups that some would like to remain hidden, like the fact that many *hijras* engage in sex work and the abuse that can occur within the families *hijras* create. To find someone whom I thought was a *hijra* at an NGO was therefore striking, and I was interested to hear more about her thoughts on these matters.

I was thus excited when the conversation turned to the organization's work with *hijras*. In what was in retrospect a very clumsy segue, I attempted to bring Priya into the conversation by asking her if she identified as a *hijra*. Before Priya could answer, Deepa jumped in, her eyes wide. "The people who are ... living in the *hammams*, following the tradition of the *hammams—they* are called *hijras* [emphasis original]," Deepa informed me. "Priya's a modern girl; she's educated, she's literate." Then she looked me in the eye to ensure she had my full attention before continuing. "She's called *transgender*." Priya looked at me seriously as she furrowed her brow and nodded vigorously in agreement with Deepa.

I realized then the mistake I had made. I mistook Priya for a *hijra*, totally unaware of the tensions experienced by trans women when they are recognized by others as *hijras*. When I reflected on this incident, I could not help but feel embarrassed to have essentially misgendered someone.

To someone like myself who did not know better (at the time), trans women and *hijras* do appear similar on the surface. However, people familiar with the context would know that there is an important distinction at play, at least for trans women. Deepa claimed the differences between trans women and *hijras* are about education (or lack thereof) and being "modern" versus following "tradition." These were not surface distinctions but signaled something deeper, as being "modern" and educated are both coded as middle-class signifiers in India. What I did not realize at the time is that the difference between who is a trans woman and who is a *hijra* is not simply about hairstyles and hemlines, but that it is actually all about class and respectability.

This mistake pushed me to explore the growing divide between trans women and *hijras*. Given the recent global attention to trans identities, particularly trans women, the appearance of groups of feminine-presenting people who identify as trans women is not all that surprising. But in India, the trans woman identity is emerging within a historical context of other recognized GNC identities—particularly *hijras*. I began to ask questions like: What kinds of economic and social changes have enabled some feminine-presenting GNC people to identify themselves as transgender women? How do perceptions about *hijras* shape the ways transgender people (and especially trans women) are understood—by themselves and by others? And why do so many trans women want to differentiate themselves from *hijras*?

This book analyzes how new economic and social opportunities allow some GNC people to identify as trans women, but also how and why these trans women are often framed in opposition to *hijras*. It also explores why many trans women disidentify with *hijras* and how the rise of the trans woman identity impacts *hijra* groups. In doing so, it describes the deepening rift between trans women and *hijras*. The trans woman–*hijra* distinction is important for many trans women I spoke to since they draw on this distinction to position themselves as more worthy and deserving of respect than *hijras*. But most importantly, the distinction illuminates at a fundamental level the workings of intersectionality—how gender and class are simultaneously at work for this group of GNC people.

Trans Women and Middle-class Aspiration in India

Transgender is a relatively new identity category in India, emerging during a time of major economic and social changes that made new sexual and gender identity categories available.[3] These changes are partly due to NGO-led, internationally funded HIV/AIDS projects, where feminine-presenting GNC people are targeted because they are considered at "high risk" for sexually transmitted infections. NGOs initially conducted outreach with working-class feminine-presenting GNC people who identified with different and oftentimes more traditional identity categories such as *hijra*.[4] Through their programs, NGOs introduced new categories, broadening the kinds of identities that people believed were available to them.[5] Yet at the same time, prevention and outreach coordinators began to distinguish between "target groups"—different sexual and GNC identities—to identify which groups were most in need of intervention and to receive funding.[6] As a result, identity categories that were once considered malleable and accommodating became more rigid and inflexible.[7]

When they first began, HIV/AIDS projects classified all male-assigned sexual minorities and GNC people (including *hijras*) as "men who have sex with men" (MSM)—a term that did not recognize this group's diverse gender identities.[8] Activists soon started to demand that HIV/AIDS interventions recognize feminine-presenting people who did not identify as men.[9] Then, in the 1990s and early 2000s, the category of transgender began to circulate through international sexual health conferences. Some Indian GNC activists began to identify themselves as transgender and translated this new category into their own languages.[10]

At approximately the same time NGOs identified male-assigned GNC groups as "high risk" for HIV transmission, a group of *hijras* "colluded" with NGOs and media to position certain *hijras* as "real" or "authentic" based on their participation in *hijra* family relationships.[11] Their efforts resulted in the notion that *hijra* kinship systems are the "bedrock" of authentic *hijra* identity. At this time, the idea that participating in *hijra* family systems determined whether or not someone was a *hijra* was yet another way that boundaries between groups of GNC people became increasingly defined and inflexible. These kinds of ideas were used to separate *hijra* and supposedly non-*hijra* identities in state, NGO, and media discourse.[12] So at the same time that "transgender" was embraced as an umbrella term that could accommodate gender variation among male-assigned people[13] (and, much less frequently, female-assigned people), the *hijra* identity became increasingly circumscribed. My research reveals that the characteristics determining whether or not someone is a *hijra* are once again changing.

Today, there are increasingly visible groups of working-class, feminine-presenting GNC people who identify themselves as transgender.[14] These trans women often position themselves as "independent" of *hijra* groups, though many have connections with them. In fact, the majority of trans women I met over age 30 had previously identified as *hijras*. However, these trans women are eager to raise awareness and promote an understanding of their identities as separate from *hijras*. As they claim transgender identities, the trans women I spoke with—the majority of whom were past or current employees of sexual rights NGOs—undertook identity work[15] to educate the public about their identities.

Recall Deepa's response to my mistaken assumption that Priya was a *hijra*. She explained that Priya was not a *hijra* because she was educated and modern, pointing to the ways that class (along with class aspirations) is central to trans women's identity work. This book focuses on how gender intersects with class aspirations for newly emerging trans women, who are now assumed to have new opportunities. To puzzle out the ways gender and class intersect for trans women, it is instructive to examine the public discourse around another group of people once believed to have new opportunities—cisgender women. This book therefore asks: How are emerging trans women identities shaped by societal understandings about (cisgender) womanhood in India? More specifically, how do historical ideas about new opportunities for cis women shape how contemporary trans women are understood, both by themselves and by others? I argue that in their pursuit of respect and opportunity, the trans women I spoke with align themselves with historical constructions of "new" middle-class (cis) womanhood. I read this identity work as signaling a desire to merge transgender womanhood with an elevated class status. This desire is rooted in historical constructions of what it means to be an "ideal" woman in postcolonial India.

I suggest the analytical construct of the "new" transgender woman helps to understand how newer identities such as transgender are connected to older categories such as class. By examining how the trans woman category has become associated with middle-class-ness in urban India, we can grasp how preexisting social hierarchies shape emerging identities. These trans women are using the gender binary and the centrality of class for womanhood in India to gain acceptance—making transgender an attractive category for working-class GNC people seeking upward mobility.

Trans Women and the Class–Caste Nexus

The trans women I spoke with express their class aspirations through claims about gender as they navigate a society infused with multiple hierarchies. Scholars have pointed out that class is often tied to notions of morality, with distinctions between class groups creating and reinforcing "moral boundaries."[16] This leads to moralizing attitudes where the attributes of some class groups are understood as more or less ethical than others, serving to legitimate the inequalities produced by unequal class systems.[17]

In India, the moralizing of class is also tied to a form of social distinction specific to South Asia—caste.[18] Recent research shows that caste identities (and biases) have been "absorb[ed]" into *class* identities (and biases).[19] For example, the ideals of cleanliness, modesty, restraint, moderation, and "decency"—associated in the past with dominant-caste identities—are now key indicators of middle-class identities.[20] In urban India, these ideals have been adopted by people of all castes who can afford to maintain them.[21] Similarly, attributes like a perceived lack of cleanliness, overt displays of emotion (including violence), and the purported disorder once associated with marginalized-caste identities are now associated (by people of all castes) with the working classes.[22] In this way, moralizing ideals previously connected to caste now manifest in the "attitudes, values, and practice[s]" associated with class, "rationalizing" the adoption of caste-based perspectives, stereotypes, and biases as class ones.[23] Thus, the meanings around class in India are inlaid with ideas connected to caste.[24]

These moralizing attitudes have far-reaching implications. For example, people from marginalized castes experience low levels of upward mobility (especially as compared to poor people in other countries) that are often attributed to caste hierarchies. Research has found that people from marginalized castes are more likely to engage in manual labor, while those from dominant castes are more likely to engage in "white-collar" work.[25] As a result of the connection between caste and class, working-class people in urban areas are generally from marginalized-caste backgrounds, while middle- and elite-class people in urban areas are generally from dominant-caste backgrounds.

The changing meanings of class and caste are also intimately linked to gender, with all three of these categories "interact[ing] with and shap[ing] each other."[26] For example, upholding caste requires marriage (and childbearing) to occur only within one's caste group; since cisgender women bear children, control of their sexuality is crucial to maintain caste boundaries.[27] In Chapter 1, we willhear about how practices once about maintaining caste through controlling the bodies of cis women (especially those of dominant castes) have morphed into practices for maintaining middle-class respectability through controlling middle-class cis women's bodies.

These connections between caste, class, and gender lead to consequences that are not limited to dominant-caste groups or middle-class cis women. For many trans women aspiring to join the middle classes, it means rising above their caste. Although caste was not something I asked trans women about specifically, many trans women spoke about caste, and everyone who brought up caste identified themselves as coming from a marginalized caste. These trans women seek to fulfil their class aspirations by aligning themselves with middle-class womanhood. As middle-class attributes in urban India are now based upon what were once considered respectable dominant-caste attributes,[28] the construction of middle-class womanhood these trans women align themselves with is based upon the ideals of dominant-caste womanhood.[29]

Hijras Past and Present

Like Priya and Deepa, many feminine-presenting GNC people I met during my fieldwork identified themselves as transgender.[30] I initially found this intriguing, given the context of GNC identity in India. That was because while in many countries people identify as either cisgender or a variation of newer non-cis identities like transgender, nonbinary, and so on, India is unique due to the historical presence of *hijras*.

Hijras are the most prominent, publicly recognized group of GNC people in India.[31] They are most often feminine-presenting GNC persons who leave their families in their teenage years (usually due to abuse) and run away to urban areas[32] to live and work with others "like them" in communities organized around the *hijra* families they create. Historical archives show that *hijras* have lived in South Asia for at least 300 years,[33] while popular and mythological accounts place them in the region for the past several millennia. Because of this history, I assumed that at least some of the feminine-presenting GNC people who identified as transgender were using the term "transgender" for my benefit, perhaps thinking that a white, middle-class, cisgender woman from the United States would not know about *hijras*. I thought if they were speaking to another Indian who was familiar with the term, then they would identify themselves as *hijras*.

Scholars regularly emphasize that *hijras* have shaped popular and scholarly understandings about gender and sexual nonconformity in India.[34] Outside of India, *hijras* have been hailed as figures that "stand for 'the Indian homosexual'"[35] and remain "the most frequently encountered figures in the narrative linking of India with sexual difference."[36] Looking back on the incident where I called Priya a *hijra*, I realized I had fallen prey to exactly these kinds of assumptions.

In India, *hijras* are associated by the non-*hijra* general public[37] with a variety of gender and sexual nonconforming practices and characteristics.[38] Despite being historically recognized in South Asia, today they are extremely marginalized as a group. *Hijras* are often "constructed in the popular imaginary as 'dirty'" and maligned for their poverty, which results in their being treated as social "outcasts"[39] who are excluded based upon their perceived "other"-ness.[40]

As a result of their perception as sexual deviants, *hijras* have experienced intense scrutiny both politically and in the media.[41] In Indian and international news, there are frequent reports about the injustices faced by *hijras* as well as documentary-style exposés centering on the troubling behaviors that can occur within *hijra* family systems. Yet despite what would seem to be their "hyper visibility,"[42] there have to date only been three book-length ethnographic studies focusing on *hijras*. Two of these[43] were conducted in the 1980s and 1990s, before many of the changes this book addresses had taken hold, and the third was conducted more recently in the 2010s in rural eastern India[44]—a very different setting than the urban context of Bangalore. Comparing my analysis about how *hijra* groups in Bangalore are changing to this study reveals the uniquely urban context this book chronicles.

A key reason for the emergence of transgender women in India is the ability of visibly GNC people to live outside of *hijra* groups. As we will hear more about in the coming chapters, *hijra* communities formed at least several centuries (and possibly millennia) ago to combat their societal exclusion. At that time, visibly GNC persons could not access necessary resources like housing and employment, but through family relationships, *hijra* groups, led by a powerful "head," provided these resources. In the past 25 years, media and political attention about gender nonconformity has led to incremental but important shifts in societal acceptance. Now that they face relatively less exclusion, some GNC people in urban areas who might have formerly joined a *hijra* family can live "independently" as transgender women. This book explores the social changes that have enabled groups of (primarily younger) feminine-presenting GNC persons to claim transgender identities, describing how these changes have impacted not just them but traditional *hijra* families.

One effect of these changes is that they have undermined the countercultural institutions painstakingly created by *hijras*. When GNC people were excluded from dominant institutions, *hijras* created their own families where they could live together by their own rules. Now that new opportunities enable some visibly GNC people to participate in dominant institutions (to a degree), they also enable them to live outside of *hijra* groups. On the one hand, we can think about these changes encouraging GNC people to embrace conformity to dominant ideas and institutions—bringing transgender women "back into the fold," so to speak. But on the other hand, now that certain GNC people can survive outside of *hijra* groups, *hijra* relationships have shifted in ways that disempower those remaining *hijra*s who depend on them for survival.

Recognition and Respect: Diverging Stories for Trans Women and *Hijra*s

Although India has a long history of recognizing feminine-presenting GNC people, it was striking to meet so many of them who, like Priya, identified as transgender and insisted they were not *hijra*s. However, during my fieldwork, there was not much awareness among "mainstream" society of the differences between *hijra*s and trans women. Among many cisgender people at that time, the terms "transgender" and "hijra" were used almost interchangeably, with *hijra* falling under an all-encompassing transgender "umbrella" within LGBTQ+ (lesbian, gay, bisexual, transgender, queer+) and gender rights activism. At public events like protests, rallies, and Pride parades, *hijra*s were referred to as transgender people. Official state reports, Indian publications, and NGO documents referred to *hijra*s as transgender.[45] News reporters, community activists, and even the organizers of NGO-led sexual health programs used *hijra* and transgender interchangeably. I came to realize that the only people who actively resisted equating the two identities were trans women themselves.

As my fieldwork continued, I noticed a visible (and vocal) group of feminine-presenting GNC people who wanted to claim transgender identities separate from *hijra*s. Many of these trans women had links to *hijra* groups, yet they sought to raise awareness and promote an understanding of themselves as transgender. In doing so, they emphasized (and also reified) the differences between themselves and *hijra*s. The more I heard trans women explaining how and why their identities are different from *hijra*s, the more I became intrigued by this distinction. I came to realize that the desire of these trans women to differentiate themselves from *hijra*s revolved around garnering respect, implying that the respect they sought was not available to *hijra*s.

One way to capture this idea is to recognize that trans women are emerging in India at a time when issues impacting GNC people have vaulted to the forefront of global media and public visibility. Across the world, GNC persons and their allies have come together to demand a diverse array of rights, from legal recognition via government ID cards and inclusion in anti-discrimination laws and policies to the ability to use bathrooms that coincide with their gender identities (just to name a few). The debates sparked by the media attention on these efforts brought GNC issues to the forefront of public discussion in practically every country in the world.[46] As a result, GNC people have gained new opportunities as public awareness of GNC issues has expanded.

This certainly has been the case in India, where heightened awareness has led to GNC people recently[47] gaining a degree of legal recognition.[48] In 2011, India's national census included a "third" gender option for the first time,[49] and three years later the Supreme Court of India passed a judgment (known as the NALSA Judgment) that affirmed the rights of all Indian citizens to determine their gender identities.[50] As the decade came to a close, the controversial 2019 Transgender Persons' (Protections of Rights) Act was passed by the Indian parliament, mandating legal recognition of someone's gender.[51]

When surveying the media coverage about the legal and social strides GNC people have made, it is easy to assume that these changes are on the whole positive for this group. For example, when considering the context of emerging trans women in India, it might appear beneficial (and even "progressive") that they can now access basic necessities like employment, gender affirmation surgery, and housing and can live "independently" of *hijra* groups. It might even seem unquestionably good that trans women can access middle-class markers like office employment and education, which opens up "respectable" routes for being a woman. But I ask: Is what appears to be social progress good for (or at least equally distributed among) all members of this marginalized group? Could it be that some members of the group benefit from the social changes this book discusses, while others are actually harmed by them?

"New" Transgender Women versus *Hijra* "Others"

Distinctions between groups of feminine-presenting people shaped by notions of middle-class respectability are not entirely new in India. In fact, these kinds of distinctions appeared among cisgender women in historical periods where certain groups of cis women gained increased opportunities.[52] Now that some trans women are being confronted with newfound opportunities, trans women describe themselves and these opportunities by adopting similar rhetoric used to describe cis women's shifting access to opportunity in previous eras. The narratives that trans women tell in their everyday lives and in media show that notions about empowerment and respectability that impacted cisgender women's shifting access to opportunity also impact how transgender women perceive and represent their struggles.

Middle-class cisgender women in India have confronted new opportunities for public participation at least twice in the past 200 years. These changes in opportunity have been described using the language of the "new" Indian woman. In both cases, the new woman and the opportunities available to her exist alongside a binary construct of her "other," a working-class woman whose opportunities remain constrained. The new woman's enhanced opportunities come into sharp relief only when she is juxtaposed to her "other." This new woman construct offered enhanced possibilities for middle-class women. However, new women had to carefully police their behavior to avoid being mistaken for their common women counterparts. Ultimately, these constructs both contained and circumscribed women's public participation.[53] I argue that trans women implicitly draw on notions of "new" (middle-class) womanhood in order to distance themselves from their own "other"—the *hijra*.

Today, a salient part of the new woman's identity is her unstated middle-class-ness. Her access to resources enables her to access opportunities open to a small fraction of Indians under liberalization.[54] The figure of the new woman suggests that economic liberalization empowers women to fulfill their desires and ambitions in ways that were previously impossible due to India's closed economy.[55] Yet feminist scholars have encouraged us to question assumptions about women's empowerment being connected to liberalized economic policies. They argue that upward mobility and interpreting oneself as an autonomous individual are "resources" that are distributed unequally.[56] Certain groups, such as working-class women, must remain in place, thus enabling middle-class women's mobility.[57] Similarly, the figure of the *hijra* must stay in her place to make apparent the newfound opportunities available to trans women.

Like their cisgender counterparts during the colonial, postcolonial, and contemporary period of liberalization, some transgender women have encountered newfound freedoms. In this way, some trans women's access to office employment combined with the Indian state's emphasis on empowerment through employment for cis women has paved the way for (particularly younger) transgender women to imagine fulfilling their (middle-)class aspirations. They attempt to do this by closing the gap between themselves and middle-class womanhood, symbolized by the appealing figure of the new woman. At the same time, trans women favorably contrast themselves with the figure of the disreputable *hijra*, who effectively bolsters trans women's ascent up the social hierarchy ladder.

The identity struggles among the transgender women I spoke with are inflected with notions of new womanhood at the same time that they are grounded in a discourse of enhanced possibilities for (middle-class) women in a liberalized economy. These trans women draw on similar understandings about womanhood and opportunity to position themselves as empowered. Like other new women in Indian history, they also juxtapose themselves with their disreputable "other," meaning that the power and promise of the transgender woman come into stark relief only when she is contrasted with the figure of the *hijra*.

Trans Women, *Hijras*, and Overlapping Identities

Early in my fieldwork, I regularly witnessed transgender women resist being identified as *hijras*. Consider the case of Pari, a trans woman in her twenties. When we spoke, Pari was carefully draped in a bright red sari as she sat across from me in the NGO office where she worked. In response to my question, "Do you define yourself as a *hijra*? I mean, will you say [to others], 'I'm a *hijra*?'" Pari exclaimed, "No, no, no!" Shaking her head emphatically, Pari looked at me seriously as she explained, "I am a transgender [person]. I understand myself as transgender." But later in our conversation, Pari revealed that she "ha[s] relatives in the *hammam*," meaning that she is a member of a *hijra* family.

Like Pari, oftentimes the same person who adamantly told me she is not a *hijra* would later admit that she has a *guru*, meaning she participates in a *hijra* family. This deeply puzzled me. How is someone not a *hijra* even while participating in a *hijra* family? Why might someone who takes part in *hijra* relationships decide not only to identify themselves as a trans woman, but also to disavow their identification with *hijras*? In addition to exploring how trans women align themselves with "new" (cis) women, this book also investigates the contours and contradictions of the trans woman–*hijra* divide in the lives of trans women.

Prior to my fieldwork, I would have thought that an emerging group of GNC people in the 2010s would want to challenge the negative stereotypes about gender nonconformity that are most apparent in the stigmatization of *hijras*. But what I discovered is that the trans women I spoke with were at pains to emphasize their difference from *hijras* and expressed anxiety about being identified as *hijras*. Their desire to draw hard boundaries between themselves and *hijras*[58] is partly due to their similarities in class location.

In urban India, a person's class shapes many parts of their life, like how often they eat, the "physical comfort" of their dwellings, and their health and health-related care.[59] Class also mediates the dignity and respect people can expect to be granted by others, their access to certain spaces, and their aspirations for themselves and their families. In this way, class is an important identity in urban areas of India today.[60]

In India, older GNC and sexual minority categories (especially *hijras*) are associated with poverty and the working classes. Like most *hijras*, the trans women I spoke with are working class, though many aspire to join the ranks of the middle classes. This makes transgender an attractive category for working-class people who seek upward mobility. But even as I heard trans women repeatedly distance themselves from *hijras*, I came to realize that these distinctions are not as clear-cut as many of them might imply.

In a similar fashion to Pari, Deepa revealed her distress at the thought that she could be recognized as a *hijra*, yet also acknowledged that she too had a *hijra* family. When I asked how someone could both participate in *hijra* families and also not be a *hijra*, she explained:

The new generation [of GNC people] is such that they don't want—even if they're *hijras* also—they don't want to show themselves as *hijras*. They want to live as women.... So even I don't want to tell others that I'm a *hijra*. Even my houseowner and all, they don't know that I'm a *hijra*. So people, this [younger] generation, you know, they want to live away from these *hijras*. They want to be like women.

Throughout my fieldwork, I came across many trans women like Pari and Deepa. Their ties to *hijras* reveal curious overlaps between the trans woman and *hijra* categories. These attempts to draw a firm boundary between trans women and *hijras*, despite and perhaps even *because of* these overlaps, show the transgender–*hijra* divide is an aspirational and anxious projection instead of an uncontested binary.

But trans women's desire for the respectability associated with middle-class womanhood is not the only reason they distance themselves from *hijras*. Another key reason trans women disidentify with *hijras* has to do with the difference between stereotypical ideas of what it means to be a *hijra* and the realities of their own lives. If we consider the changes in opportunity for (mostly younger) GNC people, we see that there is a significant difference between stereotypes of what a *hijra* is and the lives of these trans women who are also part of *hijra* families. When trans women who work in offices and aspire to join the ranks of the middle class consider their own life experiences, they do not fit into the stereotype of what it means to be a *hijra*. So when trans women who participate in *hijra* families emphatically state that they are not *hijras*, this is partly about seeking the respectability they do not think is available to *hijras*. However, such assertions are also about how much the recent social changes discussed in this book have impacted *hijra* relationships and the lives of (primarily younger) GNC people.

By aligning themselves with "new" womanhood, trans women distinguish themselves and their opportunities (real and imagined) over and against those of *hijras*. As a result, these trans women are pursuing the respectability denied to *hijras* by distinguishing themselves from them. In claiming "I am not a *hijra*," trans women assert their upward social mobility and their similarity to respectable middle-class cisgender women, and distance themselves from the negative associations of gender nonconformity most evident in the stigmatization of *hijras*.[61] The rise of the trans woman in India is therefore more than a simple story about expanded opportunities for feminine-presenting GNC people.

Some "new" trans women have experienced a measure of acceptance that might, at first glance, appear distinctly positive. It is also undeniable that the social changes described in this book have made a positive impact on some trans women's ability to live as they want. However, there are also several unintended consequences of these changes, including some trans women's desire to penetrate class hierarchies. The work trans women engage in toward this end results in outcomes that are distinctly less positive for other GNC people and are even predicated on the exclusion of *hijras*. Instead of "lifting as they climb" the social hierarchy ladder, some trans women reinforce the inequality and stigma attached to *hijras* for their inability and/or refusal to conform to middle-class womanhood. In doing so, these trans women implicitly support the marginalization and exclusion of *hijras*.

I understand "new" trans women as seeking to be included in the category of ideal womanhood, voicing an inclusionary politics similar to Higginbotham's notion of a "politics of respectability."[62] Under this politics of inclusion, marginalized groups seek to remake and recast themselves in ways that allow them to be included within dominant systems of power. As they pursue middle-class lives, some trans women "inadvertently reproduce the discourse which governs them," [63] since many seek to conform to (and thereby reinforce) patriarchal constructions of womanhood. The identity work trans women engage in as they align themselves with "new" womanhood and "other" *hijra*s also circumscribes their lives. This is because trans women must police their behavior carefully to avoid being misrecognized as *hijra*s, even as many of them participate in *hijra* families.

As they pursue upward mobility, these trans women demonstrate the importance of the gender binary and an elevated class status for feminine-presenting GNC people's intelligibility and acceptance in urban India.[64] Their actions not only reinforce the gender binary but also highlight its intersection with class hierarchies. What appears as a positive social change for marginalized groups who seek inclusion is actually predicated on participating in dominant institutions and reproducing the very marginalization they are trying to escape. Specifically, I show that this supposedly progressive change is not available to all GNC people, is embedded within struggles to penetrate class hierarchies, and ultimately is predicated on the exclusion of *hijra*s. My research reveals these kinds of narratives of social uplift for certain members of marginalized groups can actually serve to reinforce inequality for other group members. This is a story then about how more privileged people within marginalized groups can use their resources to fit in, and about how those who have less access to resources cannot (or refuse to) conform.

The Power of Conformity: Creating "Ideal" Trans Subjects

Of course, this situation where trans women are perceived as having increased opportunity is not specific to India. Though this story is set there, it is also a case study of a broader phenomenon that is relevant for other places. The larger narrative is about social change that enables new opportunities for marginalized groups and how marginalized groups react to this change.

GNC people (and particularly trans women) around the world are gaining increased recognition, if not broad acceptance. To understand what this recognition actually entails, it is instructive to think through the experiences of another group that recently gained societal recognition and acceptance in some parts of the world—lesbian and gay people. A concept activists and scholars use to think about this group's experience is homonormativity. But to understand the term "homonormativity," we need to first think through another concept, heteronormativity.

Heteronormativity refers to the ways that heterosexuality is often positioned as the only "normal" way to be and live.[65] When something is held up as the only valid way of being, this means experiences that fall outside of it are positioned as "other" and usually disparaged. When someone who falls outside of what is considered normal is othered, they face serious repercussions, like exclusion, violence, and even death.[66] By emphasizing heterosexuality as the only legitimate way of expressing sexuality, heteronormativity implicitly reinforces the gender binary and its resulting gender expectations.[67] It is easy to grasp how this harms those who are not heterosexual and/or who do not fit within the gender binary. But heteronormativity even harms people who *are* heterosexual and who *do* fit within the gender binary by limiting the kinds of practices, behaviors, and desires available to them.[68]

Homonormativity applies this same logic to gay and lesbian people. It upholds a certain set of expectations for what it means to be a "normal," valid, or "good" lesbian or gay—a set of ideas that do not oppose the key values and institutions that support dominant heterosexist culture. Homonormativity (and those who endorse it) instead confirms, supports, and pursues inclusion within these institutions and values.[69] The result is that lesbian and gay people feel pressured to support and reinforce heteronormative expectations by presenting themselves as "just like" straight people.[70] In this way, homosexuals who have access to certain forms of privilege (mostly due to their gender, class, race, ability, and so on) are tenuously included in mainstream heteronormative society.

Like heteronormativity, homonormativity rests on gender conformity, which means that "good" lesbians and gays need to present themselves in highly gender-conforming ways. In this way, homonormativity recognizes (and even celebrates) gay and lesbian people who do not challenge dominant gender expectations. Homonormativity is criticized for harming people who do not fit homonormative expectations (for example, that gender-conforming gays should be attracted to other gender-conforming gays within monogamous relationships). These expectations obviously harm bisexuals, people engaging in nonmonogamous relationships, and people who fall outside the gender binary. But like heteronormativity, homonormativity even harms people who *are* homosexual, monogamous, and whose identities *do* fall within the gender binary by (once again) limiting the possible practices, behaviors, and desires available to them.[71]

Whether or not certain gay people are eligible for inclusion also hinges on the degree they can sync with the cultural ideals of late capitalism, particularly the importance of consumption. People who can do this become "good" gays who are worthy of inclusion, whereas those who do not are viewed as not worthy of being included. As one queer activist puts it, homonormativity "tells us that we all should be building this 'Gaylandia' where everyone can shop in comfort and buy the right cocktails and the right accessories and the right [car] and the right kind of dog."[72] In this fantasy land, assimilated gay people inhabit a "depoliticized gay culture anchored in domesticity and consumption."[73] They become part of a "demobilized constituency" of gays who support the spread of global capitalism and its cultural ideals in ever more facets of daily life.[74] In this way, homonormativity is criticized because it threatens to incorporate LGBTQ+ people who might otherwise align themselves with movements for social justice that critique consumer culture.[75]

In recent years, activists and scholars have noticed that something similar is occurring around public understandings of emerging transgender identities. This is partly related to how GNC people feel compelled to position themselves and their identities when speaking to wider (cisgender) publics. To make their experiences intelligible to cis people, GNC people often draw on what is known as the "wrong body" story. This "wrong body" story emphasizes cross-gender identification and dressing from a young age and a pervasive feeling of being "trapped" in a body that does not match their gender identity.[76] The popularity of this story shows that it resonates with cis people trying to understand the experiences of GNC people. Unfortunately, the resonance of this story has led to a situation where only certain kinds of transgender experiences become socially recognized (at least among wider cis publics). An unintended consequence is that certain "ideal types of transgender selfhood" have emerged.[77] For the GNC people who can mold their experiences to fit within these recognized forms that shape what it means to be trans, these ideal types offer potential social acceptance. Unfortunately, they enable even greater marginalization for people who cannot fit their experiences into these forms.[78]

Scholars also assert that, like the "good" gay, the "ideal" trans subject is connected to late capitalist notions about economic productivity. In the North American context, requests for the public to accept trans people as "legitimate" citizens have historically highlighted "their valuable contributions to society through their labor."[79] The "wrong body" story that catalyzed the ideal trans subject includes a discussion of the person's gender transition.[80] Within this story, ideal transgender subjects[81] are positioned as in sync with the cultural ideals of late capitalism, particularly the "demands of liberal individualism."[82] Trans subjects are said to demonstrate their ability to sync with liberal individualism by completely "reinventing" themselves through their transitions.[83] Ultimately, ideal trans subjects are positioned as respectable people seeking to ascend the social class ladder. This "provincial" and often US-centric interweaving of transgender subjectivity with the cultural ideals of late capitalism[84] has since traveled far beyond its origins. This book investigates the "ideal types of transgender selfhood"[85] that are emerging among some middle-class aspiring trans women in urban India.

My Path to Trans Women and *Hijras*

This project has taken some unexpected twists and turns since I began my fieldwork. I came to India intending to study the dynamics of sexual rights activism.[86] My interest was partly due to my own involvement in LGBTQ+ communities and activism in the United States. I became interested in sexual rights NGOs after realizing that was where the bulk of advocacy happened. I was curious about how NGOs both enabled and constrained activism and how international funding shaped what happened on the ground.

I began my ethnographic fieldwork in the office of a large, well-known, internationally funded NGO in Bangalore. Through its activism and advocacy beginning in the late 1990s, this organization had steadily built up a working-class "community" of gender and sexual nonconforming people in Bangalore. Indeed, many people reported migrating from other states and/or rural areas in South India specifically because they had heard there was such a community in Bangalore.

I initially spent most of my time at the NGO office interacting with staff and "community" members and observing their day-to-day activities while writing copious field notes. I quickly realized that there were many NGO employees in the office who seemed to be assigned little work. For a researcher wanting to casually chat with people without being too much of an imposition on their time, this was an ideal scenario. While hanging around the office, I would often ask broad questions to get a sense of what kinds of issues were salient in people's lives. I also helped staff members write emails in English, located grants the organization could apply for, taught conversational English classes to a small group of sex workers, and compiled a lengthy report documenting current projects.

In an NGO setting where foreign visitors are not uncommon, I was usually met with only mild curiosity, and my presence soon seemed unremarkable. Yet my position as a white, American, middle-class, cisgender woman undoubtedly shaped my interactions in the field and with trans women. It is essential to acknowledge that these interactions were shaped by colonial legacies, historical imbalances in power, and current global power dynamics that perpetuate intersecting inequalities. When asking trans women to reflect on their identities and scrutinizing media featuring trans women, it is also important to carefully consider their presumed audience. This book delves into the ways trans women portray themselves when they interact with outsiders; other studies have revealed the complex ways feminine-presenting GNC people in India discuss and present their identities within their insider circles.[87]

As my fieldwork progressed, my language skills improved, allowing me to converse more fully with community members. Most importantly was simply being present; as one participant observed, I "kept on coming back." I slowly gained people's trust and even became friends with many people working there. During this time, I also attended and participated in all of the NGO's sexual-rights-focused events, rallies, and protests. As a result, I met other activists (including many *hijras*) whom I started meeting with regularly. I soon observed the growing divide between trans women and *hijras* and became increasingly curious about the emergence of the trans woman identity, especially in light of the overlap between trans women and *hijras*. It seemed to me that even working-class trans women who were never part of *hijra* groups would very likely have joined a *hijra* family in a time before there were increased opportunities available to GNC people. The tensions between the two groups were therefore all the more remarkable.

After honing in on key dynamics through fieldwork, I conducted over 75 semi-structured interviews. The interviews lasted between 45 minutes and 5 hours, and most interviews took place at the participant's home, an NGO office, or, on occasion, a restaurant or coffee shop. I conducted approximately half the interviews in Kannada, half in English, and three additional interviews in Hindi. The majority of participants self-identified as hailing from working-class backgrounds, while a minority of people identified themselves as having middle-class origins. Most of my interviewees were people I met during fieldwork; occasionally someone would arrange for me to interview someone they knew. Except in two cases where the person declined to be recorded, I digitally recorded each interview after obtaining consent (I took careful notes during the non-recorded conversations). After each interview was complete, I hand-wrote detailed notes about the experience. I then transcribed the interviews and typed out my notes.

During this time, I collected and analyzed over 200 English-language news articles about sexual minority rights and GNC people's identification struggles. While I would occasionally search for news articles and videos online, I often found relevant media through social media. Using social media to gather these reports allowed me to access a pool of media representations that circulated among my participants, influencing the way they understood and voiced their identity claims. Analyzing ethnographic data alongside online media representations offers a contextualized picture of how transgender women at my field site represented themselves in daily interactions and in materials that circulated to a wider online audience. During the analysis phase, I compared these media representations, my fieldnotes, and the line-by-line coding of my interview transcripts to form the key foci my analysis is based upon.

Plan for the Book

In the first chapter, I lay the groundwork for my conceptual framework of the "new" trans woman. This chapter explores a popular construction of womanhood in past and contemporary India—the "new" middle-class (cisgender) woman. It investigates how notions of new womanhood shape trans women's understanding of what it means to be transgender and how they are leveraged in creating the "new" transgender woman. These new trans women emerge in relation to both ideal (meaning middle-class cisgender) womanhood and in relation to *hijras*—their "other" counterparts. The "new" transgender woman framework helps to understand how the category of transgender is being incorporated into social hierarchies in India.

This sets the stage for the rest of the book, which traces the similarities between historical accounts of "new" middle-class (cisgender) womanhood and how contemporary trans women speak about their lives. As trans women align themselves with respectable (cis) womanhood, they strategically distinguish themselves from their disreputable "other"—the *hijra*. The rest of the book will also address how these tactics trans women use to seek inclusion into the category of "ideal" woman implicitly reify the exclusion of *hijras* who cannot or will not align themselves with middle-class cisgender womanhood. By conforming to established ideas about class and gender that shape idealized notions about womanhood in India, the trans women in this book uphold and perpetuate social hierarchies rooted in postcolonial experiences.

In Chapter 2, I show the importance of middle-class employment options for "new" middle-class aspiring trans women's understanding of themselves as respectable women. I emphasize how new possibilities for GNC people to work in offices pave the way for some trans women to imagine fulfilling their middle-class aspirations. When these trans women discuss their newfound employment opportunities, they explicitly and implicitly compare themselves to *hijras*, who are assumed not to have such opportunities. I will show that their aspirations for social mobility are connected to their desire to be recognized as "ideal" women who are respectably middle class. These trans women actively participate in shaping their identities, as they introduce subtle modifications to the gender binary. These modifications collectively contribute to a remaking of the binary and the inequalities it upholds.

The next three chapters will explore how increased opportunities for "new" transgender women impact *hijra* groups. Chapter 3 focuses on how GNC people's enhanced access to housing has led to major shifts in *hijra* relationships, particularly an increase in what I think of as "nonresidential" *guru–chela* relationships. In addition, it explores the disconnect between new trans women's lives and stereotypes about *hijras*. I show that these dynamics cause trans women to insist that they are not *hijras*, even though many participate in *hijra* families. When people speculate about what is causing these shifts, they often reference the ability of younger GNC people to make their own choices. I argue that this narrative of enhanced choice positions younger feminine-presenting GNC people as empowered "new" women who can effectively participate in globalized marketplaces through their ability to make choices.

This chapter builds on my argument that transgender is not merely an alternative label that offers other (equal) ways of being a GNC person. It is a category that is so new that it has not yet been fully incorporated into social hierarchies, unlike the stigmatized category of *hijra*. Thus, some people who take on trans identities seek to influence not only what it means to be transgender, but also *how* and *where* the category of trans might eventually be incorporated.

The rise of the "new" transgender woman has had a major impact on *hijra* families. Chapters 4 and 5 examine changing behaviors within *hijra* groups and how people interpret these transformations. Chapter 4 traces how the mutual need for resources that once brought *hijra* families together has been disrupted by social changes that enable some (usually younger) GNC people to become "new" trans women. This chapter shows how *hijra* relationships and behaviors have been reimagined as a result of shifting opportunities for some GNC people. This has impacted relationships of authority within traditional *hijra* families, empowering younger GNC people and disenfranchising older *hijras* who depend on these families for survival.

Chapter 5 focuses on how people interpret and frame these transformations in *hijra* families. I argue that the changes in *hijra* families are being measured and explained using rhetoric about the "decline" of the (cisgender, heteronormative [cishet]) joint family, a mainstay in popular culture in India. Like the discourse around "new" women is being leveraged to explain changes in younger GNC people's lives, the transformations in *hijra* families and households are being interpreted through discourses about younger GNC people's "choice" and newfound "freedom" from (supposedly) traditional family arrangements. While people often compared *hijra* families to joint families, I argue that a more relevant comparison is between *hijra* families and changing ideals for middle-class cishet couple relationships. These changes are part of wider societal shifts in power relationships that impact the relationships GNC people create.

In the conclusion, I turn to an example of how trans people in other parts of India distinguish themselves from *hijras*. As my analysis of the 2016 "I am Not a *Hijra*" photo series will show, many trans women outside of my field site of Bangalore also favorably contrast themselves with the figure of the *hijra* as they align themselves with respectable middle-class womanhood. These photos illustrate a key argument of this book, that some trans women attempt to climb the social hierarchy ladder by stepping on the *hijras* just below them. Instead of "lifting as they climb," these trans women reinforce the inequality and stigma that plague *hijras* for their inability (and/or refusal) to conform to the dictates of middle-class womanhood. The book ends on a cautionary note about the perils of seeking inclusion, instead suggesting other strategies to combat marginalization.

Notes

1. I employ the broad category of gender non-conforming (GNC) to refer to people whose dress, demeanor, and comportment are recognizably at odds with the gender they were assigned at birth. This is a term I use as an umbrella category and placeholder for anyone who is essentially not cisgender, rather than a category that I heard people identify themselves with. While generally considered a neutral term, GNC has been criticized by some trans people who do not appreciate being referred to as "non-conforming." As Serano (2014) points out, the language used to describe marginalized groups can quickly become subject to contestation. Recognizing that this term is imperfect, I emphasize Serano's point that language is not the problem per se, but that it is the existing marginalization which causes negative connotations to adhere to the terminology referencing marginalized groups (Serano 2015).
2. Reddy 2005; see also Cohen 1995; Nanda 1990.
3. Valentine 2007.
4. Cohen 1995; Boyce 2007; Reddy 2005; Hall 2005; Dutta 2012a; Dutta and Roy 2014.
5. Cohen 2005; Boyce 2007; Dutta 2012a.
6. Misra 2006; Cohen 2005; Boyce 2007; Dutta 2012a.
7. Cohen 2005; Boyce 2007; Dutta 2012a.
8. Boellstorff 2011: 296; see also Dutta 2012b.
9. Dutta 2012b: 3.
10. Dutta 2013: 505.
11. Dutta 2012a: 832.
12. Dutta 2012a: 832.
13. Dutta 2012b: 3.
14. In India, transgender most often denotes male-assigned people.
15. Snow 2001.
16. Dickey 2016: 16; see also Liechty 2003; Lamont 1992.
17. Dickey 2016; Liechty 2003; Lamont 1992.

18. For an overview on caste in India today, see Vaid 2014.
19. Dickey 2016: 38.
20. Dickey 2016: 40.
21. Dickey 2016: 40.
22. Dickey 2016: 210.
23. Dickey 2016: 40.
24. Dickey 2016: 16.
25. Vaid 2014: 398.
26. Chakravarti 2003: 26.
27. Chakravarti 2003: 26.
28. Dickey 2016: 40.
29. These representations of womanhood in India are implicitly characterized by "normative experiences of Hindu, middle-class upper-caste (and, often, North Indian) women" (Mankekar 1999: 161).
30. I use transgender or trans to denote people who self-identify in this way. But it is important to remember that any identity claim is probably shifting and does not necessarily prevent people from identifying with other terms (Cohen 1995; Reddy 2005; Dutta 2012a; Dutta and Roy 2014). However, in media and state discourse, transgender often refers to GNC people (usually those assigned male at birth), including *hijras* (Dutta 2012b, 2013; Dutta and Roy 2014). But as I shall show, there are also times when media serves to reinforce distinctions between transgender women and *hijras*.
31. Reddy 2005; see also Cohen 1995; Nanda 1990.
32. However, recent research by Saria (2021) has shown that there are also rural-based *hijras*.
33. Reddy 2005; see also Cohen 1995; Nanda 1990.
34. Reddy 2005; Cohen 1995; Nanda 1990.
35. Cohen 1995: 279.
36. Reddy 2005: 2.
37. In North India, there is a prevalent myth that children born with forms of intersex variations resulting in ambiguous genitals belong with *hijras*. It is suspected that the parents of such children would contact the nearest *hijra* clan, who would then raise the children. I heard of a group of elder *hijras* in North India who had been with the community since birth; they had recently had genetic testing performed and were diagnosed by doctors as having intersex variations, so there is some evidence of this occurring.
38. Puri 2015.
39. Reddy 2005: 257; see also Hinchy 2014.

40. Hinchy 2014.
41. Reddy 2005: 2–3.
42. Reddy 2005: 2–3.
43. These monographs are Gayatri Reddy's (2005) book, *With Respect to Sex: Negotiating Hijra Identity in South India*, and Serena Nanda's (1990) book, *Neither Man Nor Woman: The Hijras of India*. Nanda's work, following decades of pathologizing research about *hijras'* "deviance," was pathbreaking in her emphasis on *hijras* as "full human beings." Reddy's work was similarly influential, as she challenged the understanding of *hijras* as "third gender," arguing instead for analyses that examine sexual–gender identity alongside other identity categories. Reddy's (2005) work is based on research conducted in the 1990s. Since this time, *hijras* have come into contact with global LGBTQ+ (lesbian, gay, bisexual, transgender, queer+) activism, and India has undergone vast social changes connected to liberalization that have impacted GNC people. This book offers a timely update that takes into account new GNC identities that now exist alongside (and in competition with) the *hijra* category.
44. Saria 2021.
45. Dutta and Roy 2014: 329.
46. When speaking to *Time Magazine* in the United States, Laverne Cox famously referred to this recent change as a "tipping point" in transgender representation (Steinmetz 2014).
47. Activism for sexual minority rights undertaken as a result of the global HIV/AIDS crisis paved the way for these successes.
48. However, many transgender activists express disappointment about the impacts of these laws on their lives (S. Ghosh 2021).
49. Cohn 2011.
50. However, this judgment has also faced intense criticism (see Dutta 2014).
51. However, the process of mandating legal gender recognition it requires has faced sustained criticism (Knight 2019).
52. Oza 2006; Rajan 1999; Thapar 1993.
53. Thapar 1993: 83.
54. Fernandes 2015; see also Bhatt, Murty, and Ramamurthy 2010.
55. Oza 2006: 27.
56. Skeggs 2004.
57. Massey 1994; see also Bhatt, Murty, and Ramamurthy 2010.
58. Mount 2020.
59. Dickey 2016: 11.

60. Dickey 2016, 2012; Bhatt, Murty, and Ramamurthy 2010; Fernandes and Heller 2006.
61. Mount 2020: 642.
62. Higginbotham 1994.
63. Berry 2008: 19.
64. Though this story is set in India, it is also a case study of a broader phenomenon that is relevant for other places.
65. Warner 1999.
66. Haritaworn, Kuntsman, and Posocco 2013.
67. Warner 1999.
68. Warner 1999.
69. Duggan 2002, cited in Stryker 2008: 145.
70. Warner 1999.
71. Warner 1999.
72. See Ruiz 2008: 238.
73. See Duggan 2002: 177.
74. Duggan 2002: 177.
75. Stryker 2008: 147.
76. Lampe, Carter, and Sumerau 2019: 869.
77. Lampe, Carter, and Sumerau 2019: 869.
78. Lampe, Carter, and Sumerau 2019: 869.
79. Irving 2008: 40; see also Aizura 2018.
80. Aizura 2018: 32.
81. Lampe et al. 2019: 869.
82. Aizura 2018: 31.
83. Aizura 2018: 31.
84. Aizura 2018: 35.
85. Lampe, Carter, and Sumerau 2019: 869.
86. When I began my fieldwork in 2009, the sexual minority or LGBT movement in India had a strong and growing presence. Since the 1980s, a smattering of activist organizations focusing on nonnormative sexualities were active in India. In the 1990s, the number of groups focusing on sexuality and queer rights substantially increased (Shah 2014; Dave 2012; Narrain and Bhan 2006; PUCL-K 2004). These groups wrote and circulated publications, and created spaces where participants could question heteronormativity (Shah 2014; Dave 2012; Narrain and Bhan 2006; PUCL-K 2004). These groups emerged partly due to economic liberalization that increased international funding for development and social justice work. By the early 2000s, a large

group of well-connected sexual-rights-focused organizations ran helplines, wrote newsletters, provided health resources, and offered social spaces for sexual and gender minorities in major metropolises and in some smaller cities (Shah 2014; Dave 2012; Narrain and Bhan 2006; PUCL-K 2004).

87. See especially Saria 2015; Dutta and Roy 2014; Dutta 2012a; Reddy 2005.

1

"New" Women and Old Hierarchies

Gender, Class, and Women's Opportunity

To understand the context in which "new" trans women align themselves with middle-class cisgender womanhood as they distance themselves from *hijra*s, we need to return to the NGO office where I spoke with Deepa, Priya, and their friends. Indu, a soft-spoken trans woman in her fifties wearing a coral-colored sari, looked serious as she said, "I don't want to tell others that I'm a *hijra*." Though Indu was part of a *hijra* group for many years, now she does not want to be associated with *hijra*s at all. Indu considered herself lucky as her facial features do not mark her as visibly GNC; in her words, she appears "feminine, *very* feminine." She remarked that most people initially recognize her as a cisgender woman.

Nodding toward Indu, Deepa observed, "If she says to the [other] passengers [she encounters] on the bus, 'I'm a *hijra*,' nobody will want to sit beside her on the bus. But looking how she looks, very feminine, the other passengers will sit beside her on the bus." Shaking her head, Deepa continued, "If she's looking like a *hijra*...." and she trailed off, looking uneasy. For trans women like Indu and Deepa, the costs of being perceived as a *hijra* include being excluded and ostracized.

Indu nodded seriously, remarking, "So what's the use in telling people that I'm a *hijra*? ... It's better you present yourself as a woman and just be on your own. Then you'll be—" and at that point, Deepa jumped in, saying, "— For respect. For self-respect. See, we want to give respect to ourselves also." For Deepa and Indu, aligning themselves with cisgender womanhood[1] offers the potential of being regarded with dignity by the people around them—and a form of self-respect they do not think is available to *hijra*s.

This interaction also indicates the deeper meanings around *hijra*-ness and womanhood in economically liberalized India. Indu points to a connection between *hijras* as a collective and "new" women as individuals "just ... on [their] own." Someone who once identified herself as a *hijra* and now identifies as a woman is therefore autonomous and not limited by her association with a particular group. In this chapter and the next, we will hear more about how this notion of womanhood as synonymous with independence and autonomy aligns with recent economic and cultural shifts in India.

Indu's comment also reveals the complexity of GNC identification. Indu implied that she is actually a *hijra*, but she does not see any benefit in directly acknowledging this (at least in public). When I asked why, she said it is because *hijras* experience "a lot of discrimination" and "there's no rights for *hijras*" in this part of India. Like other older GNC people I spoke with, Indu perceives that recent legal advances for GNC people in India do not have much of an impact on the lives of *hijras*. This is something we will hear more about in Chapter 5.

As Deepa and Indu spoke, I realized that being recognized as a *hijra* by those around them was a familiar (and often distressing) experience for feminine-presenting GNC people. Deepa remarked,

> If somebody [upon seeing my group of friends] calls out, "the *hijras* are coming!," I'll feel very bad. See, they don't know the relationship between transgender, trans woman, *hijra*. If [a person] is [a] man-to-woman [GNC person], they [that is, the general public] all call us *hijras* only. If I look like a female, but I have [facial hair/stubble], they call me a *hijra*. It's like that.

To avoid being perceived as a *hijra*, Indu and Deepa said they pointedly ignore *hijras* in public. Indu explained, "If I see a group of *hijras* outside, you know, I won't come—" She paused before eventually continuing. "I'm not comfortable going and talking to them. I'm not comfortable. Their dressing, the way of their loudness—I'm not comfortable. I really avoid them." Deepa then jumped in to reinforce Indu's position: "Sometimes I want to hide my identity in front of them. I want to give money to them and...." She offered a series of dramatic hand motions that suggested sending them away.

These interactions between Indu and Deepa hint at the role class plays in the growing divide between trans women and *hijras*. Indu described the *hijras* around her as boisterous and unattractively dressed, implying that their dress and demeanor mark them as working class. This sounds a lot like everyday media accounts positioning *hijra* behaviors as improper and threatening to disturb properly behaved middle-class cisgender people. When she encounters *hijras*, Deepa wants to "hide [her] identity" so they do not assume she is one of them. These actions suggest Deepa's fear that if recognized as a working-class GNC person, people will assume she is a *hijra*. The thought of being perceived as a *hijra* provokes her to slip them a few rupees so they leave quickly and she does not have to face what she sees as such a potentially embarrassing dilemma.[2]

Like Deepa and Indu, most trans women I spoke with expressed palpable anxiety about being misrecognized as *hijras*. This anxiety is partly because, like most *hijras*, these trans women largely come from working-class backgrounds. Due to their visible gender nonconformity combined with their similar class status, the trans women in this book are liable to be recognized as *hijras* by people who are not aware of the transgender–*hijra* distinction and its importance for many trans women. In their quest to avoid this scenario, these trans women seek to distinguish themselves and their identities from those of *hijras*, aligning themselves with "new" middle-class cisgender womanhood to emphasize how they differ from *hijras*.

Trans Women, Opportunity, and Identity (Work)

Scholars refer to identity work as when people adjust aspects of their identities (and behavior) to gain social approval, recognition, and/or respect.[3] In this chapter and the next, we will explore the identity work engaged in by emerging trans women. As they speak about their lives, trans women implicitly draw on historical narratives about middle-class cisgender womanhood and opportunity. Today, there is a strong sense that like their middle-class cis women counterparts in past eras, trans women in India are presented with enhanced opportunities. When they speak about these opportunities, many trans women draw from narratives of "new" womanhood that were originally applied to middle-class cis women. To understand the emergence of these "new" transgender women, it is important to explore how and why the new woman construct initially emerged to describe middle-class cis women. Specifically, we need to analyze the rhetoric used to describe middle-class cisgender women's access to increased opportunities in the past. This chapter traces the history of the new middle-class cisgender woman in India to argue that emerging trans women are also embracing "new" womanhood.

But ideas about new womanhood are not just about new middle-class cis women or new trans women—they also tell us about the relationship between new trans women and *hijras*. That is because the new woman figure requires an "other" against which she and her opportunities are contrasted. For new middle-class cis women in previous eras, their other was the figure of the working-class woman whose opportunities remained constrained. For new trans women, their other is the figure of the impoverished, disreputable *hijra*.

This, then, is a story about the intersectionality of gender and class aspirations as they are voiced through claims about gender. These trans women draw on a similar discourse to position themselves as empowered, like other "new" women in Indian history, while juxtaposing themselves with their disreputable "other," the *hijra*. In this way, trans women position themselves as deserving of the respect accorded to middle-class cis women, instead of meriting the stigma and discrimination faced by *hijras*. These trans women engage in identity work as part of a symbolic class project that connects being a trans woman with an elevated class status. The trans women I spoke with bolster their symbolic positioning as middle-class, respectable women by differentiating themselves from *hijras*, who either cannot or will not conform to these class and gender mandates.

Social Change, Class, and Respectability: The "New" Indian Woman

To understand how and why "new" trans women emerged, we need to locate contemporary trans women within patriarchal and postcolonial histories that shape notions of ideal womanhood in India. We will investigate two key moments in recent history when, like their trans women counterparts today, middle-class cis women confronted new opportunities.[4] In both cases, the new woman and her newfound opportunities were brought into sharp relief when juxtaposed against the binary construct of her "other," a working-class woman who could not access such opportunities. Understanding how these opportunities were discussed contextualizes the emergence of the new trans woman and how people interpret her opportunities.

The first of these opportunities emerged at the end of the 19th century when women's status in India was elevated to an important national concern, as it signaled India's level of "modernization" to the British colonizers.[5] At the time, there were opportunities for men of dominant-caste and middle-class backgrounds to participate in English-medium education and serve as "intermediaries"[6] in the colonial government.[7] Women were not allowed to attend the same educational institutions or to serve in these administrative roles, but middle-class and dominant-caste women family members of government officials advocated for greater opportunities, and many were able to enter into other professions (particularly medicine and teaching).[8] Since women's public participation marked India as "modern" in the eyes of the British, nationalist leaders made efforts to increase participation from educated middle-class women. To this end, they created the construct of the "new" woman alongside her working-class counterpart—the "common" woman.[9] The new woman was educated and could swiftly adapt to shifting political contexts like independence, while, by contrast, the common woman was uneducated and likely to encounter difficulty responding to political change. The new woman embodied the purported virtues of "cleanliness, companionship, discipline and self-control," whereas the common woman was "coarse, promiscuous and vulgar."[10] Common women engaged in manual labor, whereas new women were associated with proper femininity and motherhood. Because they hailed from middle- and elite-class backgrounds, the majority did not work outside of their homes.[11]

On the one hand, the new woman construct gave middle-class women increased access to the public sphere, including paid middle-class employment for a select group. In this way, new women made significant contributions to the "modernization" of the nationalist movement.[12] On the other hand, new women had to carefully monitor their behavior to avoid being mistaken for their common women counterparts.[13] So at the same time that the new woman construct opened up opportunities for some women, it also led to new constraints that circumscribed women's public participation.[14]

After India won independence from the British Empire, the middle classes were empowered to control and maintain the "political and administrative machinery" of the state.[15] They gained a kind of "moral legitimacy" to envision and manage the nation by participating in state politics and administration and dominating the professional sector.[16] Despite some loosening of caste constraints at the time, the new state administration largely hailed from dominant-caste backgrounds. But changes also came to the middle class— in particular, women's ability to work outside the home improved. This was partly due to a constitutional prohibition against gender discrimination in employment, which expanded their opportunities, especially in the already women-friendly sectors of education and healthcare.[17]

As middle-class women's ability to engage in paid work outside their homes increased, they were confronted with increased pressure to uphold certain "criteria of respectability."[18] Middle-class families were often concerned about "the respectability of the occupation" undertaken by the women in their families.[19] It was implicitly understood that low-status employment would be "unacceptable" and that "professional" jobs were preferred, while high-status jobs were the most sought-after employment option, partly because these jobs reflect well on the status of their families.[20] These criteria were coded as middle class, yet they also resonated with expectations for women's appropriate behavior among dominant-caste groups.

The "New" Liberalized Woman

When India's economy began to liberalize in the 1980s, another "new" woman appeared. This new woman had resonances with her pre- and postcolonial counterpart, yet the context of liberalization also distinguished her from her predecessor. To understand this avatar of the "new" woman, we need to turn to the social and economic context of India's post-Independence period and how that shifted during the transition to a liberalized economy.

In the early years of independence, India was understood as a developmentalist state operating under socialist ideals, a managed economy, and centralized planning. The state supported its growing industry and technological advances, while the middle class continued to supply the specific knowledge and administrative skills needed to develop the nation. But after economic liberalization started in the late 1980s, groups that benefitted from these new policies began to push India toward the ideals of globalization.[21] To this end, these groups collaborated with the state and advocated for opening economic markets to ensure India's spot as a key player in the global economy.[22] They emphasized its potential for growth due to its large number of "English-speaking, technically-qualified" workers combined with "low production costs, a relatively stable, reform-oriented government, and rising consumer aspirations."[23]

Liberalization profoundly impacted class systems and hierarchies in India. Following liberalization, the "new" middle classes began to enjoy financial benefits from economic policies[24] that supported technological growth and the privatization of industry.[25] In Indian popular culture and in global news coverage, there was a lot of rhetoric about these "new" middle classes,[26] who were assumed to signify the "benefits and values of liberalization."[27] Today these middle classes are widely recognized, and more and more people identify themselves as middle class,[28] making them more socially significant than other class groups in the past.[29] The recent global recognition of India as a major economic player is generally understood to have increased the confidence of the middle classes.[30] This legitimized a desire by more powerful groups within the middle classes to rearticulate their own "class interests" as "universal" to all class groups in India,[31] enhancing what the middle classes see as their ability to effectively represent all of India[32] despite their relatively small numbers.

Although those who benefitted from India's entry into the global economy are few in number relative to India's entire population,[33] the cultural ideas that support liberalization presume that anyone can benefit as long as they work hard and embody the correct attitudes and values.[34] As a result of the increased visibility of the middle classes, larger segments of the population—what I call middle-class aspiring—began to dream of joining the "new" middle classes[35] despite lacking the standard markers like income or class background.[36]

Following liberalization, the Indian economy experienced high rates of growth in the service sector.[37] This expanded middle-class employment opportunities, especially for women,[38] whose participation in the service sector nearly doubled between 1977 and 2017.[39] At the same time, consumption was becoming an important part of what it meant to be middle class. This made an additional income important for the economic security and comfort of middle-class cishet families.[40] Thus, in these middle-class households, women's employment became seen as increasingly "necessary" to maintain the family's lifestyle,[41] seemingly increasing the opportunities available to middle-class and educated urban women.

In the wake of these economic and cultural changes engendered by liberalization, another "new" woman appeared. She appears "aggressive, confident, urban" and embodies a sexuality that was previously reserved for the "vamps" in Bollywood films—a far cry from her opposite, the "traditional" Indian woman who is often described as "docile and homely."[42] This new woman is portrayed as "assertive, in control and particularly modern," in contrast with the portrayal of traditional

Indian women as "oppressed, burdened, and backward."[43] Media outlets embraced and propped up this construct of the new woman, especially through gendered representations in advertising and television.[44] As an executive for a popular women's magazine explained, the "persona" of the new woman was not just widely accepted but had become "even an aspirational one."[45] This avatar of the new woman "quickly became iconic" of a liberalized India.[46]

Like her nationalist-era counterpart, this new woman's supposed freedoms were not uncontested. She became the ground on which anxieties about India's newly opened borders and the cultural changes engendered by liberalization were voiced. This sparked public and media debates about the place of women in a rapidly globalizing society.[47] The outcome of these debates was ultimately a reworking of the new woman construct, which remained connected to opportunity and modernity while simultaneously giving her domestic role in "the patriarchal household—as mother, wife, and sister"—increasing emphasis.[48] Through this reworking, the new woman's relationship with men was foregrounded, making her less independent.[49] Today, the new woman's opportunities are circumscribed by her participation in the cisgender heteronormative family.

Similar to the nationalist-era new woman, a key part of the new liberalized woman's identity is her middle-class status, and within urban middle-class families, there is intense "concern with respectability" associated with "new" cis women.[50] Their families maintain respectability partly by stressing the economic and social benefits of their employment,[51] where women often work for pay outside of their homes. Yet this is a highly gendered form of respectability as well, where a family's honor rests on the behavior of the women who are obligated to maintain the family's respectability.[52] This emphasis on upholding certain "criteria of respectability"[53] is also related to caste hierarchies. In dominant-caste families, women are secluded[54] from the outside world, making concerns about middle-class women's movements and behavior also rooted in the maintenance of caste inequalities. The result is that the benefits of liberalization are in tension even for a group that would seem to benefit from it, like middle-class, educated, urban cisgender women. Liberalization promises this group greater access to economic opportunities, and some have experienced more opportunities. However, these opportunities have also opened them up to additional scrutiny from their families and, ironically, narrowed what would have been a wider array of employment opportunities.

In spite of these complexities, popular discussions about liberalization and opportunity often presume that liberalization fully empowers women. These discussions suggest that economic liberalization enables women to fulfill their ambitions in ways that were impossible in a closed economy.[55] Feminist scholars have questioned these assumptions, arguing that the supposed effects of liberalization for women, such as upward mobility and the ability to interpret oneself as an autonomous individual, should be viewed as "resources" that are more accessible to women from privileged groups than from marginalized groups.[56] As privileged women obtain upward mobility, feminist scholars point out that marginalized women often remain in place, suggesting that working-class women's lack of opportunity partly enables middle-class women's upward mobility.[57]

"New" Trans Women: Opportunity and Symbolic Class Projects

When we consider the new opportunities for transgender women alongside historical narratives about cisgender women's changing opportunities, we see that trans women are becoming connected to opportunity in ways similar to generations of cisgender and middle-class women before them. As we will hear more about in the next chapter, some trans women have experienced substantive changes in opportunity. Yet we will see that trans women's (and other GNC people's) opportunities are constrained by the resources available to them. Even within working-class (and middle-class-aspiring) groups, there is considerable variation in income levels and perceived opportunity. My conversations with trans women and other GNC people (like *hijras*) revealed that those who grew up in families with relatively more money and/or who managed to progress further in their education perceived themselves as having more opportunities. By contrast, people who grew up with relatively less money or who had to stop going to school (due to abuse, harassment, poverty, and so on) saw fewer opportunities on the horizon. This means that for working-class GNC people, their access to resources like education and financial security at least partly determined whether they could imagine living as "new" trans women. In addition to these actual changes in trans women's lives, there is also a media discourse connecting trans women to opportunity. This discourse assumes these opportunities are equally available to all trans women (which is not the case). What is driving this "leveling" discourse is how people—when discussing trans women's newfound opportunity—frame these opportunities and trans women's ability to access them. Trans women's opportunities are positioned in ways similar to how new opportunities for cis women were historically framed.

Media coverage of transgender women increasingly focuses on their new (middle-class) employment and educational opportunities, as we will hear more about in the next chapter. These reports emphasize trans women as having a greater ability to pursue educational qualifications and employment pathways[58] than GNC people in the past. Many trans women also reported to me that they enjoy increased opportunities, which we will hear more about in the coming chapters. And there are several prominent examples of trans women "firsts"[59] in their chosen (middle-class) professions and higher education programs. These examples show that there *are* increased opportunities for some trans women today.

In sum, the ability to live outside of *hijra* communities combined with access to education and respectable office employment paves the way for (particularly younger) feminine-presenting GNC people to envision fulfilling their (middle-)class aspirations, symbolized by the appealing figure of the "new" woman. In the face of media attention to trans women's new opportunities, trans women (and others around them) implicitly draw on notions of "new" womanhood when talking about their lives. In doing so, trans women position themselves as empowered like other groups of "new" women in Indian history. In this way, they seek to close the gap between themselves and respectable, middle-class womanhood. We will hear more about exactly how they do this in the next chapter.

Similar to the contrast between "new" middle-class, cisgender women and working-class women in previous eras, the opportunities available to trans women become most apparent when they are contrasted with their "other"—the *hijra*. Media coverage of trans women's opportunities (implicitly and explicitly) distinguishes between trans women's new opportunities and the lack of opportunities for *hijras*,[60] and trans women themselves juxtapose their opportunities with those of *hijras*. Instead of aligning themselves with other feminine-presenting GNC people, these trans women align themselves with the ideals of middle-class, cisgender womanhood because they seek the kind of respect that middle-class cis women can expect, but that is often denied to *hijras*.

This means that for middle-class aspiring trans women seeking respectability, the figure of the *hijra* needs to stay marginalized and excluded to make apparent their newfound status.[61] Without the figure of the *hijra*, it might be more difficult for these trans women to make the case that they are aligned with middle-class cis womanhood. Similar to the predicament of the new woman from previous eras, who had to regulate her behavior to avoid being mistaken as a "common" (working-class) woman, trans women have to navigate the trans woman–*hijra* binary and distinguish themselves from *hijras*. But just like the demand for respectability actually constrained the opportunities of the "new" woman, the demand that trans women similarly regulate their behavior and appearance to ensure they align with respectable, middle-class womanhood actually serves to circumscribe the possibilities for "new" trans women.

Ultimately, for the trans women I came to know, being transgender is in part about aligning themselves with respectable middle-class womanhood. Their aspirations for upward mobility are tied up in their ability to be (ideal) women, which means being recognized as respectably middle-class. In this way, they seek incorporation into existing class and gender hierarchies within heteronormative systems of power. In the coming chapters, I describe how these trans women emphasize the importance of middle-class status for the respectability they seek and argue that the identity work these trans women take on is a symbolic class project that connects being transgender with an elevated class status for feminine-presenting GNC people.

The Context of Bangalore: A "New" Aspirational City

In some ways, it makes sense that I would observe these connections between gender and class aspirations in a city like Bangalore because this urban environment shapes trans women's aspirations in particular ways. That is in part because the city of Bangalore is itself an aspirational place. In fact, Bangalore exemplifies these ideas about connections between economic liberalization and new opportunities that the new woman construct is based upon.

Bangalore is the capital city of the state of Karnataka, which sits atop the Deccan Plateau in South India. The city boasts a mild climate, a network of lakes, and beautiful public parks. These amenities earned Bangalore its former reputation as the "Garden City" of India, once known as one of the nicest places to live in or visit.[62] But today the city is known on the global stage for its advances in information technology (IT) and computer software. The growth of the IT industry in Bangalore began on a small scale in the

1980s, expanded exponentially in the 1990s, and continued to grow (albeit at a reduced pace) since the 2000s.[63] As the city developed into an important center for business process outsourcing work, Bangalore became notorious for its traffic,[64] pollution,[65] and high cost of living.

These changes impacting Bangalore are part of the larger economic changes affecting urban India. Following liberalization, India witnessed a shift from "state-directed" strategies of development and urban planning toward market-driven and *laissez-faire* policies,[66] with its urban areas reshaped as "world class cities."[67] Even as urbanization intensified, bringing increased numbers of people to reside in cities,[68] city planners and municipal governments faced constraints like the privatization of basic services, the withdrawal of state support, a fervent embrace of "public–private partnerships" with limited accountability, and increased gentrification with the goal of "expand[ing] space for elitist consumption."[69]

As the avatar of Silicon Valley in India, perhaps no city has been subjected to these processes more than Bangalore. In fact, at one time urban planners and government officials hoped to recreate another Singapore in Bangalore's place.[70] The desire to remake and recast Bangalore as a "global city" is evident in the many infrastructure projects[71] at various levels of completion—new or expanded highways and flyovers, older commercial and residential areas being demolished for "redevelopment," and the city's much-anticipated "Namma Metro" railway. This landscape of aspiration has impacted the lives and imagination of the city's residents, including the trans women who are the subjects of this book.

When first seeing the city, visitors are often struck by the amenities catering to the prime movers behind its transformation: IT multinational corporations. Their offices (known as "campuses") rise above the city skyline: tall, gleaming metal skyscrapers encircled with glass windows. Near these offices, IT professionals live with their families in large, lush apartment complexes organized in grid-like symmetry and set back from the road behind high walls. The executives live in even more luxurious gated complexes with high-end villas surrounded by exquisite landscaping, exclusive clubhouses, and large swimming pools. The city also boasts several luxury malls with large movie theatres where affluent families and teenagers hang out on weekends and holidays. These areas of Bangalore are only a small part of the entire city, but images of these parts circulate widely, creating the impression that Bangalore's economy orbits around the IT sector.[72] In contrast, the surrounding urban area is marked by small shops and older, more modest residential and commercial neighborhoods, as well as areas that were once villages but have since been absorbed into the "urban sprawl" of the city.[73]

Bangalore has experienced incredible levels of urban growth in the past several decades. A report by the Indian Institutes of Science found that Bangalore has grown by more than sixfold—the greatest increase among the ten major metropolitan areas they studied.[74] This accelerated process of urbanization has utterly transformed Bangalore, forcing it to abandon its "Garden City" reputation as its green spaces rapidly shrink to accommodate wider roads while additional buildings and metro stations are constructed. In the years between 1973 and 2016, urbanization led to over a 1,000 percent increase in newly paved surfaces in the city and a concomitant 88 percent decline in vegetation. Along with the loss of green spaces has come a severe reduction in the size of the city's bodies of water—an 85 percent decrease between 2000 and 2016.[75] Residents of working-class neighborhoods are the most affected by these changes. A survey of four working-class neighborhoods in Bangalore found high dissatisfaction with water availability from public water taps, toilets, and underground drainage. Concerns about the ability of Bangalore's municipal government to effectively and efficiently manage basic services like garbage removal are rife as well,[76] with the title of a *Times of India* article pithily summing up the issue: "How India's 'Garden City' Became a Garbage City."[77]

Bangalore's economic growth is almost entirely due to the IT sector, and so it is unsurprising to learn that the people who benefit most from this growth are the "new" middle classes who work in IT.[78] This group makes up only a small proportion of Bangalore's population, yet they occupy "an outsized role in global, national, and urban imaginations."[79] On a symbolic level, the IT boom "captured the imagination of the nation and enhanced India's image within the global cultural economy."[80] It also created new kinds of aspirations and novel routes toward social mobility. Though the IT industry created tremendous wealth for only a few citizens, this reinforced a popular perspective that globalization and open markets hold the keys to India's future growth.[81]

In Bangalore, the economic mobility of the middle classes relies heavily on the labor of the poorest residents of the city,[82] who build and maintain their homes, collect their garbage, and take care of their children. Most people imagine that migrants to Bangalore are largely middle-class IT workers.[83] However, working-class and formerly rural-based groups have migrated to the city in large numbers in the past decades.[84] It is true that migrants can expect a higher income, increased educational opportunities, and enhanced "business prospects."[85] Yet Bangalore has also earned a reputation for its high cost of goods and services, so these same migrants often struggle to make a sustainable living.[86]

In addition to these economic changes, Bangalore has also witnessed a steep increase in moral policing, often tied to the rise of Hindu nationalism[87] as well as local forms of linguistic and regional nationalism.[88] In Bangalore, the right-wing Bharatiya Janata Party (BJP) enjoys considerable support,[89] though the city was historically considered "liberal and tolerant."[90] Today, left-wing politics occupy a small space that is mostly disconnected from elections, and the social sector faces accusations of being overinfluenced by NGO-ization and its "technocratic" ideals.[91] As one resident put it, Bangalore is "a city that's struggling to accommodate an expanded identity."[92]

The changes Bangalore has experienced are due to its rapid yet unequal economic growth; as a result, the city has attracted considerable amounts of international funding from NGOs.[93] At the same time, metropolitan areas like Bangalore that experienced population booms also became important sites for sexual minority activism and community building.[94] It is in this context that activism for sexual rights and the rights of GNC people in Bangalore emerged.

From its inception, activism for sexual minorities and the rights of GNC people in Bangalore has included the voices of working-class people. This is unusual, since middle-class sexual minority concerns dominated activism in other large Indian cities in the 1990s and early 2000s.[95] This unique situation is partly due to the work of a small group of middle-class sexual rights activists. While this group was conducting field research to document abuse against sexual minorities, they began to uncover and raise awareness about how sexuality- and gender-based discrimination are compounded by other axes of identity such as class, caste, gender, religion, and ability. These activists made a point of reaching out to working-class people and encouraging them to become involved.[96] Many of these working-class people were *hijras*, and as a result they became increasingly active in sexual rights groups and movements in Bangalore. As sexual rights advocacy and activism became more prominent, a recognizable and vocal "community" of working-class sexual minorities and GNC people began to cohere, leading to the city also becoming a destination for sexual minority and GNC migrants from different parts of South India.[97]

Bangalore is home to several well-known sexual rights NGOs. During my fieldwork, the majority of trans women I met were connected in some way to these organizations—many were even current or former employees.[98] In the next chapter, we will see how this new ability to obtain respectable, middle-class office employment is especially important for these trans women's understanding of themselves. Of course, the number of GNC people who obtain paid positions at NGOs is very small in relation to the estimated number of GNC people in Bangalore. However, trans women associated with NGOs are highly visible in various media and speak openly about their identities. In this way, they have an outsized impact on public perceptions about transgenderism and gender nonconformity.

"Middle-class Aspiring": The Complexities of Class in Trans Women's Lives

The vast majority of people in this book hail from working-class backgrounds. I characterize these trans women as "middle-class aspiring" to mark the class aspirations they voice through claims about gender. However, it is important to acknowledge that a person's social class can be difficult to pin down. This is especially true in urban centers in India today, where economic liberalization has produced many middle-class aspiring groups.[99]

Social class is important in GNC people's lives for several reasons. A key reason is that their social class determines the pathways available to them. As we will hear about in the next chapter, people who can access more resources tend not to join the *hijras* upon leaving their families, whereas those who need social and financial support can find it upon joining the *hijra* system. To illustrate how class shapes GNC people's pathways when they leave their families, I will relay a conversation I had with Sanya, a trans woman in her late thirties who initially joined a *hijra* group as a young GNC person.

After enjoying a delicious lunch she cooked, Sanya and I chatted as we sat on the floor of the living room in the cozy flat she shared with her boyfriend. These surroundings were quite a departure from how she grew up—in an impoverished family from a marginalized caste in a rural area. When Sanya was young, she identified as GNC and left her family, but her options for earning a livelihood were limited by her class background: "At that time, like when I was 20 years old ... I just—I was ready to [join the *hijra*s and] be a beggar. I started my career as a beggar, I begged, I earned some money." Because Sanya came from a poor family and *hijra* communities provide employment options for people who are willing to solicit money and engage in sex work, she did not think twice about doing anything differently. But according to Sanya, the story plays out differently for better-resourced middle-class GNC migrants to the city:

> I've seen some people who are from upper-class or like middle-class [backgrounds] … they definitely don't want to do begging work … they don't want to identify themselves as a sex worker or a beggar [and therefore wouldn't join the *hijras*]. They'd never want to become a beggar. They could never imagine it!

When I asked specifically about how class has influenced her life, Sanya pointed out that her class identification is complex. "My parents are working-class. I'm coming from a Dalit [marginalized caste] background, very much from the poorest class." However, despite Sanya's background, she does not "think I'm exactly working-class because I'm not working like, you know, I'm not working as like a … laborer, that kind of work. I'm a [radio] disc jockey." Despite the fact that she grew up in a working-class family, as an adult Sanya would situate herself closer to the middle class. Sociologists refer to the distinction between the social and economic context someone grew up in and their current social and economic context as the distinction between social class and socioeconomic status.[100]

For Sanya, her socioeconomic status is partly related to the prestige of her occupation in media. "I may not earn very much money, maybe less than a working-class person, but still, you can't exactly say I'm working-class." She positions her job as situating her outside of the working class, despite the fact that her salary is comparable to (or even lower than) that of a manual laborer.

Now that Sanya interacts with GNC people from different class backgrounds, she has realized how much someone's class shapes their life. As she remarked,

> I came from a working-class community and that's why I lack a lot of information and exposure. Like for example … I just got a very ordinary, like 10,000 Rupees (approx. 170 USD at the time) [gender affirmation] surgery for about two hours [in total, but the actual operation was done] in 20 minutes. And the next day, I left the hospital [as compared to people who recover in a fancy hospital for several days]. So it's like that.

Unfortunately, Sanya has suffered from repeated health problems that she attributes to the quality of her surgery. In contrast, "some upper-caste, upper-class [GNC] people" she knows had a very different experience:

> They have … exposure about like where do you get the surgery, where do you get the high-class surgery, you know, like facial [feminization surgeries] and all that. So those kinds of things, they know a lot about. You know, they have their own circle to figure out those things and they can even travel to, like, Thailand or [somewhere] like that, so they get a … very good surgery. But for us, people who don't have this much exposure, what do we know? … I had no idea about [going to get surgery in] Thailand!

There is not that much information available about middle- and elite-class GNC people in India. It is assumed that they do not publicly identify as GNC for fear of losing family or financial support—as has been confirmed in a few instances where GNC people from higher-class backgrounds have publicly identified themselves.[101] Sanya explained, "For upper-class people, it's hard for them to come out to their family because they won't get their inheritance money or something like that. Maybe they'll be victims of honor killing or something." Thus, it may be partly due to their marginalized-class backgrounds that working-class GNC people can publicly claim GNC identities, while middle- and elite-class GNC people's privilege blocks them from doing so. However, Sanya observed that there is an alternative pathway for them:

> There are some [middle- and elite-class] people who are very smart and they can escape. Since they got a good education, they can get a very good job and then they can come out…. They can leave their family and then they can find their own way.

As Sanya suggests, people with access to resources like education may be able to independently maintain their middle- or elite-class lives and even as "out" GNC people maintain their privilege.

By contrast, people from working-class backgrounds who do not have access to resources like education cannot access the same kinds of resources when they leave their families. This was Sanya's experience:

> For me, when I left my family, I had to start from zero, you know? Obviously, being a beggar or a sex worker [with a *hijra* group], like that … I may have come out from my family easily, but my lifestyle, my life is at the same [class] level … In terms of employment, I'm not working-class, but my income is still less than many working-class people, so it's like that.

Despite the fact that Sanya no longer considers herself "exactly working class," she acknowledges how her working-class background curtailed her aspirations as a young GNC person (for work and surgery, among other things) and how it continues to influence her current economic and social situation.

This is all to say that the category of "middle-class aspiring" that I am referring to is quite broad in terms of its members and encompasses different kinds of working-class backgrounds. This is intentional. Like Sanya, I spoke to several trans women who situated themselves in a higher class than the one they grew up in. From the outside looking in, these stories might appear as straightforward examples of upward social mobility. However, as we will see in the coming chapters, when we dig a bit deeper, we uncover a more complicated picture in which some trans women have increased opportunities and have experienced forms of class mobility while others (and other GNC people) experience constraints on their ability to take advantage of these opportunities.

Conclusion

This chapter offers context for how and why trans women like Indu, Deepa, and Sanya align themselves with middle-class womanhood and distance themselves from *hijras*. Instead of telling a story about trans women's desire to avoid the social stigmatization faced by *hijras*, I have presented how a specific way of understanding and discussing opportunities for women from India's past shapes the present. These understandings position "new" women as benefitting from increased opportunity at the same time they emphasize that their "others" do not have (or deserve) such opportunities. These "new" woman discourses shape the identity work emerging trans women engage in, making them what I refer to as "new" trans women.

Ideas about women's empowerment and respectability that impacted middle-class cisgender women in late colonial, postcolonial, and liberalized India now impact how trans women understand and discuss their struggles and newfound opportunities. The notion that trans women have increased opportunities is grounded in ideas about enhanced possibilities for middle-class women in a liberalized economy. The perception that trans women now have opportunities enables them (and others around them) to perceive themselves as new women. And just like some of their cis women counterparts from previous eras encountered new opportunities, the same can be said of some contemporary trans women. Accompanying these new opportunities is a media discourse claiming that such opportunities are widely available for all trans women. These ideas that connect trans womanhood with opportunity allow some trans women to imagine fulfilling their class aspirations as they align themselves with the figure of the new woman.

But these new woman discourses that some trans women draw on also posit an "other" against whom new women can favorably contrast themselves. In the colonial, postcolonial, and liberalized eras, "new" middle-class cis women contrasted themselves with their disreputable "other," the working-class woman. Similarly, "new" trans women favorably contrast themselves against their own "other," the disreputable *hijra*. The power and promise of being a new transgender woman come into stark relief when contrasted with the figure of the stigmatized, impoverished *hijra*. In drawing this contrast, these trans women voice a "politics of respectability"[102] as they seek to conform to middle-class womanhood. They bolster their symbolic positioning as middle-class women by differentiating themselves from *hijra*s, who cannot (or will not) conform to these class and gender mandates.

This complex picture of trans women as "new" women (and *hijra*s as their "others") will come up throughout the book, though it will be particularly prominent in the next chapter and the book's final chapter. In the middle three chapters of the book, we will explore how understandings of feminine-presenting GNC people as "new" women impact *hijra* groups and the families they create. But for now we will turn to focusing on how trans women talk about their newfound opportunities to work in respectably middle-class office employment. This discourse shows the importance of middle-class office employment for trans women's understanding of themselves as respectable women. We will see that trans women narrate their experiences (and perceptions) of opportunity by drawing on these "new" woman discourses from the colonial, postcolonial, and liberalized eras.

Notes

1. However, they recognize that some trans women are more successful in claiming similarity with respectable cis womanhood, based on how closely their physical traits align with stereotypical notions of femininity (Schilt 2011: 141).
2. This conversation, occurring in a sexual rights NGO, is illustrative of Dutta's point that "even at the moment of protesting against transphobia, a division emerges between the innocent and victimized transgender and unruly trans-people who behave badly in public" (Dutta 2012a: 132).
3. Watson 2008.
4. It is important to note that like other representations of womanhood in India, the "new" woman is implicitly characterized by "normative experiences of Hindu, middle-class upper-caste (and, often, North Indian) women" (Mankekar 1999: 161).
5. Thapar 1993: 82; see also Bhatt, Murty, and Ramamurthy 2010; Rajan 1999.
6. Beliappa 2013: 46.
7. Liddle and Joshi 1986: 71; see also Beliappa 2013.
8. Liddle and Joshi 1986: 72.
9. Thapar 1993: 82.
10. Thapar 1993: 83.
11. Thapar 1993: 83.
12. Thapar 1993: 81.
13. Thapar 1993: 83.
14. Thapar 1993: 83.
15. Liddle and Joshi 1986: 72.
16. Deshpande 2003 cited in Beliappa 2013: 47.
17. Liddle and Joshi 1986: 72.
18. Liddle and Joshi 1986: 108.
19. Liddle and Joshi 1986: 110.
20. As they enter into high-status professions, middle-class working women can become economically independent, offering possibilities to challenge patriarchal power relations within their families. At the same time, the woman's family may "appropriat[e] the social status of the woman's profession"

in order to enhance the class status of the family. Thus, middle-class women's employment is "far from being peripheral or incidental" to the social status of their family and community. In fact, women's employment "holds a central place in the definition of the group's social identity" (Liddle and Joshi 1986: 110).

21. Beliappa 2013: 47.
22. Beliappa 2013: 47–48.
23. Beliappa 2013: 48.
24. Bhatt, Murty, and Ramamurthy 2010: 129.
25. Belliappa 2013: 15.
26. Dickey 2012.
27. Fernandes and Heller 2006: 501.
28. Dickey 2016: 123; see also Bhatt, Murty, and Ramamurthy 2010; Fernandes and Heller 2006.
29. Dickey 2016: 123.
30. Beliappa 2013: 48.
31. Fernandes and Heller 2006: 502.
32. Beliappa 2013: 48.
33. Fernandes 2015; see also Bhatt, Murty, and Ramamurthy 2010.
34. Bhatt, Murty, and Ramamurthy 2010: 135.
35. Fernandes and Heller 2006.
36. Dickey 2012.
37. About 33 percent of women in India are employed; of these women, only a fraction work in the organized sector (Beliappa 2013: 92).
38. Bhat, Murty, and Ramamurthy 2010: 132.
39. Nikore 2019: 1.
40. Beliappa 2013: 61.
41. Beliappa 2013: 80.
42. Oza 2006: 22; see also Rajan 1999.
43. Oza 2006: 29; see also Rajan 1999.
44. Oza 2006; see also Munshi 1998; Ganguly-Scrase and Scrase 2008.
45. Munshi 1998: 39.
46. Oza 2006: 22–24.
47. Oza 2006: 22–24.
48. Oza 2006: 30.
49. Oza 2006: 35.
50. Liddle and Joshi 1986: 108.
51. Liddle and Joshi 1986: 108.
52. Mankekar 1999: 114.

53. Liddle and Joshi 1986: 108.
54. The degree to which families can maintain their women's seclusion is reflected in their social status (Liddle and Joshi 1986: 108). Within high-caste families, men's social position is gleaned partly from the status of women in the family, which means that "the women's respectability determines that of the men [and] the family" (Liddle and Joshi 1986: 110).
55. Oza 2006: 27.
56. Skeggs 2004.
57. Massey 1994; see also Bhatt, Murty, and Ramamurthy 2010.
58. Almeida 2021; *India Today* 2018; Kathuria 2018.
59. Mount 2020.
60. *The Hindu* 2015; *India Today* 2017; Salaria 2017.
61. For similar examples of these processes, see Massey 1994; Bhatt, Murty, and Ramamurthy 2010.
62. *Times of India* 2017.
63. Upadhya 2016: 2.
64. Vijayalakshmi and Raj 2020.
65. Iyengar 2019.
66. Shaw 2012: 45.
67. Bannerjee-Guha 2009: 96.
68. Shaw 2012.
69. Bannerjee-Guha 2009: 95.
70. Nair 2005: 79.
71. Nair 2005.
72. A. Ghosh 2005: 4914.
73. Upadhya 2016: 1.
74. *Times of India* 2017.
75. Ramachandra and Aithal 2016.
76. Shaw 2012: 59.
77. *Times of India* 2017.
78. Vijaykumar 2021: 71.
79. Khubchandani 2020: 12.
80. Upadhya 2016: 2.
81. Upadhya 2016: 2–3.
82. Khubchandani 2020: 164.
83. Films Media Group 2009.
84. Mount 2020.
85. Keshava 2006.

86. Mount 2020
87. Upadhya 2016: 4.
88. Vijaykumar 2021: 72.
89. Vijaykumar 2021: 72.
90. Reuters 2015; see Vijaykumar 2021: 72.
91. Vijaykumar 2021: 72.
92. Reuters 2015.
93. Vijaykumar 2021: 71.
94. Shah 2014: 8; see also Dave 2012.
95. Mount 2020.
96. Mount 2020.
97. Mount 2020.
98. This is partly because sexual rights NGOs often hire visibly GNC people to authenticate themselves as "community"-focused organizations (Mount 2020).
99. Dickey 2012.
100. Rubin et al. 2014: 196.
101. Semmalar 2014: 287.
102. Higginbotham 1994.

2

Sex Work versus Office Work

Gender Nonconforming Identities and Employment

Introduction

One bright, warm afternoon, I sat across the desk from Akrithi, a trans woman in her thirties who has a *guru*[1] and is also an NGO staff member. As sunlight streamed in through her office window behind her, she excitedly related her experience of a recent advocacy project for transgender people. What struck me was how her perception of her abilities and potential shifted as a result of her participation in this kind of activist work:

> I never knew that I would achieve such great success in my leadership.... I have learned a lot, I have learned a lot through all this ... my skills and capacity have gone up. I'm here to prove to any of the society [that is, public] that I can do what you're doing.

From Akrithi's perspective, the skills she developed through her employment at an NGO caused a dramatic shift in how she perceived and understood herself and her place in the world.

Akrithi's employment history also includes sex work. With a note of pride in her voice, she relays how she "got out" of sex work and into office employment at an NGO:

> When I just look back at my way of life, how I came up, from [engaging in] sex work and then joining [an NGO] as a peer educator, field supervisor, then division coordinator, then program manager of the organization,

this shows the levels of growth in my life, that [my position now] is a big achievement.... I have proved what I am.

Akrithi frames her employment history as a linear progression, moving "up" from engaging in sex work at a public park to a career as an office worker in an NGO. Her pride is evident in how, upon becoming an office worker, she steadily climbed the NGO employment ladder to her current position. Tellingly, Akrithi does not simply think of her career trajectory as an alternate source of employment and income compared to sex work; rather, it symbolizes the transformation her life has undergone. According to Akrithi, the changes in her employment have "proved" that she has accomplished something truly remarkable.

I met Akrithi on one of my first days of fieldwork in the summer of 2009 in the NGO office where she worked. By then she had been at the NGO for a few years. My impression of her from that first meeting was of a demure, even shy, feminine-presenting person wearing a bright yellow tunic top with a white scarf draped elegantly over her chest. She seemed hesitant as she spoke quietly to me in English, explaining that she was new to speaking English and that I should approach her with any questions. During my fieldwork, I watched as Akrithi steadily obtained promotions in this NGO, eventually becoming one of the most influential people in the organization. As a result, her public and media profile rose considerably, and by the end of my fieldwork period she became one of the most well-known trans people and social justice activists in the region.

As she took on increased responsibility, Akrithi became involved with transgender rights initiatives at the local, state, and national government. I remember the excitement she expressed about her first ever trip to Delhi. She proudly showed me pictures of herself dressed in a bright red and pink *sari* as she stood in front of several monuments and government buildings. I often heard her relay how she was invited to the swearing-in ceremony for the president of India, and since my fieldwork ended, I have seen several pictures posted online of her with government officials from India and other countries—including the president of Korea. These interactions with state officials have made a tremendous impact on both the way she perceives her capabilities and herself as a human being:

From ministers [of parliament] to other department chairpersons to the Chief Minister [of the state of Karnataka], to the Chief Justice [of

Karnataka], I have contacts.... What I thought eight years ago [that is, when I was a sex worker] was I'm unfit to be a human being in this world. *I'm unfit to be a citizen of this nation.* But after meeting such high-level people, I came to know that I am able to be here, I can prove what I am. (Emphasis original)

Akrithi's sense of self-worth is deeply entrenched in her employment. She considered herself contemptible when employed as a sex worker, but her ability to penetrate hierarchies of social and political authority has led to a sense of self-validation as both a human being and a citizen.

As Akrithi's story indicates, office employment (often in NGOs and sometimes in multinational companies) has had an important impact on the experiences of a small group of GNC people in India. Of course, NGOs are not able to hire all (or even a majority) of GNC people in India, so these employment options are available to only a select few. However, these trans women are highly visible in various kinds of media, and they use these opportunities to educate the general public about themselves through identity work.[2] While these opportunities directly impact only a small group of trans women, the media image of trans women's enhanced opportunities for livelihood, education, living conditions, and so on, is quickly reshaping public understandings of trans women in India.

In this chapter, I focus on the connection between transgender identities and office employment, which reveals the intersection of gender and class projects in the lives of trans women and (by contrast) *hijras*. I begin by exploring how gender and class intersect in the context of the postcolonial history of (cisgender) women and employment in India, which is essential to understanding how office employment became associated with middle-class womanhood. In contrast to soliciting money and sex work engaged in by *hijras*, respectable office employment is constructed in state discourse as "empowering" and enabling "independence" for middle-class women and is also recognized as an important marker of urban middle-class femininity.[3] I argue that the perception of possibilities for GNC people to obtain "respectable" office employment paves the way for working-class transgender women to imagine fulfilling their middle-class aspirations while also confirming the propriety of their gender identities. But these possibilities are not open to all GNC people—*hijras* are excluded and generational differences among trans women also complicate the story.

(Cis) Women's "Empowerment through Employment"
for GNC People

There is a widespread conception in India today that while *hijra*s are confined to stigmatizing jobs like sex work and soliciting money, trans women have enhanced employment options that include respectable office work. To understand this emphasis on trans women's access to office employment, we need to explore the history of employment for cisgender women in India and the postcolonial emphasis on cis women's "empowerment through employment."

"Empowerment" is a key concept that drives advocacy in the development sector, particularly in the NGO sphere. Empowerment refers to processes wherein people who were denied "the ability to make choices" gain this ability.[4] Notions of empowerment focus on inequalities that impact people's ability to make choices.[5] Development scholars and practitioners place particular emphasis on the empowerment of cisgender women, whose ability to make choices is often constrained, especially "strategic life choices" like the "choice of livelihood."[6]

In India, the ability of cisgender women to engage in paid employment has often been tied to issues surrounding respectability.[7] During the nineteenth century, women's employment was only acceptable for poor women and widows participating in manual and household labor for wealthy people and upper-class women engaged in high-status professions. The public had few qualms about impoverished women in the labor force because of their obvious economic needs, while upper-class working women were understood as fulfilling their "moral obligation" to the public.[8] For women who fell between the categories of poor and elite, any engagement in the workforce signaled a loss of respect for the women and a loss of status for their families.[9]

After India gained independence, cisgender women were expected to participate in developing the new nation through their paid labor, and since then women's "empowerment through employment" has been a key goal of the postcolonial state.[10] Today, middle-class people are expected to encourage the cis women in their families to participate in the public sphere and offer them the option of pursuing careers.[11] Young middle-class cis women position employment as "a road to independence," sometimes rejecting the idea that women work out of financial necessity.[12] These cis women emphasize the potent meanings that work holds for them, like the "confidence" they feel from working and how they equate paid employment with autonomy.[13] Women's white-collar employment has become an important marker of middle-class femininity, especially in urban areas.[14]

NGOs advocating for the rights of GNC people and sexual minorities also participate in the "empowerment" mandate by offering respectable employment to GNC people and sexual minorities who would otherwise struggle to support themselves. Research about HIV/AIDS outreach indicates that people from the affected group are best suited to encourage their peers to make the behavioral changes that could protect them from infection.[15] NGOs thus increasingly hire people from the groups thought to be most "at risk" of HIV/AIDS transmission, like feminine-presenting GNC people. Equally important is authenticating the NGO as a trustworthy organization that serves the community. This too drives sexual rights NGOs to hire "community people"—in this case, GNC people and sexual minorities—to represent the NGO to funding organizations and the public. And then there are their underemployed constituents, who increasingly expect NGOs to offer them respectable office employment.[16] All of these factors contribute to NGOs offering office employment options to GNC people.

However, critics of NGOs point out that the benefits of NGO employment are not equally available for all GNC groups. Specifically, they emphasize that primarily dominant-caste and middle-class people and sexual minorities are employed in higher-level NGO positions with high salaries and the opportunity to participate in international conferences. One reason driving this distinction is because fluency in English is required for high-level positions, and working-class and marginalized-caste people often do not have access to an English-medium education.[17] Thus, the supposed opportunities offered to GNC people through NGO employment are not equally available to everyone.

Nevertheless, the public perception of GNC people is that they have opportunities to pursue an education and a career outside of soliciting money or sex work. It certainly is the case that some "mainstream" multinational companies in large Indian cities present themselves as LGBTQ+-friendly workplaces. A few local companies in Bangalore have also claimed inclusivity for LGBTQ+ employees, in addition to the employment opportunities at NGOs. Thus, it would appear that being a GNC person alone would not necessarily block someone from working at such companies, though there are very few cases of openly GNC people working at these companies. But in reality matters are more complicated, pointing to a complex interplay of class, gender identity, and (to a degree) age as driving employment opportunities and how people understand these opportunities.

Office Employment and Contemporary Womanhood:
Trans Women's Middle-class Aspirations

Trans women's social class aspirations are reflected in how they describe themselves and their gender identities. This is not particularly surprising since gender ideals serve as markers of social class. In India, the opportunity to work in an office is constructed as an "empowering" way that middle-class women exercise independence.[18] Thus, working in an office is a way that working-class feminine-presenting GNC people can identify themselves as middle-class (aspiring) women.

Research has shown that the social environment of NGOs impacts how transgender (and cisgender) women NGO workers discuss their identities. Working in NGOs allows transgender women to "inhabit gendered respectability"[19] in ways that are not available to sex workers or people soliciting money—occupations associated with *hijras*. In the NGO environment, trans women learn to emulate "respectable embodiment" by dressing modestly and speaking softly,[20] attributes generally associated with middle-class femininity. The respect this confers on trans women NGO workers allows them to successfully navigate the public sphere by "blending in"[21] with other middle-class (aspiring) women—the opposite of how *hijras* present themselves when soliciting for money or sex. Office employment also offers trans women the ability to control their income, which was not traditionally the case for GNC people living in *hijra* families.

The trans women I spoke with implicitly compared the status their newfound employment opportunities conferred on them to occupations associated with *hijras*. Sex work and soliciting money are undesirable forms of employment for the majority of the *hijras* and trans women I spoke with because of the stigma associated with them. Since *hijras* are denied entry into dignified professions, for GNC people and trans women seeking alternate employment, an important consideration is whether their work is considered "dignified."

In the words of Suma, a trans woman in her early thirties, "everyone has to work, but dignity is very important. Begging and sex work are not bringing you any dignity." Girish, a GNC queer feminist activist, similarly observed that when "all [is] said and done, there is a certain *dignity* to walking into office in the morning for a trans woman and sitting in an office space and, you know, doing some paperwork" (emphasis original). Both argued that the more trans women obtain jobs outside of sex work and soliciting money, the less GNC people will be associated with stigmatized employment. These shifts in employment opportunities are especially important when considering how one's birth family will react upon realizing that their child is GNC. As Suma pointed out,

> if a family comes to know [their child is] a trans woman, they might feel bad, [as] ultimately their idea is that one day my son is going to be a beggar or one day, my son is going to be a sex worker. How can a parent accept it? But if they think, "OK, you are a trans woman, but still if you're working with dignity, if you're working in a mainstream job, that is different." The *feeling* is different.

These working-class trans women's desires for respectable employment are also connected to their social class aspirations, which mediate how trans women describe themselves. The opportunity to work in an office, which is constructed as "empowering" for middle-class women, opens up possibilities for working-class feminine-presenting GNC people to identify as middle-class women. When trans women discuss their employment options, they draw from discourses promoting women's independence and from popular rhetoric connecting office employment to the middle classes. Manisha, a transgender woman in her fifties, mentioned that as a teenager when she joined the *hijra*s, she refused to do sex work. Even today, she explained that she does not want to engage in sex work. "I want to work in a *nice* job. I want to work how *all* the ladies are working. Ladies and gents [that is, men and women], all are working now, right? Like that, I want to work in the world. [And with] that money only, I want to live." In expressing her desire to support herself through middle-class office employment, Manisha draws on notions of women's independence, autonomy, and empowerment through paid (office) employment.

Many trans women I spoke with emphasized their desire to engage in jobs that "normal" women undertake. Kanika, a trans woman in her forties who once identified as a *hijra*, remarked that she does not like sex work and that this was her least favorite aspect of being part of a *hijra* family. She earnestly explained, "I want to be like *normal* girls, study and get a job, like *normal*

girls," referring to the options available to "normal" educated, middle-
(and elite-) class girls. Kanika was at pains to align herself with respectable
middle-class femininity during our conversations, assuring me that she
is a very "peaceful" person who "doesn't like to get into any conflicts." She
contrasted these qualities to those displayed by *hijras*, who, she explained,
"have to be rude, rough, it's like that." During the ten years that she was part
of *hijra* groups, she was "not comfortable with those people" because she
viewed herself as "totally feminine." She explained, "I always wanted to be a
girl from the time I was very young, *that's it*," widening her eyes in an attempt
to highlight her difference from *hijras*.

Working-class trans women's desires for "respectable" employment are
connected to a desire to demonstrate appropriate (middle-class) femininity
through their paid work. Like many working-class people in urban India,
most of the trans women I met aspire to join the ranks of the middle class.
Employment is an important marker of class identity among those aspiring
to become middle class, and working-class trans women demonstrate their
middle-class aspiring identities by emulating characteristics associated with
cisgender women in the middle classes.

Akrithi's Shifting Class–Gender Identities

I observed more and more GNC people identifying themselves with the
transgender category throughout my years of fieldwork. This was partly
related to the global media attention given to transgender issues in the 2010s
mentioned in the Introduction. In addition, the language of transgender was
in wide circulation through NGOs and sexual health programs. But I also
observed a correlation between the amount of time GNC people were engaged
in office employment and whether they took on a transgender identity. This
correlation is best exemplified by returning to the story of Akrithi.

During the time I knew her, Akrithi's identity underwent important
changes that were related to her changing class status as a result of her
employment at an NGO. When we met, Akrithi identified herself as a *kothi*,
a working-class sexual minority identity. The term *kothi* denotes a "male-
born" person "with feminine characteristics" who is attracted to people "with
masculine characteristics." Akrithi also clearly articulated her working-class
background by her consumption habits. For example, one day she asked me
where I got my tunic top (*kurta*) from. I replied that I bought it at FabIndia,

a popular middle-class store.[22] She clicked her tongue and remarked, "Expensive!"

However, in later years I regularly saw her wearing FabIndia clothing that was far more decorative, fancier, and (presumably) more expensive than mine. She also mentioned shopping there in conversation with me and others on multiple occasions. Akrithi's perceptions about which kind of clothing is expensive changed over the period of time I knew her, likely propelled by a rise in her salary as she climbed the employment ladder at the NGO where she worked. Consumption habits are one way that the heterogeneous groups of "new" middle-class Indians differentiate themselves from lower classes and from members of different strata within the middle-class.[23] Akrithi's clothing choices—enabled by her increasing financial independence—helped drive her increasing identification as middle class.

A few years into my fieldwork, Akrithi began identifying herself as transgender while still retaining her *kothi* identity. This shift in her identity coincided with the current NGO discourse around *kothi*s as a subset of people falling under the transgender "umbrella." Akrithi also began to make statements suggesting that she no longer identified herself as working class (for example, sternly warning me to "take care of your things" at a community event since the majority of people there will be "from the working classes"). She also began to differentiate herself from lower-tier staff members whom she would often point out are "from the working-class sections of society." This was especially the case when anything would go missing in the office where she worked.

In the last stages of my fieldwork, Akrithi stopped altogether identifying herself as a working-class *kothi* and began instead to introduce herself as a transgender woman (and then later simply as a woman). The changes that I witnessed in Akrithi's identification illustrate how her evolution into a higher-class status was accompanied by her evolving gender identity. Akrithi's NGO employment enabled her upward class mobility, which allowed her to disassociate from her former working-class status. Her rising class status also impacted Akrithi's ability to see herself as a middle-class trans woman.

Does Transgender Have a Class Identity?

Like Akrithi, the trans women I spoke with were keen to position themselves in proximity to middle-class respectable womanhood. As I witnessed people identifying as transgender, I wondered what this increased identification with transgender identities meant for other GNC categories, especially *hijra*. Scholars have begun to emphasize processes in which "certain transgender bodies are valued, counted, [and] recognized ... while others are marginalized, rendered abject, [and] excluded."[24] As they differentiate themselves from the maligned category of *hijras*, these trans women employ the transgender category to mark themselves as closely aligned with and aspiring to middle-class womanhood.

Other scholars working with GNC groups in the Global South have also observed this phenomenon. In the Philippines, transgender women are incorporated into global labor markets when "their gender expressions (appearance, conduct and dress) remain within certain limits deemed respectable."[25] These processes of becoming "respectable" implicitly privilege middle-class markers like education, fluency in English, and upward mobility, and position other GNC people as less respectable.[26] Feminine-presenting GNC *waria* in Indonesia claim transgender identities to signify their "productivity, [and] normative middle-class aspirations," implying that *waria* are marginalized, abject subjects.[27] In Brazil, working-class, feminine-presenting GNC *travesti* find themselves pressured to claim respectably "anglophone" and middle-class transgender identities, rendering the *travesti* who are not members of the "palatable" middle-class category of transgender "illegitimate and undesirable" in comparison.[28] These studies show that transgender is becoming connected to a kind of middle-class-ness (and respectability) in countries of the Global South, while other GNC categories are becoming more marginalized. My ethnographic data from India suggests that transgender is similarly connected to the middle-class respectability sought by some trans women, while the category of *hijra* is connected to backwardness, poverty, and stigma.

Hijras' Limited Employment Options

As a socially marginalized[29] and economically disempowered group, *hijras* often face employment discrimination. This discrimination has historically blocked them from entering occupations other than soliciting money and sex work,[30] which as stigmatized forms of employment merely reinforce the negative stereotypes of the people who engage in them. Employment status is therefore an important factor distinguishing "respectable" trans women from *hijra*s, especially given the growing perception that trans women have increased opportunities to pursue respectable middle-class employment while *hijra*s remain confined to working-class and stigmatizing occupations.

Throughout India, *hijra*s are highly visible when soliciting money (often in large groups).[31] In big cities like Bangalore, *hijra*s can be seen moving from store to store in commercial areas as they request money from the shopkeepers or at busy traffic intersections where they walk among the waiting vehicles soliciting funds. *Hijra*s are also quite visible on trains throughout India requesting money[32]—an intricate exchange that requires the asking *hijra* to carefully balance aspects of "coercion, placation [and] humor."[33]

However, people who engage in the kind of work *hijra*s typically do are vulnerable to state violence and incarceration. Several anti-"beggary" laws have been passed in metropolitan areas of India[34] that explicitly prohibit soliciting money in public—including informal street-based work engaged in by poor people, such as "singing, dancing, fortune telling, performing tricks, or selling articles."[35] In 1975, Karnataka state passed its own Prohibition of Beggary Act that "prohibit[s] persons from resorting to begging and to provide for the detention, training and employment of beggars, for the custody, trial and punishment of beggar offenders and for the relief and rehabilitation of such persons in the State of Karnataka."[36] In fact, *hijra*s do not even need to be publicly soliciting money to be targeted.[37] There are reports of police entering *hijra*s' homes and arresting them.[38] In several cases, *hijra*s called fellow *hijra*s to the police station for help, only for them to also be arrested and detained.[39] As the advocacy group Orinam has argued, "Clearly the objective of the police was not merely to pick up those who were begging, but in effect all persons who answered to the description of being *hijra*."[40]

I saw firsthand the law in action one day at the beginning of my fieldwork. I was in an NGO office on the outskirts of the city, chatting with a *hijra* in her twenties named Abhilasha. Her wide eyes were accented with carefully applied makeup and she was dressed in a light blue blouse with a decorative border and matching skirt. After asking questions about what I was doing in India and what my life was like in the United States, she stood up and asked if I would come with her and Varun, a *kothi* staff member in their twenties, to a police station. She explained they had confiscated her phone the night before and she had to get it back from them.

We left the building and Varun hailed an autorickshaw, and soon thereafter we found ourselves traveling on a large highway. I had assumed we were going back to the city, but as the air became clearer and we passed fewer and fewer buildings, I realized we were headed in the opposite direction. After some time, we stopped in front of a large gate with high cement walls on either side. A guard dressed in a navy security suit standing outside observed us curiously. When Varun explained why we were here, the guard opened the creaky gate door to reveal a lush, green area with lots of large trees. As we walked up a small hill toward a group of buildings, I remarked that I had never seen a police station like this before. Varun then explained that this was a Beggar's Colony run by the state of Karnataka to "rehabilitate beggars" by teaching them skills so they have other ways of earning income.

As we walked, Abhilasha remarked that the police are required to pick up a certain number of people to bring them here. Varun nodded, explaining that police often go around picking up anyone on the street who "looks" poor to fill their quotas.[41] And indeed, the Karnataka State Prohibition of Beggary Act defines a beggar in part as "having no visible means of subsistence" and who "wanders about or remains in any public place in such condition or manner as makes it likely that he [sic] exists by soliciting or receiving alms...."[42]

As we continued up the small hill, I could not help but remark that the setting was beautiful. Abhilasha shook her head and set me straight: "First thing, you can't leave, you're stuck there." Varun added that people usually do not know how long they will be forced to stay there. And then there were the meals. "You don't get enough food, so some people try to steal your rations," Abhilasha remarked. And indeed the facility has repeatedly come under scrutiny. In the early 2010s, volunteers affiliated with religious organizations reported overcrowded facilities and malnutrition among inmates, while news reports noted that 2,500 people were housed in a facility intended for only 750.[43] In one eight-month period in 2010, at least 286 inmates passed away under "mysterious circumstances,"[44] with the dead not being removed from the dormitories for two or three days.[45] In 2015, the High Court of Karnataka tried three officers who managed the Beggar's Colony for "causing death by negligence."[46]

As the courtyard came into view, we could see a stage set up and some sort of meeting going on. In the audience area were probably 100–150 very thin women in plain blue saris sitting on the floor ("the beggars" Abhilasha whispered), while on stage were eight women sitting in chairs dressed in stylish, colorful, and distinctly middle-class clothing. Abhilasha said they were having a meeting where the staff would aggressively scream at the women, demanding, "Why were you begging?!"

Abhilasha, Varun, and I went around to the back of the courtyard area and walked over to a group of people dressed in staff uniforms. Varun asked them where the head office was, and they pointed to a nearby building. As we walked over there to finally retrieve her phone, Abhilasha fell behind to flirt with one of the staff members. As I watched, Abhilasha smiled as she entered her phone number into his mobile. When Abhilasha returned, I looked quizzically at her, and she whispered that maybe he would contact her for sex work. The irony was not lost on me: Abhilasha was placed in this facility for looking poor while conducting street-based sex work, yet she also solicited customers among the staff while we were inside the facility.

Ethnographic research shows that *hijra*s have engaged in sex work for at least the past 30 years.[47] While the association between *hijra*s and sex work may have been less obvious in the past, today it is more explicit, in part due to sexual health research collected and disseminated through NGO-led HIV/AIDS outreach projects. Indeed, I often heard that sexual rights NGOs are accused of spreading information linking *hijra*s to sex work through HIV/AIDS interventions. As a result of NGO outreach in South India combined with *hijra*s' lack of employment options, the *hijra* category is often exclusively associated with sex work.[48]

Many *hijra*s express frustration that sex work and soliciting money are their only means of employment. Some even stated that they should not have become *hijra*s, which they believe effectively foreclosed other avenues of employment. During my fieldwork, I heard many people lament the person they could have become if only they had not joined the *hijra*s. Their regrets are best expressed by Johan, a trans activist in their fifties who has heard many *hijra* friends express regret that they joined the community because of the lack of a comfortable daily routine and the fear and violence associated with unregulated sex work. As Johan related,

sex work is not easy; it's quite difficult and it takes so much of your energy, so much of your time. And your whole life cycle changes and then you're not comfortable with that change.... Where you used to sleep for eight hours in the night, now you are not able to sleep [because you are working]. And you can't sleep in the day also because other people are [living] with you, right? And they will be going for day work, for begging in the morning. So you can't be sleeping.... And then, you go for sex work, and there is so much harassment, there is so much violence, there is so much fear [while] standing on that spot. The first fear is whether I'm going to earn the money that I require. The second thing is how long am I going to stand here and how many people am I vulnerable to?

The risks associated with sex work coupled with the difficulty in establishing a comfortable daily routine are understandably frustrating.

However, I also heard of *hijra*s who prefer sex work to other more "respectable" forms of employment. Monika, a trans woman radio personality in her thirties, remarked that for most of the *hijra*s she knows,

> [t]hey are simply OK with sex work. And they are OK with the abuse [sex workers are subjected to] because their defense [in favor of sex work] is that, even if you go to work [that is, office employment], you get paid much less [per hour] than you would from sex work. On top of that, you would have to work some ten hours, twelve hours under bosses who are often lusting after trans women. So sexual abuse often also has the possibility of occurring within employment [other than sex work].

For Monika's *hijra* friends, the benefits of respectable employment do not outweigh its drawbacks. While they acknowledge that they face the threat of violence while engaging in sex work, they point out that GNC people working in more respectable forms of employment are paid less while also being vulnerable to sexual harassment and abuse. In addition, these *hijra*s appreciate the degree of autonomy that sex work offers. Monika posited that her *hijra* friends "don't want to be working as slaves because ... they see sex work as free work. And they see this kind of [office] work as slavery. I mean, having to go to work at specific times and listening to crap [from their supervisors], you know? Which is true!" At least for some *hijra*s, sex work offers them control over their working hours that they do not think is available to office workers.

Media Accounts of Trans Women's Newfound Opportunities: Available for All?

In contrast to the lack of employment options for *hijra*s, news reports increasingly portray transgender women as having multiple avenues for work and possessing the ability to pursue many different types of employment that were unavailable to trans women in the past. As I examined media reports about trans women in the past several decades, I noticed that the breadth and tenor of this coverage has shifted over time. In the late 2000s and early 2010s, there were limited reports of a few trans women hired in "mainstream" middle-class occupations such as talkshow host,[49] radio disc jockey,[50] and newsperson.[51] These first reports appeared in news outlets such as an ILGA[52] report that would reach a relatively limited readership likely comprised of people already interested in trans issues. But by the mid-2010s, the number of these stories had increased significantly and they began to appear in more mainstream media sources such as the newspapers *The Hindu* and *India Today* with a much wider readership. Many of these stories refer to the transgender women featured as the "firsts in their field"[53] in India: the first transgender pastor,[54] news anchor,[55] college principal,[56] police officer,[57] legal assistant to the Delhi High Court,[58] even judge of the People's Court.[59]

These reports align trans women with newfound employment opportunities, promise, and social progress, framing trans women as "transgender icons"[60] who are "trailblazers in their fields."[61] They often read like "rags to riches" stories of heroic outcasts who eventually triumph in their professions, encapsulated in titles like "How a Homeless Graduate Became Andhra Govt's First Transgender Employee."[62] But the language of "firsts" also paints an optimistic picture of the opportunities available to transgender women, suggesting that other trans women will soon follow in their footsteps.[63] Notably, the portrayal of trans women's opportunities stands in stark contrast to the reporting on *hijras*, who are confined both in reality and in print to the stigmatizing occupations of soliciting money and sex work.

This kind of media coverage of trans women's enhanced employment opportunities has impacted how both GNC people and the general public think about trans women. Deepa, the trans woman in her thirties who characterized trans women as "modern girls" in the Introduction, excitedly recounted how trans people now have more employment options: "Lots of trans people are working in NGOs and in multinational companies like Google and Facebook. They're not limited to begging and sex work." Monika, who spoke earlier about her *hijra* friends who prefer sex work over office work, explained how the employment conditions have changed for trans women:

I don't want to say [there is] no discrimination [toward GNC people]. I would say a much-reduced level of discrimination. Now if a trans person wants to get into a corporate job, like an MNC [multinational company] job or even a regular job, if they're well qualified and if they present themselves in a good way, they won't face that much of an insult. Many of them get employed.

According to many of the trans women I spoke to, GNC people who are qualified for middle-class employment options are increasingly less likely to be excluded from workplaces on the basis of their gender nonconformity. However, for GNC people marginalized by their class background, "mainstream" jobs (that is, outside of working in NGOs) are often out of reach, since these kinds of jobs require a skill set and an educational background that are not generally available to working-class people. Monika conceded that the majority of GNC people "are not educated and don't dress nicely," which makes them less desirable candidates in occupations that employ middle- (and upper-middle) class people.

Johan pointed out that access to resources often determines which GNC people join the *hijras* and which GNC people live "independent" of *hijras*:

If you look at maybe the more educated [people], the more independent, financially independent especially, they don't become part of the *hijra* system, right? They become transgender or they take identities as women or whatever they feel like. But they don't need to follow this system because they don't depend upon the income generation that exists within this system.

Deepa also links joining the *hijras* to whether or not a GNC person has access to resources like education:

There is a large group who want to call themselves *hijras* because then, they can have a source of income. They want to be *chelas* in the *hammams* for sex work and begging. See, because there is no other way for them to get income, they want to be *chelas* in the *hammams*. A lot of illiterate people attempt to do that. Not the educated ones because they have a broad community to work for [through NGOs, and so on], you can work for the broad community. But illiterate people can't.

While the majority of trans women that I interacted with hail from working-class backgrounds, Johan and Deepa allude to differences in the education levels and degree of financial security among working-class people. For many of them, access to these resources determines whether or not they are able to live "independently" of the *hijra* system. Those with limited resources would need to earn money immediately, leading them to probably join the *hijras*.

"This [Opportunity] Was Not There": Age and Trans Women's Perception of Opportunity

Another important factor that determines whether GNC people see themselves as having enhanced employment options is age. I found that age is the most important factor determining whether GNC people consider that they have enhanced employment options. Older GNC people do not often say that their choices have increased in the past decades; instead, they say that younger GNC people have options that they do not.

This distinction was reflected in a conversation I had with Kanika, a trans woman in her late forties who was part of a *hijra* group for over 10 years. Kanika is the person who said she felt uncomfortable around *hijras* due to their aggressive behaviors, which clashed with her "totally feminine" behaviors. That day, she was showing me a social media page where there had been a recent discussion about an activist project I was inquiring about. Then Kanika smiled and asked if I had seen the pictures from the "Bangkok trip" that several Bangalore trans women activists had recently taken to attend a conference on transgender rights and activism in Asia. Without waiting for an answer, she eagerly clicked over to one of the conference attendees' social media pages and quickly navigated to the set of pictures they had posted from the trip. As she was talking, Kanika showed me 15 or so pictures of five to six 20-something trans women from Bangalore dressed in elegant saris and wearing elaborate makeup. The backdrop of the photos was a large marble staircase in the elaborately decorated interior of what appeared to be a very fancy hotel in Bangkok with the women standing regally or laying in model-like poses as they smiled coyly at the camera.

During this exchange, I was intrigued by how Kanika explained this trip as an opportunity reserved for younger trans women. She mentioned several times what an exciting opportunity this trip was for the "new generation" of trans women who were able to travel "outside India" to a place like Bangkok and meet activists from other parts of the world. Wistfully, Kanika said she would have loved the opportunity to attend these kinds of events. But shaking her head, she explained, "When I was growing up, this [opportunity] was not there." As she continued to click through the photos a second time, Kanika remarked again how fortunate the "new generation" of trans women was to have access to such opportunities, implicitly suggesting that such opportunities are for the young generation of GNC people and not middle-aged (or older) trans women like herself. She again shook her head as she stared at the images, repeating, "When I was growing up, this [opportunity] was not there. It was not there."

Kanika spent her youth in a coastal village where she endured merciless harassment and abuse by family members, schoolmates, community members, and co-workers. She was only able to complete up to 10th standard (a grade in high school) due to bullying from her classmates. After experiencing similar levels of harassment and abuse in the working-class jobs (like mining) that she took there, Kanika decided to leave her village and her family. When she came to Bangalore, she struggled to find sustainable employment and social support in the city. "There was not much awareness [about gender nonconformity] at that time," she remarked. "NGOs were not there, nobody supported you." Kanika found herself subjected to similar kinds of abuse that she suffered at the hands of her family and community members in the village. After speaking to a friend who was planning to move to Mumbai and join the *hijras*, Kanika decided to join her and then lived with her *hijra* family for about 10 years.

After leaving her *hijra* family and returning to Bangalore, Kanika used the money she earned from sex work to enroll in computer classes, earning an advanced diploma in multimedia. Armed with her degree, Kanika "tried to get a job in many places. I tried my *level best* to get a job," but no one wanted to hire a GNC person. Even though "sex work is not my thing," Kanika was forced to sustain herself through such work. After many years, she was finally able to get a work-from-home job doing freelance graphic design through a friend at a multinational company. She enjoyed working using her design skills, but shortly after her boss found out that she was GNC, Kanika was fired. Reluctant to return to sex work but with "no job, no nothing!," Kanika struggled to pay her rent. Fortunately, she soon learned about an NGO that was looking to hire GNC people. She felt incredibly lucky to receive an office job there, where she had been working for several years at the time of our conversation.

When Kanika was growing up, widespread discrimination and abuse of GNC people constrained the decisions she could make about the course of her life. But when she sees the kinds of opportunities available to younger

GNC people today, she cannot help but compare their opportunities to the situation she faced as a young GNC person. While she considers herself fortunate to work in an office, she also perceives that some opportunities seem to be reserved for the "new generation" of younger trans women. When confronted with the kinds of opportunities that are now available for younger GNC people, Kanika voiced complicated emotions, but the one that stuck out to me the most was something almost like regret—not that she had done something wrong in the past, but rather that she came of age as a GNC person in the wrong era.

Conclusion

In India today, gender intersects with class in ways that increasingly align transgender womanhood with middle-class-ness. This intersection of class and gender occurs against a postcolonial backdrop that emphasized cisgender women's "empowerment through employment" that opened up middle-class employment opportunities, enabling "independence" for middle-class cis women. GNC people's newfound access to respectable, middle-class office employment follows a similar path, and the rhetoric of empowerment used to narrate cis women's shifting access to opportunity shapes how trans women perceive and represent their struggles. The opportunity to engage in office employment combined with the ability to identify as transgender are key factors enabling trans women to align themselves with respectable middle-class womanhood. Employment is also a key characteristic that trans women draw on to distinguish themselves from *hijras*.

This research emphasizes that class aspirations are inseparable from and also supportive of gendered subjectivities.[64] Trans women's identity claims are part of a symbolic class project. In their pursuit of respect and opportunity, the trans women I interacted with align themselves with respectable middle-class womanhood as they pursue entry into middle-class employment. Middle-class markers like office employment enable trans women to access respectable ways of being women while also providing the kind of economic stability, upward mobility, and independence that they do not think are possible for *hijras*. For trans women, claiming transgender identities is about symbolically positioning themselves in proximity to middle-class women who are deserving of the kind of respect trans women seek. Thus, class aspirations are inextricably connected to trans women's desires to more fully be women and to do this in ways that are respectable.

These newfound opportunities available to some transgender women who move into office employment may appear to represent positive, progressive social change. However, I argue that within the GNC community there is ambivalence about this because not all GNC people can take advantage of these opportunities and thus fulfill the standards associated with middle-class womanhood. On the one hand, generational differences mediate whether trans women believe they can take full advantage of these opportunities. But even more pronounced is that the same narrative valorizing this pathway to respectability and upward mobility also reinforces the stigmatization of GNC people who cannot (or do not want to) access this path. *Hijras* face employment discrimination that confines them to the disreputable and unsustainable occupations of sex work and soliciting money,[65] and partly as a result of their employment, *hijra* identities are stigmatized and tainted with a pronounced lack of respect. It is this lack of respect that trans women hope to sidestep by emphasizing their difference from *hijras*, which we will hear more about in the Conclusion. In the next chapter, we will consider how the new possibilities for younger GNC people to live independently impact *hijra* groups and the families they create.

Notes

1. In *hijra* families, a *guru* is a parent figure who is also the head of the household (Nanda 1990; Reddy 2005; Saria 2021).
2. Snow 2001.
3. Waldrop 2012.
4. Kabeer 1999: 13.
5. Kabeer 1999.
6. Kabeer 1999: 437.
7. Misra 2006.
8. Ganguly-Scrase and Scrase 2008: 81.
9. Ganguly-Scrase and Scrase 2008: 81.
10. Ganguly-Scrase and Scrase 2008: 81.
11. Ganguly-Scrase and Scrase 2008: 82.
12. Ganguly-Scrase and Scrase 2008: 89; see also Vijaykumar 2013 and Radhakrishnan 2008.

13. Ganguly-Scrase and Scrase 2008: 82, 91.

14. Waldrop 2012: 166.

15. UNAIDS 1999.

16. While NGO employment can be lucrative for educated English speakers, the majority of NGO staff members are fieldworkers from the working classes, whose work is poorly compensated and precarious (Bano 2012; Abdelrahman 2007; Ahmad 2002). Despite this, NGO employment offers a degree of respect often denied to GNC people; thus, NGO work is desirable.

17. Ahmad 2002: 3.

18. Ganguly-Scrase and Scrase 2008; see also Vijaykumar 2013 and Radhakrishnan 2008.

19. Vijaykumar 2021: 88.

20. Vijaykumar 2021: 95.

21. Vijaykumar 2021: 95.

22. Srila Roy (2022), in conversation with Sarhar Romani's (2016) work, has deftly analyzed the role of FabIndia clothing among Indian feminist activists in Kolkata. Roy points out wearing the ethnic cotton styles associated with FabIndia "became a shorthand for denoting choice in values, and not merely dress and style," especially among dominant-caste and middle-class feminist and queer activists (2022: 92). Romani suggests that this manner of dress "serves to conceal any wealth," while simultaneously "reveal[ing] wealth, class and, most importantly, respectability" (2016: 373). Indeed, FabIndia clothing serves to signify one's "political belonging" with progressive feminist activists and NGO workers "whose political ideologies and beliefs were [thought to be] legible simply by virtue of their taste in clothes" (Roy Romani 2022: 93). As a researcher trying to gain the trust of and "fit in" (Roy 2022: 93) with a similar NGO and activist crowd in Bangalore, my own clothing choices were unquestionably impacted by this dynamic.

23. Fernandes 2015: 235.

24. Kunzel 2014: 287; see also Haritaworn 2015.

25. David 2015: 189.

26. David 2015: 189.

27. Hegarty 2017: 91.

28. Jarrin 2016: 367, 369.

29. Cohen 1995: 25.

30. In some parts of North India, *hijra*s earn respect for their supposed asexuality. Some of these groups can expect to earn considerable sums of money by performing at special functions such as festivals, weddings, births,

and other important occasions. This option is less available to *hijra* groups
in South India, who tend to be confined to earning an income through
soliciting money and sex work.

31. Puri 2015.
32. Saria 2019, 2021.
33. Saria 2019: 148.
34. Ramanathan 2008: 33.
35. Karnataka Prohibition of Beggary Act 1975: 4.
36. Karnataka Prohibition of Beggary Act 1975: 4.
37. The Transgender Persons (Protection of Rights) Bill 2016: Responses From
    the Trans & Intersex Communities.
38. The Transgender Persons (Protection of Rights) Bill 2016: Responses From
    the Trans & Intersex Communities.
39. The Transgender Persons (Protection of Rights) Bill 2016: Responses From
    the Trans & Intersex Communities.
40. The Transgender Persons (Protection of Rights) Bill 2016: Responses From
    the Trans & Intersex Communities.
41. Ramanathan 2008: 33.
42. Karnataka Prohibition of Beggary Act 1975: 4.
43. UCA News 2010.
44. Long 2014; see also Yasmeen 2010.
45. S. Prasad 2015.
46. S. Prasad 2015.
47. Nanda 1990; Reddy 2005.
48. *Hijras* have been associated with nonnormative gender and sexual practices
    since at least the colonial era. As a result, British rulers characterized *hijras*
    as "agents of sexual contagion," believing that *hijras* represented "persons
    who physically infected others with the 'disease' of 'unnatural' sexual
    behavior" (Hinchy 2014: 281). As a result, *hijras* have been subjected to state-
    sponsored curtailments of their rights. *Hijras* were classified as a "criminal
    tribe" by their nature, and positioned as in need of surveillance to protect
    the masculine public space they threatened with their feminine dress and
    performance style (Reddy 2005: 26; see also Puri 2016; Narrain 2013).
49. Nolen 2009.
50. Christy 2011.
51. ILGA 2012.
52. ILGA, once the International Lesbian and Gay Association, is now known as
    the International Lesbian, Gay, Bisexual, Trans and Intersex Association.

53. *India Today* 2018.

54. UCA News 2013.

55. Qureshi 2014.

56. *The Hindu* 2015.

57. *India Today* 2017.

58. Salaria 2017.

59. Acharya 2017.

60. Almeida 2021.

61. Kathuria 2018.

62. Aranha 2018.

63. There is some truth to that belief: a year after Chennai's first transgender police officer was hired, 27 trans women signed up to take Chennai's Police Recruitment Examination. See *Times of India* 2017.

64. Vijaykumar 2013; Bhatt, Murty, and Ramamurthy 2010; Ganguly-Scrase and Scrase 2008; Lukose 2009; Walkerdine 2003.

65. While *hijra*s in areas of North India engage in ritual singing and dancing during festivals, marriages, and birth ceremonies, known as *badhai,* as an important source of income, the ability to earn a livelihood through *badhai* appears to be decreasing due to the shrinking size of urban families (Nanda 1990) and the changing living arrangements of upper-middle-class people, who often reside behind guarded gates where *hijra*s are not permitted. The ability for *hijra*s to earn an income through *badhai* is significantly reduced in South India, apart from in the city of Hyderabad (Reddy 2005).

3

Hijra Families Today

Social Change and "Choice"
for "New" Women

Introduction

Mariyamma sighed, looking briefly around the large room in the NGO
office where she works before glancing back at me. She paused and looked
away for another moment before responding, "See, *everything* has changed."
A transgender woman in her sixties, Mariyamma is also involved in *hijra*
relationships and previously lived in *hijra* communal homes. Initially, she
struggled to respond to my question about the changes in *hijra* groups she
has witnessed throughout her life. But once she began to think out loud
about what her life was like as a young GNC person, she talked excitedly,
emphasizing the transformations in *hijra* family relationships.

Mariyamma left her birth family as a teenager, approximately 50 years
before I spoke with her. As a young, feminine-presenting GNC person,
Mariyamma was in a vulnerable position, and joining the *hijras* was
essential for survival. *Hijra* communities are organized around family
relationships between *gurus* (teachers or mothers) and *chelas* (disciples or
daughters). In traditional *guru–chela* relationships, *gurus* and *chelas* live
in the same household. Looking back, Mariyamma remarked, "You *had* to
have a *guru* and your *guru* used to guide you *every single day*.... See, you
had to be under the wing of your *guru*." She needed daily mentoring and the
protection that living in a *hijra* community and being "under the wing" of
her *guru* offered.

Throughout our conversation, Mariyamma consistently emphasized the
reciprocal nature of the *guru–chela* relationship when she was a young *chela*.
"You had to give them [your *guru*] all your earnings. Then, they used to take

you for [surgery] and they used to look after you." *Gurus* at that time had access to important resources that younger GNC people needed, like surgery, housing, and a means to earn an income. In exchange for the financial support *chelas* offered to their *gurus*, *gurus* provided these resources for their *chelas*.

Until about the mid to late 2000s, the majority of young GNC people who joined the *hijras* lived in *hijra* residences in Bangalore. Most often, *chelas* lived with their *gurus*,[1] and these communal living arrangements enabled the daily mentoring that *gurus* provided. I came to think of these kinds of relationships as "residential" *guru–chela* relationships (though people commonly referred to them as "traditional" *guru–chela* relationships); both terms differentiate from the situation today where *gurus* and *chelas* do not often reside in the same household. As a result, what I came to think of as "nonresidential" *gurus* and *chelas* generally spend much less time with one another.

This move from residential to (largely) nonresidential *guru–chela* relationships marks a major shift in *hijra* relationships. Mariyamma indicated there are some people who still abide by the traditional *guru–chela* relationship, "but only [in relationships] where they stay [in the same household] together." Looking around at the eight other people seated in small groups in the office, she pointed to an older *hijra* named Romilla and said, "She stays [in the same household] with her *chelas*. So there are a few people like that." But according to Mariyamma, Romilla was the exception. "Nowadays, there's [*pause*] no such relationship like traditional *guru* and *chela* relationships." Then, she paused to think, adding, "The younger generation, maybe they are—are not like that. See, [*pointing*] she's not [living] with a *guru*. She [*pointing*] is not [living] with a *guru*. Deepa [*pointing*] is also not [living] with her *guru*. So they are all [living] away from *gurus*." The three *chelas* she points to are all in their twenties. Instead of living with their *guru*, Mariyamma explained, they would instead "occasionally ... go and meet them [*gurus*], saying '*paam padti*,'[2] and we give them something [gifts and/or money] and then we leave." This kind of formalized relationship marks a dramatic departure from the kind of close mentoring Mariyamma received from her *guru* when she was a young *chela* trying to survive.

To understand this change, it is important to explore two related strands of social change. Before the 2000s, I was told that joining a *hijra* group, living in a *hammam*, and engaging in sex work and/or soliciting money was the only path younger, visibly GNC people had to access surgery, housing,[3] and employment.[4] Today, traditional *hijra* housing, families, and livelihoods are increasingly restricted (and even criminalized) by the state. At the same time, opportunities for GNC people to access housing, employment, and gender affirmation surgery have increased outside of *hijra* groups. Now, many younger GNC people no longer have a pressing need for resources that could at one time be fulfilled only through becoming a *chela* in a *hijra* group.

These many different social changes paved the way for visibly GNC people to imagine life outside of *hijra* groups. But instead of explaining the change based on these factors, people consistently explained the changes in *hijra* relationships by drawing on discourses about the "choices" that younger GNC people (including *chelas*) have. The language of choice was pervasive—every single person I spoke to attributed the changes in *hijra* groups, the *guru–chela* relationship, and their lives in general to the choices *chelas* and younger GNC people now have. According to Mariyamma, young GNC people's ability to choose today is vastly different from the time when she was in their shoes:

> When I was growing up, the only place for any [GNC person] to go was to a *guru* or a *hammam* [*hijra* household] or somewhere [like that]. That was fifty years ago, but now, it is *veeery* different. You have *lots* of options. You can have a *guru* or you don't need a *guru*. It is left to you [to choose or decide].

Tellingly, the language of choice used in describing the options GNC people enjoy today draws on a familiar association between feminine people and consumption. In an economically liberalized modern-day India, cisgender women are positioned as newly emancipated, in part due to their ability to make their own purchasing decisions. In light of the influence that the discourse about "new" women has had on transgender people, it is perhaps not surprising that similar "emerging consumer discourses of a woman exercising choice"[5] have found their way to describe the increased opportunities available to younger feminine-presenting GNC people. Aligned with the discourse about "new" (cisgender) women and the evolving nature of consumption in India, younger GNC people are now seen as empowered feminine people exercising choice.

Before we explore this discourse and its impact on *hijra* families, we need to explore why *hijra* families were created in the first place. Why would this marginalized group choose to create family relationships, and how did the social context of family relationships in India influence *hijra* support systems?

Hijra Families: Creating Resistant Institutions

In India, families provide crucial social and financial support in the absence of an organized, accessible, government-provided social safety net.[6] Because the social services available through the Indian government are limited and difficult to access (especially for GNC people), most people tend to access resources and support through their family networks. This means that GNC people encounter major problems when they are forced out of or willingly leave their birth families. Prior to the changes this book discusses, it was difficult to impossible[7] for young GNC people to survive on their own, so they needed an alternate support system.

As a marginalized group, *hijra*s are frequently "isolated or segregated" from dominant social groups and cannot access social and financial support outside of these communities.[8] *Hijra*s therefore created their own social systems that offered support and material resources,[9] with communal living pursued out of recognition of the "public violence, discrimination, and vulnerability" faced by GNC people.[10] This "strategy for survival" enabled them to "live, work and occupy public space together."[11]

But in addition to the crucial material support families provide, they also offer members social support, which is important in a family-oriented society. In popular culture and academic scholarship, "the family" is often positioned as the "solid foundation" of Indian society and "a strong, cohesive, integral and fundamental unit" within Indian social structures.[12] There are communities in India where a person is understood as "primarily a member of the family before anything else."[13] The importance of family for social support and as a reference point for someone's place in society is also part of the reason *hijra*s organized themselves into family systems.[14]

*Hijra*s traditionally lived in communal houses known in Bangalore as *hammams*.[15] Their communities are organized around *guru* and *chela* relationships that are based in part on non-*hijra* kinship formations. In these families, the *guru* is considered as a parent and the *chela* as her child; a *guru* typically takes on multiple *chela*s.[16] As time passes, *chela*s are expected to take on their own *chelas* (with their *guru*'s permission), thus extending the lineage, bringing new members into the household and making the person both a *guru* and a *chela* simultaneously.[17] When *hijra* households would grow too large (or new opportunities for sex work or soliciting money would become available, like a new train station opening[18]), *gurus* may ask their more senior *chelas* to start their own households.

Reciprocal exchanges of material support are at the heart of the *guru*–*chela* relationship. In the past, younger GNC people often ran away from their birth families, so they lost their family support system. They needed housing and access to a means of employment, and as GNC people, many also sought assistance to obtain gender affirmation surgery. In the past, these resources were only accessible through connections controlled by *hijra* groups. To access these resources, younger GNC people had to affiliate with a *guru*. In return for these resources and support, *gurus* expect their *chelas* to contribute the bulk of their wages (usually from sex work and/or soliciting money) to the household. In addition, *gurus* are expected to teach *chelas* the kinds of behaviors that enable them to rise in stature within the *hijra* community. In return for this guidance, *chelas* attend to the cooking, cleaning, and other household duties for their *gurus*; if they neglect these duties, they are liable to be verbally or physically abused.[19]

The dynamics of the *guru* and *chela* relationships were illustrated in one interaction I witnessed one morning between Vandana, a tall *hijra* in her late twenties, and her *chela*. I was in the kitchen of a *hammam* waiting for Vandana when a petite *hijra* who looked to be in her late teens or early twenties came in. She removed the long scarf covering her head to reveal short, curly hair, a likely indication that she was new to the community. Noticing me sitting there, she greeted me and explained that she had just returned from soliciting money. She pulled out a small plastic bag and opened the newspaper-wrapped parcel inside, revealing a small stack of pancake-like set *dosas* that she placed on a white ceramic plate. Then she pulled aside a curtain covering a doorway in the back of the kitchen to reveal a closet-sized room that she entered, followed by a man who had just appeared.

Vandana soon entered and sat down in a cross-legged position next to me, chatting as she hungrily ate her set *dosas*. With a nod of her head she indicated that the younger *hijra* was one of her *chelas*. Soon, Vandana's *chela* came back into the kitchen, sat down near us, and silently removed a dozen

10-rupee notes from her purse and about 80 rupees in coins and handed the money to Vandana. Vandana counted the money carefully and then gave her *chela* about 10 rupees in coins, putting the rest into a pouch that she put in her pocket. Her *chela* then said she would continue with her work, smiled at me, and left.

After Vandana finished her breakfast, I asked her about the relationships between *gurus* and *chelas*. She offered this telling reflection:

> The *guru–chela* relationship is just like any mother–daughter relationship.... We must obey our *guru*. I am the *chela* of my *guru* and I must obey my *guru*. If my *guru* asks me not to cross the road, I won't.

When I asked what would happen if she insisted on crossing the road, Vandana just shook her head and said,

> She would have taken care of me since when I was young. That's why she's like a mother and we must obey her. If I run into problems she'll support me.... If we disobey her, she won't help us.

Her matter-of-fact answers indicate that these commitments are nonnegotiable, necessary, and beneficial for all parties.

As *hijras* age, their options for earning a livelihood become limited since elder *hijras* attract fewer customers for sex work and receive fewer financial contributions when soliciting money. Thus, elder *gurus* are vulnerable to financial insecurity since they lose the ability to generate their own income. This means elder *gurus* become increasingly reliant on their *chelas* to survive. Vandana shared that her *guru* is "old and she can't go anywhere [to work]. I have to take care of her. We are young." When I pointed out that she is young and able-bodied and yet has a chela, she stressed the reciprocal nature of *hijra* relationships.[20] Her *chela* must give her money and Vandana, in turn, gives money to her own *guru*, and so on. Indeed, for an elder *hijra* who struggles to earn money, one path to continue earning an income is to have multiple *chelas*. A typical household consists of 5 to 15 "relatively permanent" household members, not including *hijras* who may be visiting for a few days to a few months.[21] *Hijra* households[22] can therefore be understood as collective poverty management systems, with the *guru's* "vocation" being the management of her *chelas*.[23]

Shrinking *Hammams* and Shifting Geographies of
Wealth in Bangalore

Vandana was one of the few people I spoke to in Bangalore who aspires to maintain traditional *guru–chela* responsibilities and ideals. Today, the majority of *hijras* in Bangalore do not reside in *hammams*, a change that has shifted the character of the *guru–chela* relationship. This change has occurred very recently, starting around 20 years ago. I was told that there used to be well over 20 *hammams* in Bangalore but only between 8 and 12 *hammams* are in operation today; during my fieldwork I visited 4.

The changes in *hijra* communal living coupled with the changing geographies of Bangalore mean that *hijras'* relationships with their surrounding communities have shifted. *Hammams* were generally located in working-class neighborhoods, and the relationships between the *hijras* and their neighbors were long-standing and interpreted as largely positive and supportive. One *hammam* was located near a temple dedicated to the goddess Yellamma, and the *hijras* who lived there were entrusted with caretaking responsibilities for the temple—even performing daily rituals on the temple grounds (a clear indication of the level of respect and reverence they were accorded). Unlike *hammams*, newer *hijra* households do not have a long history in their neighborhoods, and their occupants lack long-standing social ties to these neighborhoods.

Newer living arrangements among *hijras* are also taking shape at a time when the ability of *hammams* to continue functioning in Bangalore is threatened by gentrification and the changing geographies of wealth in the city. As we learned in Chapter 1, the local economy of Bangalore has grown in recent decades, and real estate prices across the city have risen exponentially. As real estate prices increased, many inhabitants of these formerly working-class areas sold their homes to middle-class and largely dominant-caste Hindus and moved to less expensive areas. These new inhabitants usually had not had sustained contact with *hijras* prior to moving and considered themselves "respectable" people. They expressed little desire to cultivate relationships with *hijras* and possibly even felt threatened by their presence in the neighborhood.

The perceived effects of *hammams* on real estate prices in Bangalore have also led to what appears to be a state-sponsored displacement of *hijra* households.[24] In 2008, there was an instance of police evicting *hijras* from a neighborhood in Bangalore that had an old *hammam* and many smaller *hijra* households located nearby. Police officers reported that they received complaints about *hijras*' "anti-social activities" that were "bringing down real estate prices" in the area.[25] Though their neighbors only had positive things to say about the local *hijras*, the police ordered flat owners to evict all *hijras* from the area as part of an effort to "clean up" Bangalore.[26] As a result, all *hijras*—some of whom had lived in the area for decades—were forced to leave.

The shifting geographies of wealth in a gentrifying city such as Bangalore therefore can have profound trickle-down effects on *hijra* household arrangements. As areas of the city "modernize" and gentrify, the perception of who are acceptable neighbors also changes. Although there is more information and awareness about *hijra* lives and an arguably greater acceptance of sexual and gender nonconformity today, *hijras* continue to be a maligned group, with "so-called decent folks" (in the words of one participant) usually not wanting them around. The result is that at the same time opportunities for GNC people to reside outside *hijra* communities are increasing, large *hijra* households are being forced to relocate as local residents and the government "clean up" areas to attract wealthier residents.[27]

Hijra "Traditional" Relationships: The Context of Criminalization

The principle of reciprocity in *hijra* relationships and the obligations it entails are coming under fire from the state. One example of this is the Transgender Persons (Protection of Rights) Bill, passed in 2019. The stated motivation behind the bill is to codify state recognition of GNC people and ensure their rights under the law. Yet critics argue that it also transforms GNC people into an enumerable, intelligible population in the eyes of the state. This is especially noteworthy in the case of *hijras*, a group that previously existed (largely) outside state surveillance.[28]

The Transgender Persons (Protection of Rights) Bill includes a clause that has major implications for *hijra* families, livelihoods, and households. It states that anyone who "compels or entices a transgender person to indulge in the act of begging or other similar forms of forced or bonded labour ... shall be punishable with imprisonment."[29] In Bangalore, soliciting money was already criminalized under the Karnataka Prohibition of Beggary Act of 1975. But now the Transgender Persons (Protection of Rights) Bill reinterprets soliciting money (when done by a GNC person who has a *guru*) as not only a crime the person soliciting money can be punished for but also "a crime against transgender persons" that their *guru* could be prosecuted for.[30] The bill reframes soliciting money under the direction of a *guru*[31] and sharing that money with the *guru* and other members of one's *hijra* family as "bonded labour" or "forced" work—a characterization that fails to recognize that *hijras* historically engaged in such labor, which they performed in groups, and then the profit was shared among members.[32] Under this reframing, Vandana becomes the head of a "beggary syndicate" and her *chela* becomes a "forced labour[er]."[33]

The bill also enables state surveillance of the families GNC people create that fall outside of heteronormative, cisgender family forms. The bill legally prevents GNC people from leaving their birth families as minors to join other families, like *hijra* families. It states that anyone who "forces or causes a transgender person to leave house-hold, village or other place of residence ... shall be punishable with imprisonment."[34] Every *hijra* I spoke with (and many trans women) had left their birth families willingly, and almost all had done so when they were under the age of 18. This bill makes their actions illegal. But what is unrecognized here is that GNC people generally leave due to the abuse and harassment they are subjected to by their family and/or community.[35] Ultimately, the bill enables state surveillance of *hijra* forms of kinship (especially the *guru–chela* relationship), and allows for the possibility of interpreting leaving one's birth family as a kind of forced relocation, thereby criminalizing *hijra* households and relationships[36] and potentially other family forms that fall outside cishet family structures.[37]

By criminalizing the social organization of *hijras* and their livelihoods, the bill undercuts traditional *hijra* families and communities. In response to concerns expressed by GNC community groups, the Supreme Court explained that "[t]he spirit of the bill" is "primarily aimed at retention of transgender children within their immediate family."[38] GNC groups and their allies pushed back, requesting that family be interpreted in ways that protect the *guru–chela* relationship as a form of adopted family, but the final bill was not amended.[39]

New Housing Opportunities for GNC People

Although in the last two decades gentrification in Bangalore has impacted the ability of *hijras* to live together in *hammams*, at the same time visibly

GNC people can increasingly find accommodations they can rent on their own. GNC people's access to housing has been influenced by a greater perceived acceptance of gender non-conformity from the "general society" in Bangalore. Although some middle-class residents and state representatives will not accept *hijras* living in places where their presence might negatively impact real estate prices, there are strong indications that individual flat owners have become more accepting of GNC people.

Prior to public advocacy and media awareness of the plight of GNC people, finding rental accommodations for visibly GNC persons was extremely difficult. Flat owners were most often unwilling to rent to GNC people. In the rare cases where someone agreed to rent to a GNC person, they would demand prohibitively high rates for a deposit and rent. Though everyone admitted that it is still difficult to find a rental flat as a visibly GNC person, in recent years it has become considerably easier and certainly no longer impossible. Many flat owners still demand higher rent rates for GNC people than they would for cisgender people; however, those who want to live outside of *hijra* households are willing and increasingly able to bear this cost.

Of course, apartment living is by design transitory in nature, and the kind of ties to a neighborhood that used to exist when living in a *hammam* do not typically exist in such settings. As we sat sipping tea on the floor of the flat she shares with her boyfriend, Suma, a trans woman in her thirties, related an incident that happened during the festival of Diwali, when people light firecrackers outside. As she was walking back to her flat at night, Suma noticed three or four teenage boys gathered together. The next thing she knew, there was a firecracker coming straight toward her from that direction. Luckily, the boys had not aimed correctly, or the firecracker would have hit her. She turned and felt relieved when she noticed a man who had also witnessed this incident, hoping he would come to her aid. However, as Suma recounted, "he saw everything, but he's telling me, 'Go, no? go!' Like, to *me*. He didn't even ask, 'Why are you doing this, boys?!'" Instead of reprimanding the boys and by implication validating Suma's presence in the neighborhood, the actions of both the boys and the older man suggest that the ability to rent a flat does not translate into acceptance by the surrounding community members.

There is another very small (but significant) group of GNC people who do not participate in *hijra* households for an altogether different (and surprising) reason. Today, there are some visibly GNC people who are able to continue living with their birth families—surprising because most GNC people in the past reported levels of ridicule and abuse that made such an arrangement impossible. Mohan, a cisgender NGO worker in his forties, cited this as the most salient change he witnessed among *hijras*' living situations:

> There are actually a large number of [GNC people] staying with their parents now, their [birth] families. Of course, they're not very happy. They say that they don't treat us equally, they discriminate against us. But, you know, moving from living in a *hammam* and doing sex work there to your own rented space, to [returning to] your own home is a huge, huge, *huge* change ... a major change.

In spite of the potential to experience unequal treatment from their birth families, the fact that some GNC people do not feel forced to leave their families and search for a new support system marks a significant shift in the lives of younger GNC people—especially in light of the increasing cost of renting in urban centers like Bangalore.

For Mariyamma, the fact that some younger, visibly GNC people reside with their birth families indicates a major reduction in the stigma once associated with gender nonconformity. When she was growing up, "there was no place for anybody [that is, a GNC person] to go" for material and social support except to join the *hijras*. Knowing the kind of stigma and social ostracization their families would face, GNC people who became *hijras* generally would not want to disgrace their birth family by continuing to associate with them. To illustrate how unlikely maintaining relationships with one's birth family was in the past, Mariyamma shared the story of her *guru*, who had joined the *hijras* as a teenager and never returned to visit her birth family.

> Even in her last days also [before she passed away], I asked her, "did you ever go to your parents' house?" She said no. She was still scared, [thinking: if I return,] "what will my people say, what will my relations say?"

Although family dynamics are changing, there appears to be an urban-rural divide that shapes family acceptance of GNC people. Recent research on rural-based *hijras* shows that these shifts in family acceptance of GNC people are specific to urban areas. Traditionally, among urban *hijra* groups, members must sever all ties to their birth families after joining their new *hijra* families that replaced the one they left. This was not an issue for most *hijras*, who were "abandoned" by their families long before they could renounce them.[40] Despite this, some urban-based *hijras* and trans women do continue to maintain relationships with their birth families, typically keeping in touch with one person (usually a sister or their mother).[41] However, the limited research about rural-based *hijras* shows that they face a different situation. In the first ethnography conducted with rural-based *hijras*, Vaibhav Saria shows that *hijras* in rural Odisha often continue residing with their birth families[42] instead of joining *hijra* households. Instead of being seen as a disgrace to the family, the families of rural-based *hijras* value the economic contributions they make through soliciting money, collecting alms, and sex work.[43]

What accounts for this difference in how GNC people are regarded by their birth families? These different reactions by cishet families to their *hijra* members are rooted in the social contexts of class and aspiration. Working-class families residing in urban areas like Bangalore are surrounded by a social context of class aspiration. Urban areas generally witness greater class inequality because higher-class groups, from the upper-middle class to the ultra-wealthy, live in cities.[44] In addition, there are large groups of working-class people residing in cities who aspire to join the middle classes.[45] These middle-class aspiring groups attempt to distinguish themselves[46] from other working-class groups by positioning themselves as respectably middle class. One way they do this is by endorsing and upholding middle-class gender norms. Thus, middle-class aspiring groups living in cities once turned their backs on their GNC family members as a way of conforming to gender expectations within the kinds of respectable, middle-class families they aspired to become (although family attitudes are changing in light of increased acceptance of middle-class aspiring trans women in urban settings).

By contrast, rural-based families with GNC members are not surrounded by cultural ideas assuming upward mobility is possible for anyone who works hard and has the right kind of attitude.[47] These rural-based families tend to be poor and likely do not view themselves as in a position to join the ranks of the middle classes, making them less likely to endorse middle-class urban gender norms. Instead, these families value the kind of money their GNC family members can bring in, so it makes sense for them to retain their GNC family members who can contribute financially instead of abandoning them in the hopes of emulating middle-class groups.

Shifting Access to Gender Affirmation Surgery

A key resource for many GNC people is access to some form of gender affirmation surgery. Twenty-plus years ago, these surgeries were neither widely available in hospitals nor discussed in media or by members of the public. They were instead traditionally performed within *hijra* groups, and *gurus* would most often arrange for their *chelas'* surgeries. Because there was limited information about these procedures, people outside of *hijra* groups did not generally have access to them. This is a key reason that many people like Mariyamma reported that they joined the *hijras* as young GNC people. But today, both private and government hospitals throughout the country provide these surgeries, and there is ample information about them through media and online, making them possible to obtain without becoming a *chela*.[48]

There are different routes that people traditionally took to alter their bodies surgically. In *hijra* groups, such surgeries were once performed by midwives known as *dai ma* in accordance with ritual beliefs that the surgery catalyzes a rebirth for the person being operated on.[49] These traditional methods had considerable downsides: anesthesia was not used, so the procedure was very painful, and people often suffered from long-lasting complications or even died. Neelima, a trans woman in her sixties who was part of a *hijra* group as a young GNC person, recalled the era when she was a young *chela*:

> Those days there were no doctors [performing the surgery], right? See, when a person is neither a man nor a woman, being in that state, how much pain one goes through! How can anyone understand that? To overcome that pain, the *dai ma* would help us ... we would worship the deity Mata [goddess] and then she would do the procedure. If she did this operation on 10 people, there was a chance that two of them would die.

Nisha, a trans woman in her thirties, heard about the procedure from her *hijra* elders:

> The *dai ma* herself would do the surgery ... and it was done by hand [that is, without using modern medical technologies or tools]. If the person lived through the surgery, they would come back to join the community.

When I asked about the last time there was a surgery performed by a midwife in Bangalore, people estimated that it had at least been 20 years if not more.

Although gender affirmation surgery has been offered in select private hospitals and overseas for many decades, private medical care and international travel for surgery are prohibitively expensive for most GNC people in India. As a result, many GNC people in the past would seek out "quack" surgeons with limited medical training who worked out of unlicensed clinics. Since these clinics were not officially registered medical centers, information about them would circulate among *hijra*s by word of mouth.[50] But many people who had surgeries performed by "quacks" reported long-lasting complications, which often required additional (and costly) procedures.

Gaining access to surgery was an important reason that younger GNC people joined the community and became *chela*s. However, surgeries were expensive and most *guru*s did not have the means to fund these surgeries outright. They would normally offer their *chela*s one of two options: (*a*) a loan that had to be paid back (often with interest) to fund the surgery or (*b*) the *guru* would take the *chela* on for two to four years and part of the money the *chela* earned during that time would go to fund her surgery. In both cases, the *guru* was understood as taking on the risk that her *chela* would leave once she completed her surgery.

In the case of Sanya, a trans woman in her thirties who spoke about her complicated class background in the Introduction, the only reason she participated in the *hijra* system was to access surgery. After joining a *hijra* group in Mumbai as a teenager over 20 years ago, Sanya realized that soliciting money and sex work for livelihood was not for her. She planned to get her surgery as quickly as possible and leave her *guru* afterwards, but she knew that she needed to act strategically in order to accomplish this goal. She was fully aware that *guru*s fear their *chela*s will leave after completing their surgeries. As she explained, "some of the people, once they get surgery, they go back to their homeland; they do sex work by themselves." Since these runaway *chela*s do not share their earnings with their *guru*s, the *guru*s wonder "what's the point?" of looking after a *chela* for so long, asking "what do I get [from her]" if she were to leave? As a result, in the group where Sanya became a *chela*, new *chela*s were not allowed to get surgeries for at least two or three years. Sanya believes this was also a tactic *guru*s used to encourage *chela*s to stay after their surgeries were complete. "If you start living someplace for two years, then you will come to love it, right? You don't want to go to another place and start there from zero."

Upon hearing about how long it took to get surgery, Sanya began to strategize about how she could convince the senior *gurus* in the group to allow her to get an early surgery. She realized that the trick was "you have to win [the *gurus*'] heart, you have to give them that [sense of] trust, that [they think] 'OK, she will stay here with us.'" Sanya made sure to engage in behaviors she knew the *gurus* would appreciate. "I was a very, very good girl for them. I didn't speak too much, I didn't cheat them." Sanya also strove to maximize the amount of money she could give the *gurus* from soliciting money. Usually "people give [*gurus*] 300 [rupees] per day, [but] I used to give like 800 [rupees].... And I didn't drink, I didn't chase after men. I was very good for them." Indeed, Sanya pretended that one reason she wanted to get gender reassignment surgery is so she could do sex work to make even more money that she would share with them. In less than a year Sanya was able to gain the trust of her *gurus*.

> They liked me and they thought "ok, she's good, you know. Good for us, she's very obedient and she's looking pretty [so she'll earn a lot of money from sex work]." So they thought if I got my surgery earlier, then, you know, they can use me for sex work and they can get more money out of it. So that was their idea.

After she recovered from the procedure, Sanya made plans to return to her home state. However, she knew that the *gurus* would not allow this, so she had to leave in secret late in the night. Sanya escaped with the belongings she could carry and left her *guru* a note to explain her departure.

> I wrote a letter to [my *guru*], [writing] that, "Sorry, Ma. Sorry I disappointed you. I didn't want to disappoint you. I want to ... live with my family. If I can't survive with my family, I won't work with anybody else [that is, I won't enter into another *guru–chela* relationship and share my income].... I'll only come back to you. But always, I love you and ... I'm really grateful to you [for helping me get my surgery]".... So, [my *guru*] was, like, angry, but at least she was happy [thinking] that, "OK, the income is not going to someone else. She's not working, it's OK. Maybe she'll come back one day."

In rare cases, people were able to obtain surgery without becoming a *chela* in a *hijra* group. Rani, a transgender woman in her fifties, obtained her surgery when she was 17. At the time, she and her boyfriend knew many *hijra*s because they spent time in Cubbon Park, a cruising spot where many feminine-presenting GNC people and sexual minorities congregate in Bangalore. They became friendly with a group of *hijra*s who mentioned a clinic in Mumbai. Rani was unaware that she could alter her body in this way, so she asked many questions about the procedure that her *hijra* friends patiently answered. "No one [that is, outside *hijra* groups] knew where the [surgery] was done, what [the procedure actually entailed], and these kinds of things. For this, you had to have a *guru*." Fortunately for Rani, her *hijra* friends (who were themselves *guru*s) were willing to share this information.

After thinking carefully about the prospect of surgery, Rani decided that she wanted to pursue it. Rani's boyfriend began to save a portion of his salary to pay for her surgery. At that time, the surgery was reasonably priced, so Rani soon went to Bombay with one of her friends. Rani subsequently lived for almost two decades with her boyfriend until he left. It was only then that Rani became a *chela* in a *hijra* group.

As I spoke with Sanya and Rani, they both marveled about how much access to gender affirmation surgery has changed since when they got surgery. Rani attributes these changes to enhanced awareness about GNC people's lives through media. A GNC person seeking surgery today has "access to the internet"—in her words—"access to so much" information about gender nonconformity, including surgery. "Nowadays, [GNC people] go [for surgery by] themselves. And there are so many people who [undergo surgery, but] don't even join the *hijra* community at all!"

This enhanced accessibility of information about gender affirmation surgery is in stark contrast with Sanya's lack of knowledge when she was undergoing her surgery. At that time, information about the procedure was shrouded in secrecy, so Sanya was completely dependent on senior *guru*s to assist her. She explains,

When I was going for [surgery], I didn't even know the place, where it is. Only *they* [*guru*s] knew. And those doctors, if I went alone, they wouldn't even do it…. Now it is not like that, it's very open. If you have money, you don't even need to join the *hijra* community. You can even continue living with your [birth] family [and get surgery]. If you are rich, you can just save some 60,000 [Indian rupees; about 1,200 US dollars at the time] and then you can go do a surgery just like that.

Sanya even occasionally hears of people today who continue living with their families and undergo gender affirming surgery without their family's knowledge. She explained that this is possible since people can go to the clinic and then recover with the help of friends or partners. "After one week, they can simply go back and live with their family, without even telling them that 'I got surgery.'"

The Rise of Nonresidential *Guru–Chela* Relationships

The ability for visibly GNC people to obtain employment, housing, and surgery on their own (coupled with a simultaneous crackdown on *hijra* communal living and working) has enabled (younger) GNC people to imagine living outside of *hijra* groups. As a result, many *chela*s reside in smaller households away from their *guru*s. These transformations in *hijra* households were often remarked upon when I asked people about the major changes they witnessed among *hijra*s. For example, in response to a general question about the changes he witnessed while working in the sexual rights field, Mohan, a longtime sexual rights activist and cisgender man in his forties, exclaimed,

> We can't believe that so much has changed! If you take the *hijra* community, when we started [our work], 90% of them lived in *hammam*s; [they] did sex work in *hammam*s. Today, 90% of them live on their own, in their own rented housing and many of them do sex work not only in *hammam*s, but [many] even [work] outside [of the *hijra* community].

This move from residential to nonresidential *guru–chela* relationships does not always mean that *chela*s have stopped residing with members of the larger *hijra* community or even members of their own *hijra* family. In fact, when choosing the people that they want to live with, *chela*s often prefer to reside with their *gurubhai* (usually translated as "sister")—the other *chela* of one's *guru*. In the view of Rishabh, a GNC person in their fifties, *chela*s often consider their *gurubhai*s "more friendly, more progressive, more, you know, free. So [they think that] we can be more comfortable in that space." While fewer *chelas* now live with their *gurus* in *hammams*, I did hear of a few small *guru–chela* households (usually in rented flats). However, the *chelas* in these households were less likely to be responsible for all of the household chores and obey their *gurus*, which marks a major shift in the understanding of this relationship.

Several younger GNC people that I spoke with had once identified primarily as *hijras* and still loosely associated with the *hijra* community, but either lived alone or with their cisgender men partners. Andavar, who is in their thirties and identified themself as *kothi*, is one such person. Andavar explained that there are lots of trans women and other people who are associated with the *hijra* community who live with their romantic partners. Like Andavar, many also had a *guru* and even considered entering into a residential *guru–chela* relationship. These people "don't fully oppose *hijra* culture" according to Andavar; "They'll follow *hijra* culture [but] also they'll live separately, with their partners [because] they want … to live like a general [non-*hijra*] family, how they live." These people will occasionally visit their *gurus* and attend community-wide functions and celebrations, but their relationship with *hijra* groups is mediated by their participation in a "general family" living situation.

Hijras and other GNC people today therefore can be found in many nontraditional living arrangements: with other *hijras*, with their romantic partners, or even with their birth families. The increase in state interventions into *hijra* communal living, livelihoods, and families combined with new possibilities for living outside of *hijra* groups have contributed to a major transformation in "nonresidential" *guru–chela* relationships. As we will see in the next chapter, these changes impacting younger GNC people have shifted the balance of power in the *guru–chela* relationship and how *chelas* understand reciprocal care.

Chelas, "New" Womanhood, and the Importance of "Choice"

The changes that paved the way for younger GNC people to live outside of *hijra* groups are multiple and complex. They stem in part from the state's desire to manage GNC groups, ultimately restricting how *hijras* live, work, and create families. They also are a product of the wide-ranging changes that swept through urban India in the wake of economic liberalization, including gender and sexual rights activism that slowly increased acceptance for GNC people.

However, when people would describe what was causing these changes, these complex shifts were often reduced to a single lens—the rhetoric of "choice." This rhetoric of choice overlaps with and echoes discussions about cisgender women's ability to make "empowered" consumption choices in liberalized India, and I argue that this language of choice connects younger *chelas* (and other feminine-presenting GNC people) to the opportunities supposedly available to the "new" (cisgender) woman.

In describing the changes in *guru–chela* relationships through *chelas'* newfound ability to choose, people implicitly drew on "emerging consumer discourses of a woman exercising choice."[51] This kind of talk proliferated after the liberalization of the Indian economy beginning in the late 1980s, and it is linked to increased commercial advertising in India since the early 1990s.[52] At this time, marketing studies showed that (presumably cis) women were increasingly key consumers and considered as partners by their spouses in major purchasing decisions, regardless of whether they were employed outside of their homes. As a result, women have become major targets for advertisers.[53]

Notions about individual choice feature prominently in the advertising directed toward women. The bulk of these advertisements emphasize the salience of a woman's "choice" to make her own distinct consumption decisions. A key message in many advertisements focuses on a woman's unique individuality and how the product being sold will accentuate it.[54] The ability to make individual consumption decisions is positioned as liberating for women[55] and understood as a symbol of women's empowerment.[56]

When discussing the changes to the *guru–chela* system, trans women, *chelas*, and others draw from these media discourses that emphasize women's ability to exercise individual choice. Every single person I spoke with drew implicit parallels between younger GNC people's decision-making processes and consumption decisions. Prior to GNC people's enhanced ability to make choices about their lives, people viewed them as confined to living in *hijra* groups. In Mariyamma's view, younger GNC people are now less likely to join *hijra* groups because they now have so many other "options" for survival:

> See, nowadays, no one would like to go [with *hijras*] because there are so many other options! [As a young GNC person seeking support,] I can go and stay with [my friend] Deepa [in her rented flat], [or] I can go and stay with somebody else [in their rental accommodation], [or] I can even go and stay in a *hammam* [that is, join a *hijra* group].

These "options" available to younger GNC people were not available when Mariyamma was growing up. "Those days, there was no one" offering support except *hijra*s. But now the expanded options for younger GNC people mean that "it's not even necessary to become a *chela* or any such thing. You can live independently also, without *hijra*s also." For younger GNC people today, "it is left to them" to decide which group (if any) they will align themselves with.

The expanded "options" for social and financial support also include NGOs that advocate for the rights of GNC people. Rishabh positions NGOs as offering an additional space outside of *hijra* groups where younger GNC people can come to access support, belonging, and employment options:

> I think they [younger GNC people] came to th[is] organization because they felt that there was an alternate protection system, you know? Because before, there was no alternate protection system. It was only the *guru–chela* relationship, so they felt that, you know, there is a space for them beyond the *guru–chela* relationship and they could become more independent, more free to do what they like.

When describing what NGOs offer to younger GNC people, Rishabh also draws on notions of freedom and independence often used to describe the kinds of choices available to new women under a liberalized economy. Like everyone else I spoke with, Rishabh drew an implicit parallel between new opportunities for younger GNC people and for new women.

As media representations of GNC people have increased, younger GNC people have become more aware of their newfound ability to make decisions about their lives. And as they learn about the variety of ways to live as a GNC person, younger GNC people become more discerning of which groups they join and which (if any) *guru*s they choose. As Sanya observed, "they have that little exposure [and think], 'Ah ok, if you don't accept me this way, I can go to some other group. I'll manage, so I won't worry.' It's like that." Knowing that they have options for support, younger GNC people are likely to search for a *guru* who matches their own ideals of a good *guru*, as opposed to attempting to mold themselves into a *guru*'s ideal of how a good *chela* should behave. Because *chela*s are aware of their many options for support, Sanya observed, "if [the *guru*s] cross a limit, [the *chela*s] will just change," finding another *guru* or even another group outside of the *hijra*s.

This characterization of *chela*s' decision-making process implicitly reflects assumptions about how new women make consumption decisions.

The implication is that *chela*s now have access to additional information that enables them to make informed choices, similar to the kind of "information-centered shopping" that reportedly shapes middle-class consumption decisions in India.[57] Such practices are an important way that middle-class people differentiate themselves from the working classes.[58] The idea is that responsible women consumers conduct research on a variety of available products and then, considering their needs, make rational decisions—like how Sanya describes younger GNC people who make decisions about which groups to become a part of and which *guru*s to enter into a relationship with.

The ability for younger GNC people to make choices about their lives was often cited when I asked my participants to explain the changes in behavior within the *guru–chela* relationship. Neelima is a *hijra* in her sixties who has witnessed these changes firsthand. Whereas *chela*s were previously expected to obey their *guru*s without question, she observed that now "the *chela* can *choose* [whether or not] to follow what the *guru* asks her to do. It is fine if she doesn't choose to obey. The *chela*s question their *guru*s a lot." For Neelima, *chela*s' newfound ability to choose whether or not to obey their *guru*s is a major change compared to the days when questioning one's *guru* was unheard of. "Among *guru*s and *chela*s, it is like this: they [*chela*s] say [to their *guru*s], 'you are in your place and I am in mine. If I choose to give something, then you take it.' This is how it goes now." While there is a recognition that each person within the *guru–chela* relationship has a particular place within a traditional hierarchy, according to Neelima, it is up to the *chela* whether she follows these prescriptions or not. The *chela* has agency to choose her course of action, while the *guru* must accept her *chela*'s decision.

Even within *hijra* groups, I frequently heard that people now have choices about how to live their lives that were not available in the past. Sunitha, a *hijra* in her forties, pointed out that attitudes about obtaining surgery for *hijra*s have shifted. When she was a young GNC person, Sunitha observed, "one was accepted only if she got [surgery] done. Now, we also accept those who [haven't undergone surgery]." By contrast, "when I got the surgery done, I didn't have a choice. Now we give them the option."

These discourses of choice that came up over and over again in conversation position younger GNC people—particularly *chela*s who choose nonresidential *guru–chela* relationships and GNC people who opt not to join the *hijra*s—as empowered consumers who can confidently make their own decisions. They mirror the new women's ability to confidently choose among expanded consumption choices in a liberalized India enjoying economic progress. But as we will see, by applying these ideas about choice as empowering with a broad brush, *chelas* and younger GNC people become linked to the progress narrative presuming that economic liberalization provides opportunities for all—regardless of the reality on the ground.

Conclusion

The changes in *hijra* families and households are a result of two major sets of changes in the lives of GNC people. On the one hand, the state has intervened into *hijra* lives, making it difficult for them to live in traditional households, create traditional families, and engage in the kinds of income-generating activities that *hijras* pursued in the past. At the same time, younger GNC people now have access to crucial resources that were once only available through *hijra* groups. Some GNC people in Bangalore now have improved access to rental accommodation and a greater degree of acceptance from their birth families. In addition, they can access gender affirmation surgery on their own since information about these surgeries is now available through media and online.

As a result, *chelas* started living in varied arrangements, creating "nonresidential" relationships with their *gurus*. The social changes that paved the way for younger GNC people to live outside of *hijra* groups are related to the vast changes that have swept through urban India in the wake of economic liberalization. When people discuss the changes in *hijra* communities, these complex shifts are subsumed under the rhetoric of GNC people's increased ability to choose how they live. Having access to additional choices positions GNC people as emancipated, competent consumers who are now "free" to make their own decisions. This is in direct contrast with stories of their counterparts from previous eras who did not have options to access the kinds of resources that would enable them to survive outside of *hijra* groups.

At the same time, this rhetoric overlaps with and echoes the discourse around cisgender women's ability to make "empowered" consumption choices in liberalized India. By explaining the changes in *hijra* groups using the rhetoric of choice, *chelas* and other younger GNC people are now also recruited as active participants in the ideological project of liberalization. In the next chapter, we will learn how *chelas*' new ability to live "on their own" and exercise more control over their income has caused a major shift in the power dynamics between *gurus* and *chelas* in *hijra* families.

Notes

1. Less commonly, *chelas* live under the direction of other senior *hijra* family members, like their *naani guru*, the *guru* of their *guru* (Revathi 2010).

2. *Paam padti* can be translated as "I demonstrate my sincere respect and devotion to you by touching your feet." These actions are reserved for people of a very high social status, like respected elders and spiritual leaders. I observed people simply say this phrase to *gurus*, and I also observed some who bent down, attempting to touch the feet of the person they were addressing, while the *guru*, looking pleased at this gesture of respect, tried to stop them.

3. The historical record contains limited information about *hijras*' lives, though research by Hinchy (2019) shows that *hijras* were listed in nineteenth-century government records as residing in *guru–chela* households (most commonly), but also with cisgender men lovers, in live-in domestic servitude, and "in various forms of kinship" in several districts of semi-urban and rural North India.

4. There is limited historical information about the specifics of *hijras*' lives, though Hinchy's (2019) research shows that nineteeth-century rural and semi-urban North Indian *hijras* were registered as engaging in a wide range of occupations, including "animal husbandry, farming, shopkeeping and domestic service" (2019: 140), in addition to the traditional dance and alms-collection that is common among *hijra* groups in North India.

5. Ganguly-Scrase and Scrase 2008: 81.

6. In the Indian constitution, the state is tasked with guaranteeing the right to work, education, and public assistance for the unemployed (Yadav 2020: 1). However, this system does not often work in ways the framers of the constitution imagined (Yadav 2020: 1). Part of the problem is that large groups are "invisible" in the eyes of the state (Bansal 2020: 1), particularly low-wage workers in the fast-growing "informal" or "unorganized" sector of the Indian economy. People working in this sector make up over 91 percent of the Indian working population and 75 percent of these workers are paid less than 20 rupees (about 30 US dollars) per day. Despite their low earnings, only 8 percent of these workers currently access government-provided social security-type benefits (Yadav 2020: 1).

7. Nanda (1990) notes "a few *hijras* live alone" who "feel secure enough in this work to want to be independent," and some live with their husbands (1990: 39). It is important to note that these few *hijras* joined the community and

lived in communal homes before moving away. The majority of *hijras* once depended on the community for financial and social support.

8. Cohen 1995: 25.

9. Cohen 1995: 25.

10. Semmalar 2014: 287.

11. Semmalar 2014: 287.

12. Sooryamurthy 2012: 2.

13. Sooryamurthy 2012: 2.

14. Though there exists the potential for abuse within these kinds of community-based support structures (Cohen 1995: 25).

15. The word *hammam* is an Arabic word, meaning bathhouse, implying a space where men can go to bathe, though the *hammam* is most often associated with sex work. *Hammam*s as places for bathing and engaging in sex work are specific to the south Karnataka region.

16. Reddy 2005; Nanda 1990.

17. Reddy 2005.

18. Saria 2019.

19. Reddy 2005: 157.

20. Nanda 1990.

21. Nanda 1990: 38–39.

22. *Hijras* are also divided into seven different houses, which are distinct from the households where people reside, making houses more akin to "symbolic descent groups" or "clans" that do not necessarily correspond to spatial living arrangements (Nanda 1990: 39). There is no distinct advantage in belonging to any particular house, as they are not ranked or associated with particular jobs (Nanda 1990: 39). The concept of *hijra* houses exists with only "slight variation" throughout India, though not all seven houses are represented everywhere (Nanda 1990: 39). In the Bangalore *hijra* community, all seven *hijra* houses are represented.

23. Nanda 1990: 48.

24. This incident is part of a history of Indian state governments displacing *hijra* homes by refusing to recognize their claims to land (Preston 1987).

25. Menon 2012.

26. Menon 2012.

27. Menon 2012.

28. Saria 2019: 134.

29. Transgender Persons (Protection of Rights) Bill of 2016 cited in Saria 2019: 142.

30. Saria 2019: 142.

31. See Saria 2019: 142 for how *gurus* train *chelas* in the most profitable ways of asking for money.

32. Saria 2019: 142.

33. Saria 2019: 144.

34. The Transgender Persons Protection of Rights Bill of 2016 cited in Saria 2019: 142.

35. The Transgender Persons Protection of Rights Bill 2016: Responses From the Trans & Intersex Communities.

36. Saria 2019: 142; see also Dutta 2016.

37. The Transgender Persons Protection of Rights Bill 2016: Responses From the Trans & Intersex Communities.

38. Saria 2019: 144.

39. Saria 2019: 144.

40. Reddy 2005: 150.

41. Reddy 2005: 173.

42. Saria 2021: 16.

43. Saria 2021: 15.

44. J. Sengupta 2016: 1.

45. Fernandes and Heller 2006.

46. Dickey 2012.

47. Bhatt, Murty, and Ramamurthy 2010: 135.

48. In India today, obtaining gender-affirming surgery requires a lengthy process with extensive meetings and documentation from medical and mental health professionals. In many parts of India it is available in both (more affordable) government and (prohibitively expensive for most) private hospitals. In some states such as neighboring Tamil Nadu, the procedure is free in government hospitals, so cost is no longer a barrier. By and large, people report better results from surgeries performed in private hospitals, though the majority of GNC people cannot afford private medical care.

49. Nanda 1990: 26–27.

50. Some surgeries were also performed "stealthily" in licensed clinics (Revathi 2010: 75).

51. Ganguly-Scrase and Scrase 2008: 81.

52. Munshi 1998: 38.

53. Munshi 1998: 38; see also Oza 2006.

54. Munshi 1998: 44.

55. Munshi 1998: 38.

56. Ganguly-Scrase and Scrase 2008: 81.
57. As Jain et al. (2019) argue, middle- and elite-class urbanites "now treat information gathering as an integral part of the shopping experience." They find 85 percent of consumers in these social classes "check at least two data points (beyond prices and discounts)" before making purchases, while 50 percent conduct online research of some kind.
58. Fernandes and Heller 2006.

4

"You Can Do Whatever"

Shifting Authority in *Hijra* Family Relationships

Introduction

Neelima, a transgender woman in her mid-sixties, smiled thoughtfully as she gazed back at me, carefully considering my question. We were sitting across from each other at a small table in the NGO office where Neelima worked. Though she lives alone now, as a young GNC person, Neelima lived in a *hammam* with her *hijra* family. I asked about the kinds of changes Neelima had witnessed in *guru–chela* relationships as I was interested in understanding how *gurus*' expectations of their *chelas* have changed. I mentioned Vandana's relationship with her *chela* in the *hammam* that we heard about in the last chapter, asking if Neelima could think of any relationships she knew of that worked like that. She paused and focused her serious eyes on a point above me on the wall, thinking as she fiddled with the long gold chain that was tucked under her bright, patterned *sari*. Then, looking back at me, she grinned and replied, "You are talking about those olden days. But now, this is the new times."

In her lifetime, Neelima has witnessed a dramatic shift in the expectations of *gurus* and *chelas* in the "new times," as compared to the "olden days." In the past, she explained, "the *chela* was more obedient and the *guru* was more respected ... the *chela* couldn't go against the word of the *guru*; she was obliged to follow what the *guru* told her." For Neelima, a key feature of *guru–chela* relationships in the "olden days" was the level of authority *gurus* held within the relationship. As she recounts, "earlier, the *guru* had authority and she would order the *chela* to do what she was asked." Because *gurus* had a claim on authority in this relationship, *chela*s owed *guru*s this respect and were required to obey them. As Neelima observed, "the way a *chela* would behave with her *guru* has changed" because "those days the respect [expected to be demonstrated] was more."

Today, the authority *guru*s once held is shrinking, and *chela*s are no longer expected to demonstrate this degree of respect for their *guru*s. Contrary to when Neelima was a young *chela*, "now the *guru–chela* relationship is friendly and close." For Neelima, the imperative to show respect to *guru*s inhibited close relationships among *guru*s and *chela*s. But today the relationship feels more like a partnership than a hierarchy.

When I asked elder *guru*s about their reactions to the changes in *guru–chela* relationships, they spoke of how the *guru–chela* relationship is now less hands-on than it was when they were *chela*s. In the "olden days," the lives of *guru*s and *chela*s were intertwined since they lived together and their behavior was shaped by the expectations of the *guru–chela* system. As Neelima explained, "earlier the *chela* had to live within the parameters of the system and had to live under the *guru*. Now *guru*s and *chela*s lead their separate lives. They're independent." In years past, residential *guru–chela* relationships were characterized by physical closeness, financial–social interdependence, and the behaviors of both *guru*s and *chela*s acknowledged the authority of *guru*s. By contrast, nonresidential *guru*s and *chela*s now lead "separate" and "independent" lives. According to Neelima, because *chela*s and *guru*s usually do not live in the same space, everyone becomes busy with their own lives and they do not often make the time to see each other. "*Chela*s go and meet their *guru* when they feel like it, but if they don't feel like it, they will not go and meet their *guru* at all. Once in a few months, maybe four times a year or even twice in a year, they may go."

Throughout our conversation, Neelima's tone toward the transformation in *guru–chela* relationships was distinctly positive. This is usually only how younger *chela*s and other GNC people who opt not to join the *hijra*s speak about these changes, so I was surprised to hear an elder *hijra* speaking positively about this transformation. Of course, since she works at an NGO, Neelima is less dependent on the *guru–chela* system for survival than many elder *hijra*s who struggle to support themselves. Since she had mentioned the "good coordination" between *guru*s and *chela*s, I asked Neelima how she thinks *guru*s specifically feel about these changes. She paused for a moment and then replied,

Now the society is growing large and it is also changing. So *gurus* have understood that if they accept these changes, then the *chelas* would choose to be with them. If they don't accept these changes, then the *chelas* would leave their *gurus* and go away. So the *gurus* know that they have to accept these changes.

From Neelima's perspective, *gurus* understand that the changes in the *guru–chela* relationship are not under their control. Thus, many *gurus* make a point of acting in ways that would make them attractive to potential *chelas*.

As Neelima spoke about these major changes in the *guru–chela* relationship, I wondered: Why has the authority once held by *gurus* decreased? What are the consequences of *gurus*' decreased authority for individual *guru–chela* relationships? And what sorts of consequences does *gurus*' decreased authority entail for the *hijra* system as a whole? In this chapter, I show that, in these "new times," the *guru–chela* relationship has been adapted to suit the changing social landscape that younger, urban GNC people inhabit. As the last chapter explained, the social changes that allowed younger GNC people to access surgery and housing enabled younger GNC people to live outside *hijra* groups, and Chapter 2 detailed how some younger GNC people have expanded access to employment opportunities (particularly middle-class office employment).

These changes have impacted the mutual need that once brought *gurus* and *chelas* together. Now younger GNC people can access resources like surgery, housing, and employment that were once provided only by *gurus*. As a result, they have come to devalue the reciprocal support provided within the *guru–chela* relationship, and increasingly believe the support *gurus* expect from *chelas* in residential *guru–chela* relationships is unfair. Many are unwilling to provide this support.

As the support *gurus* provide is devalued, their authority within the *guru–chela* relationship is eroded. When *gurus* possessed authority within the relationship, they primarily determined the kinds of actions and behaviors considered acceptable, but as their authority wanes, they find themselves with reduced decision-making power. From Neelima's perspective, *gurus* understand that if they continue claiming authority within the *guru–chela* relationship, younger GNC people would be unlikely to select them as their *gurus*. These *gurus* would then have fewer *chelas*, which would negatively impact their status within the community. This chapter traces the consequences of *gurus'* decreasing authority for individual *gurus* and *chelas* and for the *hijra* system generally.

The "New" Woman and Shifting Relationships of Authority

The last chapter touched on how the ideology of the "new" woman emphasizes her ability to choose the kind of life she desires. Because of its emphasis on individual choice, this discourse also posits that middle-class cisgender women's relationship to authority is shifting. These newly empowered women are less likely to submit to traditional authority figures like older family members. Just as younger GNC people align themselves with this new economic model and its emphasis on choice, they too are less likely to submit to familial authority figures like *gurus*.

Around the time that middle-class cis women gained increased economic power, TV shows and advertising began to emphasize women's emancipation from the social structures that once subordinated them—particularly the family. Popular TV shows portrayed images of the "emancipated woman" who is untethered from the bonds of familial authority and the resulting social expectations that once shaped her life. Her newfound freedom from controlling family members allows her to make her own choices about her life, thus empowering her to "do what she does and be what she is out of conscious choice,"[1] instead of submitting to the wishes of her elders. It is this emancipated "new" woman figure that many trans women and younger GNC people also aspire to. As a result, the majority of *guru–chela* relationships I heard about look very different from traditional residential *guru–chela* relationships, impacting behaviors within *guru–chela* relationships and *hijra* communities more generally.

Authority and Hierarchy in *Hijra* Relationships

In "traditional" *guru–chela* relationships, the authority accorded to *gurus*— described as "the justifiable right, not just the ability, to exercise power"[2]— is reinforced by an emphasis on hierarchy, a prominent feature within *hijra* communities.[3] People who occupy higher positions in hierarchies hold authority only to the extent that they can successfully convince those below them that their claim to power is legitimate.[4] Because *chelas* are less dependent on their *gurus* than they were in the past, *gurus* now have a difficult time convincing *chelas* to recognize their claim on authority is warranted.

Although the traditional *guru–chela* relationship is based on mutual need and reciprocal support, the power structure is asymmetrical, implicitly privileging *gurus*[5] in part because they control the material resources that are shared (ideally equitably) among everyone in their *hijra* family. Because *gurus* controlled the material resources that younger GNC people needed for survival, their claim to power within the *guru–chela* relationship was not openly questioned. Although residential *gurus* and *chelas* are financially interdependent upon one another, as the head of her *hijra* family the *guru* possessed the unquestioned authority to make financial decisions. But now younger GNC people can access these resources on their own, and *gurus'* claim on such authority is increasingly called into question.

The behaviors and duties expected within traditional *guru–chela* relationships reflect each person's place within the hierarchy. To demonstrate their respect for this hierarchy and the *hijra* system as a whole, *chelas* are expected to show loyalty, obedience, and, above all, respect for their *gurus*. In addition to sharing their earnings with their *gurus*, *chelas* are traditionally expected to attend to the cooking, cleaning, and other household duties.[6] They are liable to be punished verbally and/or physically if they neglect these duties, rendering them "at the beck and call of their *gurus*."[7] *Gurus* are expected to treat their *chelas* fairly and to supply them with necessities like food, clothing, and shelter. They are also expected to teach their *chelas* the kinds of behaviors that will help them in their quest to rise in stature within the community.[8] Stature is a key aspect of *hijra* social organization, referring not necessarily to age but to the amount of time one has been involved with the *hijra* system.[9] But it is also impacted by how a *hijra* behaves, both among community members and the wider society. In addition, within the community, *gurus* are accorded higher social status, such that becoming a *guru* entails "a route to upward mobility," with a *guru's* status climbing as she obtains more and more *chelas*.[10]

While *gurus'* authority was traditionally accepted by most *chelas*, it was not completely unchallenged. Research from the 1980s and 1990s reveals that many *chelas* articulated what Scott refers to as a "hidden transcript" when they spoke with researchers, bemoaning the verbal and physical abuse they sometimes incurred at the hands of their *gurus*.[11] Nanda notes that "younger [*chelas*] often complain (to outsiders) about the restrictions and hardships of their life."[12] Similarly, Reddy reports hearing "incessant complaining" about the "burdensome obligations" that *chelas* were required to perform and the kinds of abuse they could expect if they disobeyed their *gurus*.[13] However, when Nanda asked a *chela* who complained about her *guru* whether she had considered "do[ing] without the *guru* altogether," the *chela* replied, "Never, it cannot be … you cannot be without a *guru*. How can we live like this in a *sari* [that is, as a visibly GNC person] without a *guru*? It is not possible."[14] Despite the hardships *chelas* recounted, not a single *hijra* Reddy spoke to said she would rather live independent of her *guru* or the *hijra* community.[15]

Both researchers found *chelas* arguing that breaking away from their *hijra* families would be detrimental to their survival.[16] Although becoming independent of the group would mean they would no longer be responsible for the upkeep of their *guru* and the chores that enabled her home to run smoothly,[17] *hijras* had limited access to a wider community and a sense of belonging that they sought, so becoming independent of *hijra* relationships would be self-defeating. As Nanda explains, independence does not mean "freedom, but social suicide … *hijras* hardly ever think seriously about severing their ties with the community and going out on their own."[18] Even if a *chela* felt disadvantaged within the *guru–chela* system, she did not consider abandoning those relationships.[19]

The Changing Cost–Benefit Calculus in *Guru–Chela* Relationships

When older *hijras* like Neelima were growing up, the *guru–chela* relationship was intended to fulfill the mutual needs of each party through reciprocal support. *Gurus* offered *chelas* housing, employment assistance, and access to surgery, in addition to mentorship. In turn, the *chela* was expected to contribute most of her income for her upkeep and household expenses. The reciprocal support provided through *hijra* systems enabled this economically marginalized and socially excluded group to survive.

These relationships of mutual support depend on the presence of (generally) more than one *chela* to support an aging *guru*. Therefore, this system relies on the idea that there will always be a steady stream of *chelas* to support the *gurus* above them in the hierarchy. Like "pay-as-you-go" social security systems, the younger generations contribute part of their income to support older *gurus* who cannot generate their own income. Younger *chelas* are willing to do this not just because they are getting support from *gurus* but also because they recognize that when they become elder *gurus* and struggle to support themselves, they will be financially supported by their own younger *chelas*.

Today, the material support once provided only through *hijra* support systems is increasingly available to younger urban GNC people outside of *hijra* systems, devaluing it in the eyes of *chelas*. This has led to an imbalance in the mutual need that once brought *gurus* and *chelas* together: while there is less of an impetus for the younger generation to participate in traditional *hijra* relationships, the needs of *gurus* who depend on financial contributions from *chelas* remain the same. Unfortunately for *gurus*, younger *chelas* are increasingly unwilling to fulfill their expectations of financial support, straining the *guru–chela* system.

As the costs–benefits analysis has shifted, the ways that *chelas* interpret the reciprocal support offered by each party have also changed. As a result, *chelas* and other younger GNC people increasingly characterize the reciprocal support expected of *chelas* in residential *guru–chela* relationships (that is, sharing their income with a *guru*) as unreasonable. This was the number one explanation that people reported they did not want to participate in residential *guru–chela* relationships. "Everyone wants their money and they don't want to give it to the *guru*," reported Mariyamma, the trans woman in her fifties from Chapter 3. Several other nonresidential *chelas* reported that they do not participate in *guru–chela* living situations because the financial demands of *gurus* from their *chelas* are too high. *Chelas* and other younger GNC people are understandably suspicious of a system requiring them to contribute their income to a *guru* who provides resources they can access on their own.

Chelas who were formerly part of residential *guru–chela* relationships spoke bitterly about their lack of control over their income. As Suma, the trans woman in her thirties we heard from in the last chapter who faced violence from neighborhood boys on Divali, explained, "in [traditional] *guru–chela* relationships, it was very strict … you really needed to be very honest to them, to give all your money." *Chelas* often emphasized how little money they were allowed to keep. Kanika, the transgender woman in her forties who spoke of the new opportunities for "the younger generation" of GNC people in the last chapter, joined a group of *hijra*s as a teenager. She went to live with her *guru*, earning a livelihood through soliciting money in Mumbai.

> Hardly we used to earn 300, 400 rupees [5–7 US dollars per day] from begging in Bombay. That also, we had to give. Nothing was given to us, they only used to give us [that is, allow us to keep] twenty rupees, thirty rupees, [approx. 0.50 US dollars] that's it.

Some might say that in leveling the charge of unfairness at the wider *hijra* system, *chela*s are neglecting to mention the reciprocal support provided by their *guru*s. Yet many younger GNC people and *chela*s noted questionable spending decisions made by *guru*s. The problem with giving the *guru* a portion of their income, they observed, is that they spend that money not only on household expenses or necessities (which is expected) but on extravagant personal luxuries, their own romantic partners, and even members of their birth families. Nor could *chela*s in the past demand that their *guru*s put a stop to such practices since they lacked any leverage in the relationship and depended on them for key resources. Since they now can acquire those needs on their own, the authority of *guru*s to make decisions about their shared income is increasingly questioned.

*Chela*s also often spoke about how their *guru*s would strongly encourage them not to have romantic partners. This is because *guru*s were afraid that their *chela*s would spend their income on their romantic partners instead of sharing it with them. *Guru*s worked to ensure that their *chela*s did not have boyfriends by carefully monitoring the movements of their *chela*s. These restrictions against having romantic relationships are an important reason that younger GNC people report not wanting to enter into residential *guru–chela* relationships. For example, Utham, a *kothi* in their thirties, considered becoming a *hijra* as a teenager. However, they explained, "In the [*guru–chela*] system, they have so many restrictions, like we can't have a partner … but we want to have a partner because, see, our desire is [to live] how general society people live, in a romantic relationship. We want to live like that." Utham continued, "If we have a boyfriend, that time [upon finding out], the *guru* will hit us and they will be very angry." They shook their head concluding, "All these kinds of problems will happen." Many *chela*s and other GNC people argue that *guru*s' monetary expectations perpetuate controlling and abusive behaviors toward their *chela*s. Actions by *guru*s that were once accepted as part of protecting their family's income are increasingly portrayed as aberrant and pathological.

Despite voicing strong objections about many of the dynamics around money within residential *guru–chela* relationships, some *chelas* point out that there are aspects of *gurus* policing *chelas'* earnings that can be beneficial. As Suma, the trans woman who "escaped" from her guru after obtaining surgery, observed, "it's good too because people earn money from begging and sex work, but then they fall in love with some stupid man and they give all their money to him!"[20] She explained that this is a serious problem because these cisgender men receive a lot of financial assistance from their *hijra* (or trans woman) partner yet the relationships almost always ends with the *hijra* (or trans woman) heartbroken and wishing that she had saved that money. The paternalistic guidance provided by an authoritative *guru* could prevent this from happening. As Suma points out, "after all, you are working hard to get this money, why should you waste it on some asshole?!" However, Suma does not think the *gurus'* concern stems from a disinterested desire to help their *chelas* manage their money or avoid heartbreak. She sees them as acting purely from self-interest: "Their worry is like, 'oh my God, my income is going to someone else!'"

"New" *Chelas*: Increased Authority and Financial Autonomy

As a result of the devaluation of *gurus'* contributions in *guru–chela* relationships and the resulting decrease in the authority *gurus* hold, the *guru–chela* system has been reimagined in ways that reflect the current social climate around gender nonconformity in urban India. Instead of emphasizing behaviors that reinforce the hierarchical nature of *guru–chela* relationships, the needs of younger GNC people are increasingly prioritized, with the hierarchical aspect of the *guru–chela* relationship reserved for ceremonial occasions.

Financial interdependence was a crucial aspect of residential *guru–chela* relationships that began from the time new *chelas* joined the *hijras*. New *chelas* are required to undergo an initiation ceremony, for which they must pay a sum of money to their chosen *guru*.[21] If they find themselves dissatisfied, *chelas* are permitted to change their *gurus*. However, each time they do this, they must pay their new *guru* at least twice the amount they originally paid for their initiation, so this option can quickly become a very expensive one. For example, in the late 1990s, a *hijra* in Bombay paid 80,000 rupees (approximately 1,200 US dollars at the time), an enormous sum, to change her *guru* yet again.[22] During her ethnographic fieldwork, Reddy asked her research participants why anyone would want to risk that kind of debt in order to once again become a *chela* who is obligated to obey a different *guru*. Her participants were wide-eyed with shock that she would ask such a question, explaining, "It is because we need our *guru*s, our people."[23] Because it was essential for GNC people to have a *guru* for survival, *guru*s as a group possessed a high degree of authority over *chela*s. "If the *chela* wanted to break away from the *guru*, they had to go to another *guru*," observed Rishabh, a GNC person and longtime activist in their fifties. As a result of the debts frequently incurred as a result of the initiation ceremony, "*guru*s had a lot of control over *chela*s."

But today the financial independence *chela*s now exercise has profoundly shifted the power dynamics between *guru*s and *chela*s. Neelima, the transgender woman in her fifties whom we heard from at the beginning of this chapter, has witnessed how *chela*s' financial autonomy has dramatically altered their willingness to maintain the *guru–chela* relationship. As she observed, "now the standard of living [among *chela*s] has improved. Earlier they [*chela*s] used to be poorer." As a result, Neelima explained,

> they could not [afford to] break away from the *guru*. [If there was a dispute,] the *chela* was punished [regardless of who was at fault]. That is why in the past, the *chela*s conducted themselves submissively. They feared the punishment and hence obeyed the *guru*. If the *guru* ordered them not to go and solicit money at a certain place or not to buy rice from a certain shop, they did not go there.

But now *chela*s have more control over their income, making the option of terminating their relationship with their *guru* more palatable. "Nowadays, if there happens to be some dispute between the *guru* and the *chela*, then the *chela* will end her relationship with the *guru*." There are still consequences for the dissolution of this relationship, and *chela*s must still pay a fine. However, the control *chela*s now exercise over the money they earn means they are no longer scared into submission through the imposition of a fine. As they have gained access to necessary resources and control over their own income, *chela*s increasingly act with the authority once reserved for *guru*s. Now that it is not a huge financial burden to switch *guru*s, Rishabh observed, "they don't stick with one *guru* for a long time. They keep changing their *guru*s all the time."

Perhaps the biggest cause of the shift toward financial independence on the part of *chela*s stems from the fact that many *guru*s and *chela*s no longer reside in the same household. Because they live separately, the amount of their earnings that *chela*s give to their *guru*s is often decided upon by the *chela*, based largely on her income and her own expenses and less so on her *guru*'s needs. "In [traditional] *guru–chela* relationships, it was very strict…," Suma remarked. "But nowadays, it depends. [The *guru* will say] 'You can stay with me, you can stay wherever, you can do whatever [you want].'" In rare cases, I heard that the amount a *chela* gives is decided upon by her *guru*, but even then the amount the *guru* requested was significantly less than *guru*s would have previously felt comfortable requesting.

The mobility of (particularly younger) *hijra*s combined with their ability to control their income and the changing living arrangements and employment opportunities for younger GNC people have made it difficult for *guru*s to keep track of their *chela*s, much less attempt to exert authority over them. Previously, *chela*s had to ask permission from their *guru*s to travel; now they just tell the *guru*s that they are going away and leave without seeking permission. For example, in order to earn money to pay for their surgeries, many of the *hijra*s I spoke with had lived for a few years in Mumbai to earn money through sex work or soliciting money and only then returned to Bangalore. Even when they are based in Bangalore, younger *hijra*s often travel to visit friends, see new places, and/or work, making it difficult for *guru*s to know where their *chela*s are. Others permanently move without informing their *guru*, leaving the *guru* unsure whether her *chela* will return or whether she has settled down and found another *guru* in her new home. Rishabh chuckled as they summed matters up: "The *guru*s have also now become very confused about their *chela*s."

The *Guru–Chela* System Reimagined: Impacts of Outside Scrutiny

The authority that *guru*s once held over their *chela*s and within *hijra* communities is also being eroded by the increased intervention of other authority figures, especially police and government officials. *Hijra*s have historically been subjected to state surveillance, stretching back at least to the efforts of the British colonial administration to brand them as a "criminal tribe."[24] More recently, *hijras* have been folded into nationalist projects undertaken by the state.[25] As state officials have become more willing to intervene in disputes within *hijra* groups, they have been increasingly called on by *chelas* to do so. These state officials are seen as alternate (and even superior) authority figures whose authority extends to all *hijras*—including *gurus*—by virtue of their state-sanctioned positions in government.

Because *hijras* were historically marginalized, until quite recently their communities were considered as relatively separate from "the general society," thus largely shrouding the behaviors that occurred within the *hijra* system from public view. This has changed as *hijra* representation in media increased exponentially in past decades, and as a result, there is more awareness of the *hijra* system and its structures among the general public. In turn, the police and government officials are increasingly willing to intervene in *hijra* communities when they receive reports of physical and financial abuse of *chelas* by their *gurus*.

Although traditional *hijra* communities originally came into being because gender (and sexual) nonconforming people were not welcome into any other group, these communities also generated oppressive and abusive behaviors directed against their members. A longtime cisgender activist in his forties who is now employed in a sexual health-focused NGO, Ramarajan explained that the *hijra* community "is really the one that took them in when they had no place to go; it was very nurturing. At the same time, it has its abusive strands. So, it's like a dysfunctional relationship with a lot of violence within, but also, it's been the only refuge for a lot of people."

In the past some *gurus* used violence as a means to control and demonstrate their authority over their *chelas*. Anyone who attempted to live outside of the community would have incurred extreme resistance from senior *gurus*, including physical violence. But today the acceptable levels of violence within *hijra* relationships have reduced significantly. Because there is greater general awareness about the potential for harassment within *hijra* systems, *chelas* are now more comfortable approaching outsiders (like the police) when problems arise. As Neelima observed,

> the involvement of the government is different now. See, the administration is aware of the situation now. Earlier no one went to the

police station [to lodge complaints against *gurus*]. Now they can go and complain if there's any exploitation … [and] police will enforce the law. And they'll punish the culprits…. See, if a *chela* complains at the police station that her *guru* is torturing her, then the *guru* would be punished. In the past, it was the *chela* being punished by the *guru* [regardless of who was at fault].

For Neelima, the ability to involve outside authorities such as the police in *guru–chela* disputes has profoundly shifted the power dynamic between *gurus* and *chelas*. "Now the *guru* is scared. Now, *chelas* have the support of … the government…. Earlier [*chelas*] used to obey [whatever the *guru* said]. Now they will go to the police commissioner's office [if they do not want to obey the *guru*]."

The fear of how the *guru–chela* relationship will be perceived by others has changed how *gurus* interact with their *chelas*. Utham reports that *gurus* increasingly act out of fear that their *chelas* will tell others if they are abusing them. "Some *hijra* community people are very scared because [they think,] 'if I am giving trouble to my *chela* … they will file a case [against me].'" Nodding vigorously, they added, "For some of them, that fear is real." As a result of this newfound fear, many *gurus* have reduced the expectations they previously held of their *chelas*, asking themselves (in the words of Utham), "Why should we take the risk [of possible police involvement]?" But the result is a further diminishment of *gurus'* authority, as state authority now is seen as superseding that of *gurus*.

Impacts of Shifting Authority on *Chelas'* Expected Behavior

An important way expected behaviors within the *guru–chela* relationship have shifted is evident in how *chelas* demonstrate respect for their *gurus*. As Suma observed,

in [traditional] *guru–chela* relationships, it was very strict … you really needed to be very [respectful] to them…. They were always, you know, [acting] like a father, [ordering you to] "do this, don't do that, come here, stay like that!" Now, it's not drastic control, not like [you are] a puppet nowadays…. It's a little changed, a little more free.

In Suma's experience, the head of her *hijra* family demanded the level of respect, obedience, and authority that fathers are often accorded in cishet families. However, as *gurus'* claim to authority has eroded, the respect that *chela*s are expected to demonstrate toward their *gurus* is mostly symbolic and reserved for special occasions. For Shanthi, a trans woman who is also a nonresidential *chela* in her twenties, the shift in the amount of power a *guru* holds over her *chela*s dramatically changed the amount of respect *chela*s are expected to demonstrate. Previously, some *gurus* would use the power they possessed to "torture" their *chela*s when they did not obey the *guru*. *Chela*s depended on *gurus* for the material resources they needed to survive, so the authority they held was felt on an everyday, material level; likewise, the respect for this authority that *chela*s were expected to demonstrate was pervasive in their daily interactions. But now things are quite different.

> The power is still there but there is less torture … actually, the power is just superficial. The *guru* has to sit at a higher level and we [*chela*s] have to sit at a lower level. We have to say "*Paam padti;*" we have to respect them. On festival days, we have to either give money or jewelry to them.

For Shanthi, *gurus* still possess authority, but this authority is largely symbolic, and *chela*s can satisfy the expectation that they demonstrate respect to their *gurus* in displays of subservience during ritual occasions.

The power dynamic between *gurus* and *chela*s has shifted to such a degree that *chela*s are now empowered to place demands on their *gurus*, which would have been impossible previously. Before she agreed to become the *chela* of her *guru*, Shanthi explained that she would participate in this relationship only on the condition that her *guru* would agree not to adopt any other *chela* except herself. She issued this demand because she had witnessed other *gurus* with many *chela*s depend on their income as their only source of livelihood. Shanthi did not want to enter into a relationship where her *guru* would think of her in that way. Because of the declining authority of *gurus* to dictate the terms of the *guru–chela* relationship, Shanti was able to avoid getting into such a situation by clearly articulating the conditions of their relationship before she agreed to become a *chela*. Twenty-five years ago, *gurus* still exercised enough authority that such a conversation would have been unimaginable.

"I Am Not a *Hijra*" (But I Have a *Guru*)

Hijra systems have undergone major changes as *gurus* lose the authority they once exercised and as some younger GNC people report feeling that they have greater opportunities. These changes have also impacted how *chelas* understand themselves and their identities vis-à-vis *hijra* groups.

One of the most surprising aspects of the *hijra*–trans woman divide is how much overlap I found between these two identities, particularly for the trans women who insist they are not *hijras*. To understand why trans women who are *chelas* disavow their identification with *hijras*, we need to consider both the new opportunities available to GNC people and the recent changes in *guru*–*chela* relationships.

As we saw in Chapter 2, the newfound opportunities for GNC people to engage in office employment have enabled trans women to imagine themselves fulfilling their class aspirations while simultaneously confirming the propriety of their gender identities. Engaging in office work also differentiates them from *hijras*, who are associated with the stigmatizing occupations of soliciting money and sex work. Trans women are pursuing the respectability accorded to middle-class cis women by emphasizing their proximity to middle-class femininity. Thus, identifying as transgender, instead of and even in opposition to *hijras*, allows trans women to position themselves as closer to the ideals of respectable middle-class womanhood.

However, this is not the only reason trans women disidentify with *hijras*. In addition to considering the benefits disidentifying with *hijras* offers trans women, we need to consider the difference between stereotypical understandings about what it means to be a *hijra* and the reality of having a *guru* and being a *chela* today. The stereotypical or "traditional" *hijra* is someone who ran away from their birth family to find others "like them." Upon finding a *hijra* group to join, the person takes on a *guru*, whom they are expected to unquestioningly obey. The *guru* offers her *chela* a place to live, the option to obtain gender affirmation surgery, and opportunities to participate in sex work and/or solicit money. It is understood that there are no other employment options open to *hijras*. In return, the *chela* shares her income with her *guru* and other members of her *hijra* family until she is too old to work. Then she will collect income from and offer opportunities to her own *chelas*.

For most *gurus* and *chelas* I spoke with, their relationship looks very different from "traditional" *guru–chela* relationships. These changes in *guru–chela* relationships combined with increased opportunities for some trans women mean that the lives of *chelas* today are very different from the stereotypical image most people hold of *hijras*. Because trans women can increasingly obtain rental flats, *guru–chela* relationships are largely nonresidential, and the financial interdependence that once characterized this relationship has reduced drastically. In addition, the *guru–chela* relationship has transformed from a relationship emphasizing hierarchical authority to a more relaxed friendship wherein the hierarchy is experienced as largely "symbolic."

For the trans women I spoke with, their lives differ dramatically from the lives of "traditional" *hijras*. This discrepancy between their own lives and their ideas of "traditional" *hijras* is also part of the reason that these trans women disidentify with *hijras*. The image that comes to mind when they think of a "traditional" *hijra* could not be more different than their own lives and their own self-understandings. One way that younger *chelas* react to the discrepancy between "traditional" *guru–chela* relationships and their very different relationships with their *gurus* is to characterize themselves as *chelas* "for the name's sake."

In Name Alone: *Chelas* "For the Name's Sake"

When I first met Deepa (recounted in the Introduction), she adamantly stated that she did not want to be recognized as a *hijra*. Yet Deepa later revealed that she has a nonresidential *guru*. Curious, I asked how she could *not* be a *hijra*, yet also be a *chela*. She explained that this was a common scenario and that many other trans women she knew did not want to be recognized as *hijras* at the same time that they took part in nonresidential *guru–chela* relationships. The social changes discussed in this book that enable GNC people to live outside of *hijra* communities also allow *chelas* like Deepa to enter into nonresidential *guru–chela* relationships that are very different from "traditional" *guru–chela* relationships. For her peer group, Deepa explained,

> See, we are working [outside of *hijra* groups] and we agree totally with [that is, show respect to] our mummy [*guru*] and we are earning

money from other sources. We are not begging, we are not [doing] any [occupations associated with *hijras*, like sex work]. There is no need to do all these things like traditional *hijras*. We're totally [financially] independent. For the name's sake, we are *chelas* in the *hammam*, but we [don't live there and] are earning money from other sources.

In Deepa's experience, the extent to which people follow traditional expectations in *guru–chela* relationships is determined in large part by their access to employment options. For *chelas* like her, who participate in nonresidential *guru–chela* relationships and work outside of *hijra* groups, Deepa observed, "We don't depend on *gurus*. Just for the name's sake, we have *gurus*, that's all." For Deepa and other *chelas* like her, their relationships are so different from traditional *guru–chela* relationships that they are almost unrecognizable as *guru–chela* relationships.

For younger trans women who are *chelas*, yet do not identify as *hijras*, the question of whether or not they are part of the *hijra* community is complex. Uma is a trans woman in her thirties who has been employed for about 10 years in a sexual rights NGO. As a teenager, she became a *chela* in a nonresidential *guru–chela* relationship. At this time, Uma considered becoming a residential *chela* and engaging in sex work and soliciting money but observed behaviors she perceived as abusive within the *hijra* system and decided against becoming a residential *chela*. She explained,

See, when I entered the community, at that time, I didn't know all these things [about the *guru–chela* system]. That time, I had a *guru*. Then, slowly, I realized I don't like that system. I mean, I like the system, but abuse occurs, right? I don't like abuse and all that. Then, slowly, I realized I don't like that culture. Then, I stopped following that *guru–chela* system and now I'm not part of all that. Now I'm away from all that.

As she spoke, Uma sounded confident in her decision to discontinue her participation in the *guru–chela* system as she firmly positioned herself outside of the system. However, Uma later revealed that her relationship to the *hijra* system is more complex than simply being "away from" it. She remarked, "It is very difficult [to explain] because sometimes—sometimes I'm—See, I *am* with the community, I *am* in the community, I *am* in that." Uma then explained that part of the reason she feels she cannot be fully "away from" *hijras* is that she fears negative consequences from those inside the community and that her relationships with people in the community would suffer. As Uma stated, "See, if I'm not part of the *hijra* community, they'll harass me and also they'll create problems for me, fight with me, all that…. If I'm not a *chela* in the *hijra* system, it's very problematic for me." Thus, despite her desire to self-identify as not a *hijra*, Uma continues to be "with the community" partly because she believes she will incur negative consequences if she were actually "away from all that."

Even *chela*s like Sanya who "escaped" from residential *guru–chela* relationships admit that there is some ambiguity about whether or not they are part of *hijra* groups. Today, Sanya adamantly explained that she does not consider herself to be part of a *hijra* group. However, like many other *chela*s I spoke with, she also observed that the degree to which she is part of the group is a question without clear-cut answers. Indeed, Sanya emphasized that when she "escaped" from her *hijra* family in Mumbai,

> it's not like one day I said, like, "I'm leaving the community" or something like that…. It's not like [I said,] "you are no longer my *guru*" or anything like that. I didn't say that. See, even if I actually met her [my *guru*] somewhere or something like that, I'd say "yeah, *paampadti*, Mummy," and all that. But that's it. Not very, you know, emotionally attached. Just like "hi," and all that [that is, exchanging pleasantries].

Sanya clearly stated that she no longer self-identifies as a *hijra* and she does not consider herself to be a part of the group. However, she did not directly voice these feelings to the members of her *hijra* family. In addition, Sanya indicated that she would still greet her *guru* by showing the same level of respect as if she were still part of the group. In fact, Sanya's prediction of how she would behave if she were to come across her *guru* sounds remarkably similar to how nonresidential *chela*s report that they behave on the infrequent occasions when they visit their *guru*s.

These stories touch on the different ways that trans women who are *chela*s disidentify with *hijra*s. For Deepa and her trans women friends, they do not identify themselves as *hijra*s because their status as independently employed in middle-class office jobs feels incommensurate with being a *hijra*. In the cases of both Sanya and Uma, they took conscious actions to limit their participation in *hijra* groups, which is part of why they do not identify as *hijra*s. The interesting thing is that all of these *chela*s reported that if and when they met their *guru* and/or other *hijra* elders, they would greet them politely and undertake actions that demonstrate their respect. In spite of their initial insistence that they are not associated with *hijras*, these trans women demonstrate the complexity of being *chelas* "for the name's sake" who report behaving in surprisingly similar ways to their counterparts in nonresidential *guru–chela* relationships.[26]

The Value of Being Kind and Gentle: Behavioral Changes among *Gurus*

The decline in the authority of *gurus* and the resulting shifts in expectations around the *guru–chela* relationship have also led to profound changes in the kinds of behaviors that are rewarded within *hijra* communities. This is largely due to shifts in which kinds of *gurus* are considered as desirable to potential *chelas*.

Gurus with several *chelas* have higher social status within *hijra* communities, but as noted earlier, only the *gurus* who have changed their expectations of *chelas* are likely to attract multiple *chelas* today. This reflects a complete reversal of the behaviors that previously earned a *guru* more *chelas*. According to Manjunath, a cisgender man in his forties and longtime activist employed in the NGO sector,

> See, the dominant *hijras* used to have more *chelas*. They're big, tough. Nowadays, a lot of … *hijras* are linked to what they call "weak *gurus*" who are more liberal, who don't take money from you. So suddenly, now you see all these *gurus* who don't [hold traditional expectations of] their *chelas* have a lot of *chelas*.

For Manjunath, this change in behavior preferences for *gurus* indicates that "people are shifting" their expectations about the *guru–chela* relationship. Now *chelas* question their *gurus* (as opposed to simply obeying them) and prefer "liberal" *gurus* who do not hold traditional expectations of their *chelas*. *Gurus* who have not adapted to these changes are less likely to obtain many *chelas*, which negatively affects their social status within the community.

These changes in the power dynamics of *hijra* communities are reflected in how *chelas* discuss the process of requesting that someone become their *guru*. Akrithi, the trans woman NGO worker in her thirties whose story appears in Chapter 2, was first drawn to her *guru* because of her soft-spoken nature. She explained that when she met her *guru*,

> she was so kind. She was so [pause] gentle. And … not like other *gurus*, like rude people who beat their *chela*s. Oooh, I don't want to become their *chela*s at all! But then [my *guru*] was a very soft and patient … *hijra*. So then I went and told her, "I want to become *your* daughter." (Emphasis original)

For Akrithi, the determining factor in choosing a *guru* was her *guru*'s "kind" and "gentle" manner, which was different from other more traditional (that is, demanding) *gurus*.

These shifts in *gurus*' preferred behavior indicate broader changes within the structure of *hijra* groups. In "traditional" *guru–chela* relationships, the behavior of *gurus* was intended to showcase their authority and elevated status within the relationship. Likewise, the expected behavior of *chela*s indicated their subordinate status. Because they previously held more power than *chela*s, *gurus* exerted a lot of control within the community. However, as Manjunath explained,

> the [power held] by seniors in the community has come down drastically in Bangalore. It was a very [*pause*] closely controlled community ten years ago. Today, it is not … it's changed quite a bit. They've democratized the relationships within the community.

In the 20-plus years that he has been involved in sexual rights activism, Manjunath has witnessed the transformation of the social organization of *hijra* groups. *Gurus* previously exerted a lot of control within the community—enabling them to set expectations about acceptable and unacceptable behaviors. Today, they face a dramatic loss of authority, rendering them unable to exert the same control over the community that they once could.

"My *Chela* Is My Own Hand": *Gurus* and the Loss of Authority

In general, the changes to *guru–chela* relationships are framed through the lens of "advance[ment]" and "progress."[27] For example, Rishabh emphasized that changes to the *hijra* system can actually benefit both *guru*s and *chela*s. As they explain,

> if you look at Bangalore today, I think, though the *guru–chela* system exists [and] it is quite strong … I think that the *guru*s have also realized that giving their *chela*s their independence, giving them their freedom would actually benefit them [*guru*s]… maybe they felt that, you know, if it [that is, becoming a *chela*] is done through their [*chela*s'] free will, it would be better than actually forcing them to do it.

From Rishabh's perspective, *guru*s benefit from these shifting power dynamics within the *guru–chela* relationship partly because they have the satisfaction of knowing that *chela*s are willing participants and are not being "forc[ed]" into these family relationships by circumstance. But while Neelima at the beginning of this chapter spoke positively about the changes in *guru–chela* relationships, the majority of *guru*s lamented them.

Gurus frequently expressed anxieties that their authority was negatively impacted by others' judgments of *guru–chela* relationships—even people who did not necessarily hold positions of authority within the community (like state officials). Some *guru*s reported that negative judgments of their relationships from others[28] affected the willingness of a *chela* to continue the *guru–chela* relationship. Saira, a *guru* in her forties, reported that her *chela*s severed their relationship because outsiders encouraged them to leave her. "For example, one person will incite a *chela* [to leave] by asking her why she is staying in my house and she encourages her to go away." In this way she lost all her *chela*s. "All of them ran away. They listened to hearsay from other random people and they ran away." Such scenarios where others encourage a *chela* to leave her *guru* were quite common among the *guru*s I spoke with.

For most *guru*s these changes are commonly framed through ideas about "loss" and "disappearance" that emphasize the vulnerability of *guru–chela* relationships.[29] Saira directly frames her current lack of *chela*s as a loss of her authority, and it is unclear whether she will be part of *guru–chela* relationships in the future.

Some *guru*s even willingly ended these relationships rather than experience the loss of authority. Manvi is a *hijra* in her forties. As we sat on the cement floor of her cosy, brightly decorated living room sipping milk tea, she explained that as a teenager, she left her family to join a large *hijra* family in Mumbai, where she lived for many years. Because she missed her home state and speaking her native tongue, she returned to Bangalore a few years ago to live on her own and earn her livelihood through sex work.

At the time of our conversation, Manvi had been involved with the *hijra* community for over 20 years, which afforded her a lot of seniority in the community, and she had around 25 *chela*s in Mumbai. However, when she left her *hijra* family in Mumbai, Manvi was surprised no one was willing to contribute money to help her start a new life. She decided she was better off depending only on herself. "I left them all and came away [to Bangalore]. I don't want any *chela*s. My *chela* is my own hand." Her words and tone strongly implied that *chela*s are obligated to help their *guru*s, conveying her disappointment that her *chela*s were unwilling to fulfill this duty. As a result, she no longer wants to enter into these relationships; instead, she will manage on her own. For Manvi, the changes in behaviors and obligations within *guru–chela* relationships is what has been lost, and those changes mean that the relationships are no longer valued by her.

When I asked if she considers herself as part of the *hijra* community in Bangalore, Manvi replied, "I'm with all the others and I'm also separate. I meet everyone once in a while. But I don't meet up with them much. I want to live separately." Because Manvi cannot change the behaviors now common within *guru–chela* relationships, she is fine with losing them and prefers living on her own to participating in a *hijra* family. But her decision to reside in Bangalore is about earning an income and not a rejection of family life in general. If earning money through sex work was not a concern for her, "I would have been living a good life with my parents and family" in rural Karnataka.

For those elder *guru*s who still want to have relationships with *chela*s, the only way forward is to accept the loss of their authority. Neelima offered a telling analogy to explain the state of affairs today:

> We can't go back to the earlier ways. For example, earlier, we could buy things with one rupee. Now inflation is so much that even with 1,000 rupees it is difficult to buy [items of similar value]. See, we can't go back to the past. Earlier, we could have a meal with 10 rupees. Now with 1,000 rupees we can eat a [comparable] meal. The world is like this. How can we go backwards?

Neelima suggests that, like the change in the value of currency, the changes in *hijra* families are related to wider irreversible social changes. Both the changes in the *guru–chela* system and the devaluation of the rupee are simply understood as a part of life and outside of one's control.

Conclusion

The *guru–chela* system came about through the mutual need of both parties, but now that younger GNC people can survive without relying on the material support provided by *gurus*, the need is no longer mutual. The resulting imbalance has caused younger GNC people to reevaluate the reciprocal support provided through the *guru–chela* relationship, devaluing the support of *gurus* and thereby making *chelas* and younger GNC people less willing to engage in the reciprocal support expected for *gurus*. As a result, *gurus* are losing their claim to authority within the *guru–chela* relationship, changing it from a clear hierarchy where both parties' behavior reinforced the power difference into a relationship resembling something more like a partnership. The result is that the behaviors expected of *gurus* and *chelas* have dramatically shifted, in turn shifting the behaviors valued within *hijra* groups.

Today, *chelas* increasingly voice an altered understanding of the costs and benefits associated with participating in *guru–chela* relationships. Many report an unwillingness to be part of residential *guru–chela* relationships where they would be expected to share their income. *Chelas'* ability to control their income affords them a degree of "independence" that impacts their willingness to recognize the authority of *gurus* and even to maintain the *guru–chela* relationship.

Outside intervention by state authority figures into *hijra* communities has also impacted the kinds of behaviors expressed in *guru–chela* relationships, particularly the behavior of *gurus*. As the general public has become more informed about *hijra* groups, state authorities like the police have increasingly been called upon to intervene in disputes between *gurus* and *chelas*. *Gurus* increasingly fear police intervention, and they have changed their behavior to act in ways that ensure their *chelas* are unlikely to complain.

As a result of the changing opportunities for younger GNC people, the *guru–chela* relationship has been completely reimagined. Once considered a strict hierarchy where the *guru* was expected to regularly demonstrate her authority and the *chela* was expected to submit, today that degree of deference is increasingly reserved only for ceremonial occasions. The power dynamic between *gurus* and *chelas* has shifted to such a degree that *chelas* are increasingly entering *guru–chela* relationships on their own terms by negotiating expectations with their *gurus*—behavior which would previously have been unthinkable.

These changes in behaviors within *guru–chela* relationships have impacted how *chelas* understand themselves and their identities. The identity divides between trans women and *hijras* are complex. Indeed, many of the trans women I spoke to insist that they are not *hijras*, even as they participate in *hijra* relationships. On the one hand, there is an intense desire by many trans women to disidentify with *hijras* in their pursuit of the respectability accorded to middle-class cisgender women (and denied to *hijras*). On the other hand, many of the same trans women who disidentify with *hijras* are involved in *hijra* families. Trans women who are *chelas* but do not identify as *hijras* are caught between somewhat competing identities in a time of rapid social change around gender nonconformity.

The changing behaviors within *guru–chela* relationships have also made an impact on *hijra* communities as a whole. Now, *chelas* are more likely to choose a guru who is "kind" and "gentle," and *gurus* increasingly emulate such behaviors (in direct contrast to the "toughness" that high-ranking senior *gurus* previously displayed) so that they can attract *chelas* and attain a higher status within the community. While some *gurus* claim these changes are beneficial, most *gurus* frame these changes using the language of loss. Some even withdraw from *guru–chela* relationships entirely. Older *gurus* who once depended upon this system for survival now find themselves in increasingly precarious positions. The next chapter delves deeper into the issue of how elder *gurus* are impacted by these changes to the *guru–chela* system. Specifically, I examine how people talk about all of these changes to *hijra* families—residence, authority, behavior, and so on—through the lens of the traditional Hindu joint family that is supposedly breaking apart as a result of social change related to modernity, industrialization, and India's entry into global capitalist systems.

Notes

1. Munshi 1998: 39.
2. Conley 2015: 570–571.
3. Nanda 1990; Reddy 2005.
4. Conley 2015: 570–571.

5. Reddy 2005: 157; see also Nanda 1990: 45.

6. Reddy 2005: 157.

7. Reddy 2005: 160.

8. Reddy 2005: 157.

9. Nanda 1990: 43.

10. Nanda 1990: 121–122.

11. Scott 1990; Nanda 1990; Reddy 2005.

12. Nanda 1990: 48.

13. Nanda 1990: 143.

14. Nanda 1990: 46.

15. Reddy 2005: 143.

16. However, there are occasional references to *hijra*s living alone, though they are generally supported (socially and financially) by men they call their husbands (Revathi 2010: 94). As A. Revathi observed, "living alone was not easy and brought with it a host of new problems" (2010: 99).

17. Nanda 1990: 46.

18. Nanda 1990: 48.

19. Nanda 1999: 48; Reddy 2005: 143.

20. As Saria (2021) remarks, *hijra*s are known for trying to "seduce" boyfriends and husbands through buying them expensive gifts (2021: 166). As a result, Saria (2021) and Reddy (2005) note a kind of trope in circulation of the *hijra* who spends lots of money on a husband or boyfriend, only to then feel she had been "used" when the relationship ended.

21. Reddy 2005: 143.

22. Reddy 2005: 143.

23. Reddy 2005: 143.

24. Hinchy 2014; see also Reddy 2005.

25. Saria 2019.

26. When I asked trans women why they continue to participate in *hijra* families, they mentioned social benefits like belonging and community in addition to the satisfaction of participating in rituals and celebrations (especially those around transition-related surgeries). But the fact that so many trans women actually still participate in *hijra* families suggests there could be other reasons that trans women continue to be *chela*s in their *hijra* families. It could certainly be the case that these social changes are so new that people who joined *hijra* groups as younger GNC people and now identify as trans women are somewhat caught in the middle of two different (and even competing) ways of being a GNC person. Or it could also be that

maintaining *hijra* family relationships is a way that these trans women resist some of the processes I have described. Focusing on trans women's continued participation in *hijra* groups might reveal that these trans women do not uncritically accept the premise (and promise) of "independence" from *hijra* groups or the cultural valorization of individuality that it is based on. A deeper exploration of these dynamics might reveal that even as trans women describe themselves using "new" woman rhetoric, they do not fully embrace all precepts of "new" womanhood.

27. Ramaswamy 2004: 1.
28. See also Reddy 2005: 153.
29. Ramaswamy 2004: 1.

5

A Family Resemblance

Explaining Changes in *Hijra* Relationships

Introduction

Sunitha, a *hijra* in her forties, had invited me to her home, where she lives with three other *hijra*s, for Makara Sankranti, the harvest festival. We sat together on a large blanket she had spread on the light yellow and orange tile floor in her sparkling-clean living room while her housemates—none of whom was her *guru*—prepared food in the adjacent kitchen. But despite having a nonresidential *guru*, Sunitha spoke in glowing terms about the *guru–chela* relationship. "The *guru* will give to the next generation," she said, "and the *guru* is next only to our parents in status." For Sunitha, the *guru–chela* relationship incorporates social reciprocity, generational continuity, and the respect for elders traditionally emphasized in both *hijra* and cishet family relationships. As a *guru*, she explained,

> If I fall ill, my *chela*s will care of me and also they share [about their experiences] with me. I also share about myself, my life, my [birth] family, etc. with my *chela*s. I also care for them if they have health problems, family problems or police problems when they beg. I protect them when this happens.

Sunitha was not alone in describing the *guru–chela* relationship in a highly idealized manner, similar to how people in cishet families speak about their family relationships.[1] When speaking of her *hijra* family, she and other older *guru*s I talked to drew on idealized discourses most commonly used to describe non-*hijra* families.[2] Such discourses emphasize positive emotions associated with ideal families while covering up the more practical aspects of being part of a family, such as financial and social interdependence—aspects that *chelas* and younger GNC people are keen to emphasize.

For Sunitha, the financial obligations between *gurus* and *chelas* that younger GNC people see as restrictive serve a crucial role in *guru–chela* relationships. It is essential for *chelas* to give part of their daily earnings to their *gurus* because, she explained, "a *chela* has to take care of her *guru*. That is the culture. If not, how can the relationship between *guru* and *chela* exist? It will get broken up." Just like scholars of Indian family systems emphasize the importance of financial support and obligations within cishet Indian families,[3] for Sunitha, *chelas'* obligation to give part of their earnings to their *gurus* is not only an expected duty, but the foundation that holds the *guru–chela* relationship together.

Like everyone I spoke with about *hijra* family relationships, Sunitha regularly drew comparisons between *guru–chela* relationships and cishet family relationships. For example, she observed that any problems occurring between *gurus* and *chelas* are actually problems that can occur in any family. Sunitha remarked, "On some occasions the *guru* could get angry with the *chela* and, on other occasions, the *chela* could get angry with the *guru*. That is only natural. This happens in the same manner that such things happen in a family. That happens among us too." According to Sunitha, *hijra* families experience the same kinds of tensions as cishet families.

When I asked people to speculate about what might be driving the changes in *hijra* family structures that we learned about in the last two chapters, my participants did not just note the new choices available to younger GNC people, but also cited the supposed transformations in the living arrangements of cishet families in middle-class, urban India. The language people used to discuss changing *hijra* relationships would mirror discussions around the changes in the "traditional" joint Hindu family, which includes several generations of patrilineal families living under one roof.[4] This family setup is said to be in "decline" as younger members seeking "freedom" from joint families move into nuclear family arrangements. Much like the discourse around "new" women is being leveraged to explain changes within the GNC community, the transformations seen in *hijra* families and households are being assessed and explained through discourses using the rhetoric of "choice" and "freedom" when talking about the purported decline of the cishet joint family. And just like how younger GNC people who have newly found access to resources employ the language of choice to describe their reasons for not entering into residential *guru–chela* relationships, the desire for freedom and independence from joint families is similarly voiced by those who (due to their age and/or financial status) have the means to leave joint family arrangements.

But the parallels run even deeper than rhetoric. GNC people's understanding of the families they create is shaped by the range of possible family forms they think are available to them outside of cishet family forms. Because there is limited research about GNC people and their families to draw on, I turn to the concept of "chosen families"—groups of non-biologically related people that fulfill similar roles as cishet family members.[5] Yet while *hijra* families might on the surface look like chosen families because they fall outside of cishet family forms and offer GNC people access to kinship relationships or support, they are increasingly seen (in the absence of other forms of support that are now available) as families that GNC people were once *forced* to join—in short, the *opposite* of chosen families.

Instead, a more apt and revealing understanding of the social dynamics impacting *hijra* families than comparisons with joint or chosen families can be made by comparing *guru–chela* relationships today with recent changes in middle-class cishet couple relationships. In both cases, the relationship was once recognized as a clear hierarchy, with the subordinate group (*chela*s and cis women) having constrained opportunities due to discrimination within the wider society, resulting in them relying on the dominate group (*guru*s or husbands) to access basic resources to survive. Although discrimination remains a major problem for cisgender women and GNC people, these groups have also gained opportunities that their counterparts in the past could not have imagined. This increased opportunity has enabled them to become less dependent on *guru*s and husbands, which shifts the balance of power in these relationships, enabling them to be more discerning when choosing a *guru* or husband. *Guru*s and cis men accordingly must adjust their behavior toward *chela*s and cis women in the hopes of attracting a partner, transforming power relationships in both cishet and *hijra* families.

Policing "New" Women in Respectably Middle-class(-aspiring) Joint Families

As discussed in the Introduction, liberalization increased the opportunities available to middle-class, educated, urban women. Yet at the same time that greater opportunities became available to new women, these opportunities were somewhat circumscribed by their participation in cishet families.

Middle-class aspiring groups tend to be especially concerned with the behavior of their family members. This is partly because aspiring to middle-class status goes beyond attaining a certain level of financial security. Being middle-class is also understood as a "moral virtue"[6]—as much about a person's financial status as it is about acquiring and/or maintaining a manner of respectability that is synonymous with middle-class status. This is a highly gendered form of respectability that emphasizes sexual modesty for cisgender women. A family's honor is often based upon the gendered behavior of its women. Age matters and younger women's sexuality is seen as particularly threatening to a family's honor, and in order to acquire and/or maintain the respectability they seek, families monitor younger women members closely. Cis women in middle-class and middle-class aspiring families often experience policing of their "bodies, movements, behavior, clothes and speech patterns."[7]

Living in joint family setups exposes these cis women to additional scrutiny from a larger number of family members. It is generally believed that "good" daughters-in-law must regularly defer to the patriarchal authority of the family.[8] Married cis women report feeling that their sexuality as daughters-in-law is controlled by their husband's family. They cite expectations to produce children to continue the family lineage as well as doubts about their "purity," which are perceived as bringing dishonor to the husband's family.[9]

In addition, whether a joint family runs smoothly is often placed directly on the behavior of daughters-in-law. As one daughter-in-law reported to another researcher, "the way [a daughter-in-law] respects the husband, the elders, the way she blends into his family" has a major impact on the family dynamic. "In joint families, if the daughter-in-law doesn't understand her husband, if she doesn't fit into his family and upsets his parents, then the family is shattered."[10] Though the joint family form is celebrated, it is generally recognized as a disempowering force for cis women since they are structurally disadvantaged within it.

Following liberalization, media narratives emphasized women's emancipation from the kinds of structures that once subordinated them, particularly the family. These narratives show that the idea of freedom from family expectations is especially appealing for the people who tend to be disadvantaged in families—young cis women. Thus, the notion that younger people seek freedom from joint families is particularly associated with the kinds of "new" (cis) women that trans women often seek to align themselves with.

The "Traditional" Indian Family: Colonial Categories and Perceptions of Change

In India, the most well-known family type is the cishet "traditional" Hindu joint family. Much mythologized and highly idealized, it "stands for *the* Indian family celebrated in popular culture."[11] The joint family is a household comprised of three patrilineal generations living under one roof, organized around a (presumably) heterosexual couple, their unmarried daughters, their married sons, and their sons' wives and children.[12]

Despite the emphasis on the joint family as an exemplar of Indian "tradition," historical evidence indicates that throughout history, the joint family form was followed by only a select group of elite Hindu Indians.[13] In the 1940s, British colonial scholars studied texts written and compiled by elites in ancient India that emphasized elite family structures;[14] they erroneously declared the joint family was "an ancient and unchanging institution"[15] and the key feature around which modern Indian society should be organized.[16] This family form was then codified into British colonial laws governing property and inheritance.[17]

Yet ever since it was first heralded as an essential aspect of "Indian tradition," the joint family has been understood as a dying structure, eclipsed first by modernity and now by social changes connected to economic liberalization. There is a long history of popular discussion about the "decline" of the joint family, repeatedly positing this supposed decline as a new phenomenon.[18] In news accounts, the joint family is described as "breaking apart," as sons move with their wives and children out of their parents' homes and into nuclear family setups.[19] The rhetoric has even reached the shores of foreign news outlets, with *The Guardian* proclaiming, "The extended family, in which several generations live together and care for older members under one roof, is splitting apart."[20] In truth, this has always been the case from the time the joint family was conceived as an institution on the brink of extinction by the British colonial administration. Despite this, the rhetoric of the joint family's decline is presented in popular media and culture as a new phenomenon that goes against Indian tradition and values. And within *hijra* communities, the dynamics of elder *hijras'* increasing precarity coupled with the opportunities for younger GNC people map nicely onto the changes that popular culture claims are occurring in joint families. Thus, it is not surprising that people make sense of the changes in *hijra* relationships by comparing them to the supposed changes in joint families.

Narratives of Freedom from Joint Families: Perspectives of the Young and (Wealthy) Old

Mainstream media reports of people pursuing "freedom" and "independence" by living outside of joint families have focused on highly educated young cisgender, heterosexual couples who left their parents' homes to migrate to North America, Europe, and Australia for work over the last several decades. In recent decades, Indian cities have also become major centers for those employed in medical and technical fields, and therefore sites where nuclear families are emerging as a new norm. As the *Times of India* explains,

> [t]he joint family is on a disintegrating path ever since society graduated into an age of technological advance, changing gender roles and better employment opportunities. Interdependence on each other in large families seems to have been replaced by independent living and self-sufficient attitudes.[21]

A similar article in the *UK Telegraph* quotes sociologist Ashish Nandy explaining that in Delhi, young people "want a level of independence which is not possible in a joint family home."[22] But what is it that they lack? For some younger couples, living outside of joint families means they can return to their home at any time of the day, which would likely be unacceptable to their parents or in-laws if they resided in a joint family. For others it is the freedom to live as one wants. In the words of one man living in a nuclear family:

> We are not answerable to anyone[.] [I]f we get late for home, watch TV on a high sound, scream, shout or do whatever we like, nobody bothers us and we don't bother anyone. In joint families one has to be sensitive to likes and dislikes of other members of the family.[23]

He revealingly summed up his reasons by concluding, "They curb the freedom we now enjoy."

However, younger family members are not the only ones leaving joint families to pursue freedom and independence. A group of affluent Indian seniors are enjoying a new level of financial independence fueled by the rise of the "grey rupee," a term that refers to the buying power of wealthy seniors with high life expectancies. Many of them are willing to spend their considerable disposable income on a peaceful retired life—one that does not include residing with extended family. This group of affluent seniors is fueling the growth of luxury private retirement communities resembling resorts with their banquet halls, swimming pools, and large gardens. Although they represent a small portion of Indian seniors, they are changing expectations about aging (at least among other elites) as they "aspir[e] to an active and independent old age."[24]

The Hindustan Times described one "courageous" senior as breaking with tradition and experiencing freedom for the first time, moving into a retirement village (with on-site Hindu temples and facilities that offer Ayurvedic massage) "hours away" from family members.[25] An elite-class retired man who bought an apartment for himself and his wife in a luxury gated community for seniors in the state of Rajasthan similarly couched their decision to move in terms of newfound freedom and how their presence in a joint family would affect their children:

> We did not want to stand in the way of our children's future. Let them enjoy their young life and let us enjoy our old life. We don't believe in the joint family. I don't like all that interfering in each other's matters.[26]

Both seniors offered remarkably similar observations that emphasize the role emancipation from the traditional family plays in their thinking:

> "I want to give full freedom to my child, and I want full freedom for myself." [27]
> "Everyone wants freedom these days." [28]

Freedom and Independence? Perspectives of Family Members without Access to Resources

The desires for freedom and independence said to be driving the changes in *hijra* and cishet family structures are not equally attractive to all family members. In fact, the desires for freedom and independence from joint families are voiced by family members with access to financial resources that enable them to outsource their care to medical and caretaking staff. By contrast, seniors from nonaffluent backgrounds benefit from the care and support provided within joint families, and many elders report a preference for living in joint families, in marked contrast to their younger counterparts.[29]

This is in part because the care and support of sick and/or elderly family members is a highly gender-stratified form of labor, historically performed by those with the least power and influence in families—the daughters-in-law[30] (or, in cases where there are no daughters-in-law, the daughters). But in the past several decades, norms around the caregiving of seniors in families have shifted due to women's paid labor force participation and changes in expectations about resource distribution within families. In middle-class families in contemporary urban India, younger educated women increasingly work outside the home, so they are not able or necessarily expected to expend significant time and effort caring for sick and/or elderly family members. There has also been a cultural shift in perceptions about how resources should be divided within families, impacting the willingness of families to prioritize care for elder members. One researcher describes the shift that has occurred:

> Modern Indian families, by and large, have become child-centered and focused more on the life and development of their children, and the parents are prepared to work to any extent to achieve this aim. Any sacrifice on the part of the parents is possible for this. This cuts across class and caste. The child-focused approach within families has, however, undermined other functions such as taking care of elderly members[,] including parents[,] in the family.[31]

The issue of elderly family members not receiving the care they expect and require has made frequent appearances in news reports. There are now over 100 million Indians over the age of 60 and, due to increased life expectancies, that number is projected to rise to over 300 million by the year 2050, when people over 60 are projected to comprise approximately 20 percent of the population.[32] Lawmakers have considered introducing legal measures to ensure that people are held responsible for the care and maintenance of senior family members. An article in *The Guardian* describes "frequent reports of elderly parents being turfed out of the family home, beaten up and abandoned," and civic agencies frequently "issue warnings about the rising numbers of neglected elderly people."[33] The complaints of elder abuse and neglect are especially concerning for lower-middle-class and working-class elders, who are more likely to be financially reliant on their younger family members.

Narratives of Freedom and Constraint in *Hijra* Families

When they discussed changes in *guru–chela* relationships, younger GNC people often referenced recent changes in parent–child relationships in cishet families. These changes impact how younger GNC people perceive *hijra* family structures and their willingness to participate in *hijra* families. Take the case of Violet. As a transgender woman in her twenties who works in an NGO, Violet was poised to take advantage of the kinds of opportunities available to younger GNC people. However, when she moved to Bangalore from her village, Violet had difficulty finding affordable housing. As a result, she initially rented a flat on the outskirts of the city that was a two-to-three-hour bus ride away from the NGO where she worked. After several months of undertaking this tiring commute every working day, she was excited to hear about an opening in a flat near her NGO office. The flat was occupied by a small group of *hijras* who were also associated with the NGO. To shorten her daily commute, Violet decided to move in.

But Violet quickly became distressed by her new living situation because one of the *hijras* directly stated that she wished to have Violet involved in a *guru–chela* relationship. In spite of the fact that she was earning her own income ("independent" of the *hijra* system), Violet expressed anxiety that she would get pulled into *hijra* relationships, which would inhibit her freedom. As we chatted quietly in her office at the NGO with the door closed, Violet explained:

> I'm telling you this, [glancing furtively at the door] please forgive me, but I'm very, very uncomfortable with *hijras*. Before this [living situation], I stayed with gay and bisexual men. There, we were enjoying freedom; we felt free. There were no restrictions, nothing. It was like close friendships only. Here [in my new housing arrangement], there is no freedom, actually. You know, [looking seriously at me] they're treating me like her *chela*.... For that reason, I just want to shift as soon as possible....

Actually, she told me that, "I'll make you my *chela*" and she said she told
her *guru* that soon, she will have a [new] *chela*.

For Violet, one particularly troubling part of being "treat[ed] like [a] *chela*" is
that the *hijra* who wanted to be her *guru* was placing restrictions on Violet's
personal hygiene routine. Her eyes wide, Violet declared her frustration that
this *hijra* believes that "she gets to decide if I can take a bath. It's like I want
to take a bath, but she gets to decide whether I can take a bath? See, I'm used
to taking a bath twice a day in my hometown, but here, that's not possible."
Violet was genuinely frightened at the thought that she could get pulled into
hijra relationships that would restrict the kind of freedom she sought.

Deepa, the trans woman in her twenties who in the Introduction said
she wants to "hide [her] identity" from *hijras*, likened the control of a *guru*
over her *chela* to the control exercised by cishet parents over their children.
When I asked why she did not want to have a residential *guru*, she referenced
changing cishet family roles, declaring,

> See, I'm not under the control of my parents. Then how can I be
> under the control of my *guru*? See, [when I thought about if] I want to
> [become] a transgender [person] or a *hijra* [in a residential *guru–chela*
> relationship], I'm not listening to [what] my parents [suggest to me]. So
> how can I listen to my *guru*?

In a time when children are less likely to obey their parents, Deepa implied
they would also be less likely to participate in relationships where they are
expected to obey another parent figure. This desire for independence from
both parents and *guru*s was a major factor in Deepa's decision about whether
to participate in a residential *guru–chela* relationship. As she observed,
"things are changing now. I want to be independent."

The concept of independence is a salient way that people communicate
their decision to alter or withdraw their participation from both joint families
and *hijra* residential relationships. Taken together, the emphasis on GNC
people's "choice" of whether or not to engage in *hijra* residential relationships
and the value attached to trans women's "independent" status suggests that
those who remain in the (residential) *guru–chela* system are dependent on
this hierarchical system. By contrast, "independent" trans women (like their
cisgender counterparts who leave joint families) have broken free of such
strictures. Tellingly, the opportunities for "freedom" are invoked by those

who already possess at least the promise of more resources and opportunities, such as adult children in joint families who earn their own income, affluent elders who can afford a luxurious retired life, and younger GNC people who perceive themselves as having enhanced employment opportunities that are not generally available to their elder counterparts. In contrast to their younger GNC counterparts, elder *hijras* do not voice excitement about being "free" from *hijra* family setups. Especially for elder *gurus* who are no longer able to support themselves, the prospect of becoming independent and free from their *hijra* families is considerably less appealing. Similar to dependent elders in joint families, *gurus* depend upon the support and care once offered within *hijra* families. As *hijra* family setups change, elder *hijras* have experienced reduced opportunities, and elder *gurus* speak of their lives and the decisions available to them as being constrained. The number of *chelas* opting to live "independently" of their *hijra* families in nonresidential *guru–chela* relationships coupled with the growing numbers of younger GNC people who do not become involved in residential *guru–chela* relationships have meant that elder *hijras* are losing the social and financial support many assumed that they could depend on in their old age.

For elder *gurus*, the lack of support from their *chelas* has produced a profound insecurity about their futures, particularly when their health begins to decline. Vidyamma, a trans woman in her fifties who was once part of residential *hijra* groups, observed that the elder *gurus* around her voice "this insecurity, thinking that, see, when I grow older, there's no one around [to care for] me." Many elder *hijras* have realized that they cannot afford to stay in Bangalore due to rising costs of living and that their *chelas* are not offering the support they expected. Thus, many have returned to their villages and birth families, even though this move has meant that some of them must wear "pant-shirt" attire and present themselves as men.

Akrithi, the trans woman NGO worker we heard from in Chapter 2, has an elder *guru* who recently left Bangalore to live in her natal village in Kerala. Akrithi remarked that the situation for older *gurus* is "very difficult. Till a certain age, you can engage in sex work or begging. But after [you become] 35, 40 years [old], who is going to take care of you?" She observed that there are very few *hijras* older than 40 living in Bangalore, saying, "You can count 10, 20, 30, that's it." The "big problem" occurs when elder *hijras* "assume that the *chelas* will take care of them, because how many people will actually do that? Very few. Very few. There are lots of [elder] *hijras* who are dying on the street" because no one is willing or able to take care of them.

Malika is one of only five elder *hijra*s I encountered over 50 during my fieldwork. I first met her at one of the *hammam*s on a main road in the city. The story Malika told about her life included running away from her family at the age of 11 due to abuse for her perceived femininity, working as a cook in exploitative conditions for several years, and then finally joining "this *hijra* gang" at the age of 16. Malika's story reveals the sense of constraint she felt early on in her life, which continues to affect how she interprets the decisions she makes.

At the time of our conversation, sexual rights organizations were advocating for legal measures that would offer financial support for GNC people over the age of 40. When I asked about how these measures might impact her life, Malika looked thoughtful as she mused that such measures "might help." Then, she shook her head, explaining that overall, she did not think *hijra*s like her had opportunities. She explained that due to discrimination and poverty,

> when we want a thing, when we want to go somewhere and we want to enjoy our lives, we can't do that, we aren't able to do that. This means that we don't have such freedom. We don't *have* such freedom … see, we want our own [opportunities, which are not available].

Malika voiced a sense of constraint that was often articulated by the few elder *hijra*s I was able to speak with. While younger GNC people stressed the new opportunities available in urban areas and the achievements of their fellow trans women, elder *hijra*s did not perceive these changes and opportunities as having much of an impact on their lives. As compared to younger GNC people who may have access to education (opening up the potential for them to work in NGOs and other office jobs) and may even be able to continue living as a GNC person with their birth families, an elder *hijra* whose source of income is precarious and who can no longer depend on earning the kind of money from her *chela*s that her own *guru* earned is in a structurally vulnerable position. Ironically, whereas younger trans women position *hijra* relationships as inhibiting their freedom, *hijra*s like Malika understand themselves as structurally disadvantaged due to poverty and deprivation and therefore unable to exercise the kind of freedom they desire.

Rishabh, the GNC person and longtime sexual rights activist in their fifties who said *guru*s now have the satisfaction of knowing their *chela*s are not forced to be with them in the last chapter, sums up the conundrum that younger GNC people's enhanced opportunities present for elder *hijra*s, explaining,

> I think the younger generation would see this as favorable, the older generations would see this as not favorable. I think somewhere we need to try and understand that the *guru*s have actually lost their power to generate income on their own. They can't go and do sex work. They have gotten old, right? Or they can't go for begging every day [because it is physically exhausting] … so it becomes very difficult for them to go and earn 500 or 600 or 1,000 rupees a day on their own. So then they look at what is the alternate source [of income]? So the only alternate source is to have as many *chela*s as possible and try to get some income from them.

I also spoke with several trans women who emphasized that there are *guru*s who purposely exaggerate the limited opportunities for GNC people in the hope that this tactic will enable them to acquire additional *chela*s. Vasudha, a trans woman in her thirties, said that she often speaks to *guru*s about this practice, which she perceives as dishonest. When Vasudha was a young GNC person, the person who wanted to become her *guru* implied that if Vasudha wanted to live as a GNC person, it was imperative for her to live and work within the *hijra* system. This *guru* told Vasudha, "The society does not accept you, they torture us, so you are safer staying with me. If you stay with me, you need a job…. You come with me, doing sex work and begging." However, Vasudha proudly explained that, as a trans woman, she was able to acquire training and employment outside of *hijra* groups and she can now fully support herself. Pointing to herself as an example, she tells *guru*s that they should not manipulate younger GNC people into thinking that their only options are within *hijra* groups. Nevertheless, she says the *guru*s always reiterate "the inferiority complex," saying that GNC people do not have opportunities to live and work outside *hijra* groups.

Residential *Hijra* Relationships: Families We (No Longer) Choose

As we explore the changes in *hijra* families and relationships, it makes sense to turn to the concept of "chosen families."[34] This notion refers to the "chosen" kinship networks of gay and lesbian people who may not maintain close relationships within their (cishet) birth families. Chosen families can be defined as groups of non-biologically related people who fulfill similar roles that cishet families fulfill for members.[35]

Like most of the research about GNC people and families, this concept was created based on research in North America, making it oriented around particular Euro-American conceptions of both gender nonconformity and family. However, the idea of chosen families has been an influential paradigm for thinking about families among gay and lesbian groups even outside of North America. Though this concept is not specific to the Indian context or the family relationships of GNC people, it is useful to apply it to changing *hijra* families, though perhaps in an unexpected way. That is because while *hijra* families that offer GNC people access to kinship relationships or support *and* that fall outside of cishet family forms may at first glance appear to fit within the concept of chosen families, they are better understood as the opposite of chosen families—since they are increasingly viewed as families that GNC people were once forced to join in the absence of other forms of support.

Chosen families were studied by Kath Weston, who conducted research with lesbian and gay people in the San Francisco Bay Area in the 1980s. Weston quickly noticed that her participants regularly compared the chosen families they created to their "straight" birth families.[36] In doing so, they implicitly distinguished between cishet families and chosen families.[37] These distinctions relied fundamentally on notions of freedom and choice.[38] In my research, I found that people often drew on similar notions around choice and freedom to describe the changes they witnessed in *hijra* families.

Weston's participants understood their cishet birth families as organized around social imperatives like compulsory heterosexuality, procreation, and the biologically infused notion of "blood ties."[39] By contrast, their chosen families were "subject to no constraints beyond a logic of 'free' choice."[40] In fact, a key feature of chosen families was "a total absence of guidelines" stipulating how these relationships should be organized, in contrast to the rigorous social imperatives that structure cishet families. When people described their chosen families, they often drew on "utopian visions of self-determination."[41]

Hijra families might, on the surface, appear similar to Weston's notion of "chosen families." Since the concept of chosen families describes an alternative to cisgender, heterosexual families, it would seem to apply to *hijra* families, which *hijras* elect to join after leaving their birth families. However, in contrast to chosen families, residential *hijra* families are organized around a hierarchical structure with clearly defined roles for members. This is very different from the concept of chosen families, where there is an "absence" of rules and "constraints" for how these relationships play out.[42]

Today, people speak about *hijra* families as though they are more like families that GNC people were once compelled to join due to a lack of alternative options for support. They imply that participating in *hijra* families was not a freely chosen decision and such families are distinctly opposed to the kind of freedom that chosen families are associated with. Ironically, this means that *not* becoming part of "traditional" *hijra* families is what freedom is understood to mean for GNC people in India today. Instead, GNC people (including *chela*s and trans women) are confronted with a host of other ways to satisfy their basic needs for survival, which open up new possibilities for creating different kinds of family relationships. They voice their "independence" from traditional (residential) *hijra* families (whether they live alone, with friends, with their birth families or with romantic partners) in ways that adopt the rhetoric (independence, freedom) and align with Weston's notion of "chosen families."

A Family Resemblance? *Guru* Is to *Chela* as Middle-class Husband is to Middle-class Wife

If we really want to understand what is going on with changing *hijra* families, I suggest there is a different kind of relationship that makes for a more productive and revealing comparison. Instead of comparing supposedly changing joint families to *hijra* families, I suggest a comparison between changing *guru–chela* relationships and changing urban middle-class cishet couple relationships. This comparison more aptly captures recent shifts in power that are surprisingly similar in both cases and reveals how changing social dynamics in *hijra* families are related to wider social changes that also impact intimate relationships.[43]

To be sure, there are several important ways that cishet couple relationships and *guru–chela* relationships are not similar. Among cishet couples, monogamy is often held up as an ideal, whereas in *guru–chela* relationships, the ideal is for a *guru* to have multiple *chela*s. Cishet couple relationships and *guru–chela* relationships are also different in terms of how the family lineage is continued. The ideal in cishet couple relationships is to continue the lineage through bearing biological children. By contrast, within *hijra* relationships, *chelas* eventually take on their own *chelas* as adults through non-biological means, who then become the "grand-*chelas*" (*naati chelas*) of their *guru*, thus continuing the lineage. Then there are relational differences. By definition, the *guru–chela* relationship is similar to a parent–child and teacher–disciple model, while cishet marriages are not typically characterized this way.

Gurus and *chelas* and urban middle-class wives and husbands also come together in very different ways. Before they were understood as having increased opportunities, GNC people often left their birth families (usually in their teenage years) and then became *chelas* in a *hijra* group. *Chelas* generally approached their preferred *guru* to request joining her *hijra* family as a *chela*, so this was a choice made by the *chela* in question. By contrast, middle-class women and men in cishet relationships were traditionally matched by their family and/or community members. They came together in marriage with the expectation that they would expand the family by bearing (ideally) biological children.

Another important difference between *guru–chela* relationships and cishet couple relationships lies in which person earns the money that supports the household. In traditional cishet couple relationships, cis men earned the money and often also controlled the money, deciding where it should be spent. Cis women generally had limited financial power in such relationships. In traditional, residential *guru–chela* relationships, *chelas* were responsible for earning the money that supported the household.[44] However, *chelas* were expected to give the money they earned to their *gurus*, who then had control over the household income.

But important and illuminating similarities abound as well. In both *guru–chela* and cishet couple relationships, there is often a strict division of household labor. As a parent figure, the *guru* is tasked with the social reproduction of her *chela*, teaching her how to act so that she might rise in stature within the community. In return, the *chela* should act as a dutiful child who takes care of the household chores, like a daughter-in-law in a joint family would be expected to do. In cishet couples, wives were tasked with the caregiving of the family, including the physical and social reproduction of children, and the household labor.

While cishet relationships are generally between two people of a similar age, it was traditionally preferred for the man to be older than the woman,[45] sometimes by a decade or more. The preferred difference in age for cishet couples reinforces the patriarchal ideology that the man should hold more power in the partnership. In this way, the age of partners in cishet relationships appears more similar to the generational gap between *gurus* and *chelas*. There was also a clear acknowledgment of the hierarchical nature of these relationships. Among cishet couples, the hierarchy was based on patriarchal gender domination, with the women as subordinates. In *guru–chela* relationships, the hierarchy was based upon age (which usually overlapped with the amount of time one had been part of the *hijra* community), making *chelas* the subordinates. In both cishet and *guru–chela* relationships, the subordinates were traditionally expected to obey the wishes of those above them in the hierarchy.

And then there are the recent developments within such partnerships. The less powerful person in both relationships (*chelas* and cishet women) once had difficulties accessing resources on their own, so this person needed to rely on people who had more access to resources—*gurus* and husbands—in order to survive. Both middle-class cis women and younger GNC people still face discrimination that makes their lives unnecessarily difficult. At the same time, these groups have gained opportunities that their past counterparts could not have imagined. For both *chelas* or younger GNC people and middle-class cisgender women, their opportunities for employment and education have dramatically shifted. Their increased access to education and middle-class office employment has given them additional leverage in society as well as in their personal relationships.

In the case of middle-class cisgender women, their ability to earn their own income in respectable jobs allows them to exercise more agency within their personal relationships. As one middle-class woman employed in the IT sector explained, "if you work, then everyone respects you. Even your husband unconsciously, he will respect you more."[46] Even though tension, abuse, and indifference exist in contemporary middle-class Indian marriages, women's employment works as an empowering force that helps them to mediate these issues.[47] This is similar to the experiences of younger GNC people, who now have increased access to middle-class employment opportunities and resources on their own. This makes them less dependent on *gurus*, shifting the balance of power in these relationships.

It also means that *chelas* can be discerning when choosing a *guru*, as we saw in Chapter 4. In the case of cisgender, heterosexual women with educational qualifications and middle-class employment, they can exercise increased agency when the time comes to marry, whether they engage in arranged marriages or "love marriages." As compared to women of their mother's generation, cishet women in arranged marriages today have far more say in whether to move forward with a match or not. As potential brides in marriage markets, educated and middle-class women employed in high-status occupations can refuse offers they find unsuitable, though they may face criticism that they are being "too picky."[48] By contrast, their mothers (who were less educated and less likely to be employed) were generally expected to agree to the match of their parents' choosing. Today, middle-class marriage inquiries often focus on compatibility, and everyone involved seeks to find the right "fit" for a couple.[49] This is markedly different than the expectation that the couple (and particularly the cis woman) should "adjust" to one another, which was prevalent among this group even a generation ago.

As a result of these shifts in the balance of power, *gurus* and cisgender men have had to adjust their behavior toward *chelas* and cis women in the hopes of attracting a *chela* or wife. In the case of cishet relationships, as the traditional balance of power has been disrupted, men are expected to change how they interact with women. A popular Indian dating app, TrulyMadly, takes these new expectations into account. Their "premium" services include tutorials offering men tips, advice, and even practice on how to "chat" with women. One of the app's cofounders explained, "We [men] don't grow up with [these] skills, like [how] to talk. Our purpose now is to teach them how to chat … [we have a woman who is] just sitting and chatting with guys, telling them how to chat up, just chatting with guys telling them how to make a conversation."[50] An alternative explanation of why these tutorials are necessary would be that when they were growing up, middle-class men in their twenties did not need advanced "chatting" skills in order to attract a partner. Now that power relations between middle-class men and women have shifted, cisgender men have to try harder to make themselves appealing to a potential mate, similar to how *gurus* have had to shift the way they interact with and treat their *chelas*.

At the same time that the *guru–chela* relationship has undergone the kinds of changes discussed in the first two chapters, middle-class marriage has also undergone important changes. For the middle classes, marriage is now not only about ensuring caste and class and/or religious continuity, but also about "companionship."[51] Both women and men in heteronormative relationships desire companionship, equality, and intimacy with their partners,[52] a result of the cultural idealization of romantic love combined with the ideal of egalitarianism. For middle-class people, the notion that wives should be subordinate to their husbands holds considerably less sway than it did a generation ago, though status inequalities between cis men and women in heteronormative relationships certainly persist.[53]

Comparing the changes in cishet relationships reveals that *guru–chela* relationships are changing in very similar ways. In both cases, these changes can be traced to shifts in power that result from enhanced opportunities for the people who were once subordinated within the relationship. As these once-marginalized groups gain increased power, they become less dependent, which shifts the relationship dynamic. In both cases, what was once an obviously hierarchical relationship has been transformed so that it now appears more like a partnership.

Conclusion

Sunitha's words at the beginning of this chapter strongly emphasize the heartwarming aspects of traditional *guru–chela* relationships. She was keen to emphasize the connection, caregiving, and emotional support that these relationships can foster because of the reciprocal care and obligation the *guru–chela* system requires from all members. Like everyone else I spoke with, Sunitha regularly compared *hijra* family systems that combine financial and social support to cishet family forms, pointing out similarities like how both provide a social safety net for sick and/or elderly members.

As a result, when people puzzled out the reasons driving the changes in *hijra* families, they drew on popular discussions about the supposed changes within the joint family. The supposed decline of the joint family is seen as demonstrating how "Indian traditional culture" is being eroded by economic opportunity and individualistic attitudes. As a result, they locate the precarity of elder *hijras* and the supposed promise and opportunity available to younger GNC people by connecting the changes in *hijra* families to the supposedly changing joint family. These comparisons certainly make sense in light of shifting power dynamics between younger *hijra* family members and older *hijra* family members that mirror shifting power dynamics within the joint family. Younger transgender people and *chelas* who perceive themselves as having enhanced opportunities for employment and social support are thought to desire "freedom" and "independence" from *hijra* relationships, similar to how highly educated children and affluent elders who leave joint family setups are described. By contrast, elder family members and *gurus* who depend on the resource distribution and social care that occur in joint and *hijra* families are not in a position to seek independence and freedom from these systems.

To understand what these changes in *hijra* family dynamics reveal about GNC people and the families they create, it might seem pertinent to compare them to "chosen families." Like chosen families, *hijra* families fall outside of cishet family forms, *and* they offer GNC people access to kinship relationships or support. However, I have shown that *hijra* families are increasingly considered as families that GNC people were once forced to join in the absence of other forms of support. Now that (younger) GNC people perceive other forms of support, *hijra* families are understood almost as the opposite of chosen families. However, now that they face an expansion of possible family forms, *hijra* families are actually the families younger GNC people would not choose.

In fact, I argue that there is another comparison that reveals more about how social change impacts *hijra* families. That comparison is between changing *hijra* relationships and changing middle-class cishet couple relationships. When making this comparison, we see that shifting power dynamics are the result of increased opportunities for the people once subordinated in these relationships (cis women and *chelas* or younger GNC people). When cisgender women and *chelas* or younger GNC people are no longer dependent on husbands and *gurus* for basic resources, they become less reliant on these hierarchical relationships. Their increased opportunities to access resources offer them the kind of bargaining power they can use to make these once hierarchical relationships appear more and more like equal partnerships. This comparison reveals that the changes occurring in *hijra* families are part of wider societal shifts in power relationships that are the result of social change.

Now that we have learned how ideas about new opportunities for GNC people are reshaping *hijra* relationships, let us turn to thinking about how "new" trans women think of their identities, especially in relation to *hijras*. The concluding chapter explores the identity work that trans women undertake in their quest to embody "new" womanhood while also considering what these trans women risk losing in their attempts to draw firm boundaries between themselves and *hijras*.

Notes

1. Nanda 1990: 46.
2. Reddy 2005: 157.
3. Within non-*hijra* families, money is shared between parents and adult children and sometimes among adult siblings (Singh and Bhandari 2012: 53). This "two-way flow of money between parents and children" is based upon parents' obligation to help their adult children and employed children's obligation to assist their parents, regardless of financial necessity (Singh and Bhandari 2012: 53).
4. Conklin 1976; Ramu 1972; Khatri 1972.
5. Weston 1991.
6. Mankekar 1999: 114.
7. Mankekar 1999: 114.
8. Mankekar 1999: 117.
9. Mankekar 1999: 128.
10. Mankekar 1999: 156–157.
11. Singh and Bhandari 2012: 49.
12. D'Cruz and Bharat 2001: 168.
13. Newbigin, Renault, and De 2009: 30; Uberoi 1993.
14. D'Cruz and Bharat 2001: 167.
15. Newbigin, Renault, and De 2009: 30; see also Uberoi 1993.
16. D'Cruz and Bharat 2001: 168.
17. In the colonial era, for purposes of creating culturally sensitive inheritance and property laws, elite Indian and British administrators were assigned the task of ascertaining how families were organized across the subcontinent (Newbigin, Renault, and De 2009: 30). Because the variety of family forms and living arrangements is "as diverse as the country's demography, culture and religion" (Sooryamurthy 2012: 2), these officials were essentially under pressure to "elucidate and codify a system that seemed impenetrably complex and regionally diverse" (Newbigin, Renault, and De 2009: 30).
18. Newbigin, Renault, and De 2009; Uberoi 1993.
19. Contemporary family forms in India are more diverse than they are similar; they cannot be encapsulated within a single "traditional" family structure. Indian families are characterized by a multitude of forms, including "joint families, nuclear families, single parent families, dual earner families and adoptive families" that exist side-by-side (D'Cruz and Bharat 2001: 185; see also Sooryamurthy 2012). In addition, the number of joint family

households has always been eclipsed by the number of nuclear households (Singh and Bhandari 2012: 49). However, the actual numbers of people living in joint family households may be greater than the number living in nuclear family households, especially in rural areas and conservative states (Singh and Bhandari 2012: 49). The National Census Data for 2011 revealed that throughout India, 18 percent of all households are comprised of two or more married couples (Sundararajan 2012: 2). The cultural emphasis on the joint family relative to its actual numbers has led some scholars to argue that "[t]he joint family's [cultural] importance is greater than its actual prevalence at any one point of time" (Singh and Bhandari 2012: 49). This may be partly because many individuals will spend at least part of their lives living in joint family households before dispersing into "various combinations of joint and/or nuclear family households" (Singh and Bhandari 2012: 49).

20. R. Prasad 2007: 2.

21. Mitra 2012: 2.

22. Nelson 2011: 2.

23. Nelson 2011: 2.

24. R. Prasad 2007: 2.

25. *Hindustan Times* 2015: 2.

26. R. Prasad 2007: 2.

27. *Hindustan Times* 2015: 2.

28. R. Prasad 2007: 2.

29. In a representative study of 50,000 urban and rural-based seniors, almost 50 percent reported that they would prefer to live in a joint family setup. *Hindustan Times* 2011: 1.

30. Previously, in middle-class and elite families, women were often not expected or even allowed to work outside of the home, which meant that their efforts could be devoted to the care of dependent family members.

31. Sooryamurthy 2012: 7.

32. *Hindustan Times* 2015: 2.

33. R. Prasad 2007: 2.

34. Some might think it makes sense to look at existing research about GNC people and their families, but to date there are not many studies on this topic (though this is certain to change in the coming years). We can break down existing literature about GNC people and families into three broad areas of research: studies of the intimate partnerships GNC people create (Pfeffer 2017 and 2012; Sanger 2010; Hines 2006), research about the children of GNC people who self-affirmed their identities after becoming parents (Taber

2019; Hines 2006), and studies examining the parents of GNC children (Rahilly 2020, 2015; Meadow 2018). However, these available studies about GNC people and families are not particularly applicable to the context of changing *hijra* families.

35. Weston 1991.
36. Weston 1991: 40.
37. Weston 1991.
38. Weston 1991: 28.
39. Weston 1991: 40.
40. Weston 1991: 28.
41. Weston 1991: 40.
42. Weston 1991: 40.
43. Of course, there are many different types of family forms that exist throughout India (Sooryamoorthy 2012). In singling out one particular relationship to compare with *hijra* families, I do not intend to suggest that this is the only non-*hijra* family form that might be revealing. Instead, I suggest this comparison because it reveals more about how social change impacts relationships than the kinds of comparisons with joint families that I regularly heard during my fieldwork.
44. Reddy 2005.
45. This was the case in many countries of the British Empire, including Britain, as evidenced by the existence of an "age of consent" to marriage for women and the lack of any conversation about an age of consent for men (Deswal 2019).
46. Radhakrishnan 2008: 16.
47. Beliappa 2013: 85.
48. Beliappa 2013: 80.
49. Netting 2010: 714.
50. V. Das 2019: 135.
51. Beliappa 2013: 81.
52. Puri 1999 and Netting 2010 cited in Beliappa 2013: 82.
53. Beliappa 2013: 85.

Conclusion

"I am Not a *Hijra*"

Opportunities, Inequalities, and the Perils of Inclusion

This book has explored the emergence of new forms of gender identity in India, emphasizing how ideas about modernity and economic liberalization come together to shape emerging trans women identities in Bangalore. I have traced how recent social changes connected to economic liberalization in India have enabled some feminine-presenting GNC people to live "independent" of *hijra*s. These changes are understood as empowering for younger GNC people who can access resources previously available only through *hijra* groups.

When we put these changes in the context of increased global media coverage of transgender issues, the emergence of trans women is not that surprising. What is intriguing is how trans women are being framed in contrast to *hijra*s. Unlike in countries of the Global North, where there is a pervasive idea that gender nonconformity is somehow new,[1] gender nonconformity has been recognizable (if not exactly intelligible) for centuries[2] (and possibly millennia) in India. This means Indian trans identities have emerged in a context where gender nonconformity is recognized through the historical presence of *hijra*s (and some other GNC categories). These understandings about *hijra*s shape how transgender people, and especially trans women, are understood.

Due to social change that promises greater inclusion, some trans women have gained newfound freedoms. This has meant that many of these trans women can envision themselves as "new" (and respectably middle-class) women. Like their cisgender women counterparts from the past, these trans women distance and differentiate themselves from their "other," the disreputable *hijra*. In their quest to be recognized as respectable women, the trans women in this book valorize this newly available pathway to respectability while simultaneously devaluing other pathways available to GNC people, especially those associated with *hijras*.

It might be tempting to assume that GNC identities inherently challenge the gender binary, given that these identities are explicitly "nonconforming." It would therefore make sense to think of GNC identities as encouraging *less* conformity to dominant ideas about gender. However, the actions of the trans women in this book bring such assumptions into question, since these trans women consciously position themselves within the gender binary as they strive for upward mobility. Their actions illustrate the continuing significance of the gender binary and its intersection with class inequalities in the lives of trans women.

The trans women in this book engage in identity work that makes small adjustments to the gender binary, as they seek to make space for themselves within it. This book has focused on these small adjustments because they add up to what is essentially a remaking of the gender binary and the inequalities on which it rests. As they adhere to prevailing notions about class and gender that define the idealized concept of womanhood in India, these trans women reinforce social hierarchies that are also shaped by postcolonial experiences.

Ultimately, in urban India, the label of transgender is emerging not only as an alternative identity, but as a nascent category with the potential to challenge established social hierarchies. The trans women in this book not only aim for personal social advancement, but also seek to shape how the transgender category becomes integrated into existing social hierarchies. As I will show in this concluding chapter, the identity work these trans women engage in is part of a nuanced strategy to influence social hierarchies and their place within them.

"We Will Not Do Like *Hijras* Do"

When discussing the dynamics of GNC people distancing themselves from *hijras*, it is important to note that trans women are not the only group within communities of sexual minorities and GNC people who are keen to avoid being characterized as *hijras*. However, I observed that trans women expressed the most palpable concern about being recognized as *hijras*; their fear of this misrecognition was made tangible to me on multiple occasions. One of the most vivid occurrences happened during an organizing meeting for Queer Pride Week.

This meeting was held on the top floor of a civil society organization near the bustling commercial heart of the city. As I walked toward the building, the setting sun painted the surroundings with a sepia-toned glow, and the hum of ambient traffic filled the air. I entered the room where the meeting would be held and saw about 20 people seated comfortably on floor mats, engrossed in animated conversations. As more people trickled in, familiar faces were greeted with waves, and people moved aside, making space for everyone on the mats. Notably, the attendees represented a diverse array of backgrounds and social classes, including key figures from the autonomous groups and NGOs dedicated to sexual rights in the city. As someone passed around small plastic cups of sweet milk tea poured from a gleaming steel carafe, the meeting began.

This was the first Pride meeting of the year, so several extensive discussions unfolded over the course of nearly three hours. The most intriguing conversation revolved around how to fund the Pride celebrations. When the topic was initially brought up by Roshan, a middle-class gay man and Pride organizer, someone near the back suggested collecting individual contributions. Suparna, a passionate queer feminist activist seated near me, excitedly agreed, explaining that since the festival of Divali was coming up, everyone would be going to lots of parties and betting on card games. Since people would be exchanging money, it would be the perfect time to ask if they were willing to donate. Rohit, a spirited middle-class gay man, nodded excitedly. Echoing this sentiment, he enthusiastically suggested that groups of people could get together and go around the city to collect donations in busy commercial areas.

At this suggestion, a brief hush fell over the room, followed by a chorus of cautious murmurs. Sultana, a working-class trans woman and dedicated NGO employee, sat up straight and widened her eyes. Speaking in a mix of Kannada and English, she said, "But we shouldn't force anyone to donate. Like if they say no, they don't want to donate, we shouldn't push them to." Roshan, who was moderating the discussion, concurred, saying in English, "Yes, of course. All donations should be voluntary and if people don't want to donate, then we should leave them alone." By this time, the murmuring had amplified to become loud chatter, so to make sure everyone understood, Roshan held up his hands. Raising his voice, he repeated that all donations would be voluntary, and no one would be permitted to harass anyone who was unwilling to donate. In case the subtext of the conversation was not entirely clear to everyone, he concluded his remarks by saying, "We will not do like *hijras* do."

This incident illustrates the tensions that arise for non-*hijra* sexual minorities and GNC people when they find themselves thrust into situations where they might be associated with *hijras*. The suggestion that groups of people could collect donations in public places was met with anxiety for what it portended: that raising money for Pride Week could be conflated with the purportedly aggressive behavior of *hijras* when soliciting money. Suparna and Rohit were less threatened by the possibility of being misidentified as *hijras*, probably because they are middle-class, but this was not the case for Sultana, a working-class trans woman who could be viewed as a *hijra* by people not familiar with the trans woman–*hijra* distinction. For her and other trans women present at the meeting, it was especially important to ensure that the distinction between *hijras* and trans women was understood.

A parallel incident unfolded at a different planning meeting—this time for a Queer Pride event held the previous year. As the discussion delved into orchestrating the rally and performances that would occur after the march, Leena, a working-class trans woman and NGO worker in her forties, emphasized that the skits and dance performances must include a message ("they can't be for entertainment's sake alone"), so they needed to explain this to participants. In a moment of contemplation, Leena got a thoughtful look in her eyes and asked, "Should we regulate the speeches that people can make? Because someone will come and start doing...." Here, she theatrically mimicked the distinctive clapping associated with *hijras*[3] while adopting a high-pitched voice, then firmly stated, "and we can't have that." The reaction was again split along class lines: Tahir, a middle-class gay man, offered a confused frown, saying he was uncomfortable with that idea. He also cautioned that if the group made too many rules, they might not get anyone willing to participate, but several other working-class trans women agreed with Leena. Their recognition of the misidentification she feared was not shared by Tahir, who did not feel the need to regulate people's behavior to ensure that participants would not engage in the kinds of actions associated with *hijras*.

Although working-class trans women occupy subordinate positions in hierarchies of class and respectability in public and even within the space of a Pride meeting, many are nevertheless keen to distinguish themselves from the even more marginalized position of *hijras*.[4] Transgender is therefore not simply an alternative that opens up other (equal) ways of being a GNC person. It is an alternative category that is new enough that it has not yet been incorporated into social hierarchies, unlike the maligned category of *hijra*.

Transgender's newness means that people who take on trans identities, like Sultana and Leena, seek to influence not only what it means to be transgender, but also *how* and *where* the category of trans might eventually be incorporated within social hierarchies. Thus, identifying as transgender for Sultana and Leena is an important way of seeking upward mobility and also attempting to influence the workings of social hierarchies.

Prior to my fieldwork, I thought an emerging group of GNC people in the 2010s would be interested in challenging negative stereotypes of gender nonconformity. In India, such stereotypes are most apparent in the societal stigmatization of *hijra*s, and therefore any attempt to challenge stereotypical understandings of gender nonconformity would need to involve them. But as this book shows, the transgender women I spoke with are at pains to emphasize their difference from *hijra*s. In fact, these trans women often favorably contrast themselves with the figure of the *hijra* in the hopes of aligning themselves with respectable middle-class womanhood. This point is especially obvious when we consider a recent photo project made by a group of mostly trans women from different parts of India that circulated widely online and received significant media attention.[5]

"I am Not a *Hijra*"

In August 2016, the Facebook group Transgender India, which had over 16,000 followers at the time, published a photo series entitled "I am Not a *Hijra*." This collection of 17 photos shows primarily feminine-presenting GNC people dressed in a variety of clothing (including several sundresses, T-shirts, and even a *sari*), holding handwritten signs that cover their faces (except for one, who is wearing a *burqa*). The signs all begin with the same statement, "I am trans*," followed by facts about the subjects' lives that mark them as contrary to stereotypes about *hijra*s, and they all end with the same sentence, "I am Not a *Hijra*." The people in the photos are pictured in a variety of settings, ranging from in front of a long escalator (perhaps at a mall or corporate office) and outside of a hospital to dining out at a restaurant or in a gym. Several photos look as though they were taken inside the person's home.

Like the trans women I spoke with, the trans people pictured emphasize how their employment (and, thus, class) status serves as a key marker of their difference from *hijra*s. Five of the 17 cards in the photos mention the holder's upper-middle-class occupations (including surgeon, corporate worker, and physical therapist) and the fact that one person earns a "six figure" salary and another is "not a sex worker," thus distinguishing the trans people pictured from the figure of the impoverished *hijra*. The trans people pictured in the "I am Not a *Hijra*" series also draw on middle-class standards of femininity to situate their sexuality as contrary to the supposedly unrestrained sexuality displayed by *hijras*. In one photo, the sign indicates the trans woman is "not a sex maniac" and in another that the trans woman pictured is "not loose." Two others indicate that the person holding the sign is "asexual" (in contrast with the hyper-sexuality that *hijras* supposedly embody) and "do[es]n't like makeup" (unlike *hijras*, who are presumed to enjoy wearing an inappropriate amount of makeup). These photos draw on stereotypes of *hijras* as displaying an overt, and therefore improper, sexuality in order to position the trans woman pictured, whose sexuality is supposedly restrained, as clearly distinct from *hijras*.

One intriguing photo links middle-class respectable femininity and family status to claim the trans woman pictured as distinct from *hijras*. The trans woman is wearing clothing and jewelry symbolizing proper middle-class femininity while the card she holds emphasizes her familial status, writing that she is "a daughter, sister, wife and mother"—followed by the familiar refrain "I am Not a *Hijra*." The implication is that *hijras* are doubly excluded from respectable middle-class femininity and family-oriented womanhood.

The "I am Not a *Hijra*" photo project reveals how some trans people emphasize their difference from *hijras*. These photos draw on stereotypes of *hijras*—as working-class people who do not aspire to middle-class status, as displaying an overt and therefore improper sexuality, or as unable to claim heteronormative familial statuses and therefore excluded from proper family-oriented womanhood. As one of the six organizers of Transgender India explained, their goal is to demonstrate that "there are transgender people who have regular jobs and lead ordinary lives" and "give young transgender persons 'positive role models' to look up to."[6] Implicit in these remarks is that the supposedly irregular jobs of *hijras* mean they have unusual lives that make them incapable of being "positive role models" for young GNC people to emulate.

In their pursuit of the respect garnered by middle-class cis women, the figure of the unfeminine, improper, and disreputable *hijra* is a useful one for some trans women. Like the construct of the working-class woman "other" used to differentiate between "new" (cis) women and their others, the figure of the tainted *hijra* is employed by trans women to distinguish themselves as they align themselves with middle-class womanhood. As the foil against which some trans women favorably contrast themselves, they use the figure of the impoverished, stigmatized *hijra* to contain negative stereotypes associated with gender nonconformity, thus distancing themselves from these connotations. These photos illustrate a key argument of this book, that some trans women attempt to climb the social hierarchy ladder by effectively stepping on the *hijra*s just below them. Instead of "lifting as they climb," these trans women reinforce the inequality and stigma that plagues *hijra*s for their inability (and/or refusal) to conform to the dictates of middle-class womanhood.

Like the "new" trans women I spoke with, the trans women in these photos engage in identity work to align themselves with respectable, middle-class femininity as they seek to claim respectable middle-class transgender identities. They express these aspirations through claims of being similar to respectable, middle-class "new" womanhood. For these trans women, being transgender is partly about symbolically positioning themselves in proximity to respectable middle-class "new" (cisgender) womanhood. They bolster their symbolic positioning as middle-class women by distinguishing themselves from *hijra*s, who cannot (or will not) conform to these class and gender mandates.

Yet in their desire to distinguish themselves from *hijra*s, something else is happening as well to the trans women in this book. Like their cisgender counterparts from previous eras, some trans women carefully police their behavior in the hopes of avoiding misrecognition as *hijra*s. They articulate (like their counterparts at the Pride meetings) what they position as the acceptable way of being a trans woman—aspiring for entry into the middle class, displaying modesty in their dress and sexuality, and conforming to gendered expectations within heteronormative families. This form of "new" trans womanhood thus ultimately circumscribes trans women's actions and opportunities.

It is easy to presume that GNC identities inherently challenge the gender binary since such identities are, by definition, "nonconforming," and therefore to assume that GNC identities encourage *less* conformity to dominant ideas about gender. However, in their pursuit of upward mobility, the trans women in this book position themselves squarely within the gender binary. They demonstrate the importance of the gender binary coupled with an elevated class status for feminine-presenting GNC people's intelligibility and acceptance in urban India. These trans women are actually conforming to dominant ideas about class and gender for ideal womanhood in India—ideas that exist within hierarchies of class and gender that are the result of postcolonial experiences.

I want to be clear that in making this argument, my aim is not to rehash (or support) long-standing critiques that GNC and trans people who identify with one gender more than another inherently reinforce the gender binary. Instead, my goal has been to contextualize the emergence of trans women within historical conceptions about womanhood in postcolonial and liberalizing India because without paying attention to the intersection of gender and class, it is not possible to understand what is happening with transgender identities. I have shown how some (younger) trans women's new opportunities allow them enhanced access to resources, like middle-class employment and education, which they can use to fit in with the mainstream and conform to the dictates of middle-class womanhood. But those who have less access to resources, such as older GNC people and especially *hijras*, cannot draw on (or refuse) those same resources to conform.

Contesting Categories, Remaking Inequalities

The trans women in this book conform to these class and gender mandates because they seek to incorporate themselves into existing social hierarchies that rest upon (and reinforce) them. Because newer categories like transgender necessarily emerge *outside* of existing social hierarchies, it takes time for these new categories to become assimilated into these hierarchies. This means newer categories like transgender can be perceived as offering more marginalized groups (like working-class trans women) a chance at upward social mobility. These groups may then think it is to their advantage to shape such newer identities in ways that may enable them to be assimilated farther up within existing hierarchies. For this reason, the trans women I spoke with may be especially keen to ensure that their identities are aligned with middle-class respectability. That can be seen in the final photo included in the "I am Not a *Hijra*" photo series, where a trans woman holds a sign asserting "my rights are women's rights too," explicitly connecting the rights of trans women to the rights of (presumably cis) women.

Claiming rights for trans people, including the ability to have your gender identity recognized instead of being lumped into a single GNC category, is a goal that can have liberatory potential. Transgender India's stated intention in circulating the photo series was to amplify Indian trans people's voices, carving out a space of recognition for their identities.[7] However, this demand for recognition largely hinges on differentiating trans women from *hijras*, whose stigmatization is unchallenged. The final photo ends as all the others do with the refrain "I am Not a *Hijra*"—a category whose lack of rights is taken as a given. As one Transgender India organizer explains, the photo series seeks to establish that "I am a trans person. I am as normal as you. And I am not a *hijra*."[8] This "normal[ity]" relies on an understanding of womanhood that aligns with middle-class respectable femininity through invoking middle-class signifiers and reifying the implicit understanding that *hijras* lie outside of that "normal[ity]."

The "I am Not a *Hijra*" series shows how recent social changes this book has documented have enabled new opportunities for some trans women that on their face can seem positive and even progressive. It certainly seems positive that a formerly marginalized group like trans women now enjoy access to basic necessities (like housing and gender affirmation surgery) that enable them to live "independent" of *hijras*. It may even feel progressive that trans women can access middle-class markers like office employment, which opens up respectable ways of being women. However, such seemingly progressive changes are not available to all GNC people, and indeed are predicated on the continuing stigmatization of *hijras*. Both the desire to attain the respect accorded to middle-class cis women and the incommensurability between their own lives and stereotypical understandings of *hijras* influence trans women's decisions to disidentify with *hijras*.

Disidentifying with *Hijras*: "Murderous Inclusions"

Like the trans women I spoke with, the trans women in the "I am Not a *Hijra*" photo series express a desire to be included in the category of (ideal) woman as they align themselves with middle-class womanhood and claim respectably middle-class transgender identities. They do this because they seek access to the kinds of social benefits that accrue to middle-class cis women. For these trans women, identifying as transgender opens up possibilities for upward mobility and independence they think are not available to *hijras*.

While the desire for inclusion is now often lauded as a progressive goal, some scholars urge us to look beyond "inclusion's seductive promises" so that we might also recognize the violence that accompanies some forms of inclusion.[9] Though inclusion as an idea aspires to "include the excluded eventually," this can only happen when they are deemed "deserving or human enough."[10] Marginalized groups that seek inclusion into existing hierarchies thus risk reproducing the very marginalization they are themselves trying to escape. As a result, processes of demanding inclusion often produce "deadly outcomes" for those groups that fall outside of the boundaries of the newly included.[11]

For example, the societal inclusion of "good" gays in parts of the Global North was not something that happened in isolation; scholars have pointed out that other marginalized groups were being simultaneously criminalized. Puar used the term "homonationalism" to capture how liberal gay politics (like homonormativity, which was discussed in the Introduction) create progress narratives that allow some formerly marginalized groups (like "good" gays) to be incorporated as citizens into the US state.[12] At the same time, other groups (such as young Muslim men assumed to be terrorists) faced increased surveillance and deportation. These two groups were often juxtaposed to one another so that the Muslim "terrorists" became increasingly othered as the "good" gays ascended the social hierarchy ladder.[13] Scholars express concern that such processes of inclusion "work to reify the boundaries and borders of exclusion."[14]

Scholars have made similar arguments about the inclusion of "good" LGBTQ+ people in parts of Europe. To secure their place as citizens in need of protection (instead of the kind of people respectable citizens need protection from), LGBTQ+ advocacy groups relied on a "perpetual (re) invention of a dangerous Other."[15] This criminalized person is characterized as: "the 'homophobic Muslim,' the 'working-class yob' or the 'backward immigrant.'"[16] These figures are all presumed to be homophobic based on their class, religious, and/or immigrant status, and that their homophobic sentiments will assuredly manifest through violent and humiliating acts. LGBTQ+ citizens therefore require protection from the state, which is assumed to be benevolent and LGBTQ+-friendly.[17] By characterizing certain marginalized people as unambiguously "backward" and homophobic, race- and/or class-privileged LGBTQ+ people garner state recognition and inclusion as "respectable, enlightened and worthy."[18] As a result, Haritaworn and their co-authors provocatively argue for "how inclusion can be murderous" when we shift our critical gaze from its promises to its necessary violences.[19]

In the case of trans women in India, this "murderous" metaphor includes the murder of "dangerous Others," such as the figure of the disreputable *hijra*, who enables respectable trans women to argue for their own inclusion by pointing to the supposed failures of *hijras*. Trans women who seek inclusion as middle-class women rely centrally on juxtaposing trans women's respectability, which marks them as "deserving," with the disreputability of *hijras*, thus positioning *hijras* as outside of respectable womanhood.

I also interpret the "murderous" metaphor to mean the murder of those parts of trans women that must be hidden, silenced, or covered up when they do not mark them as "deserving" of inclusion. This means that in differentiating themselves from *hijras*, trans women must also murder those parts of themselves that are likely to open them up to misrecognition as *hijras*. This impetus to "murder" parts of themselves that could be associated with *hijras* is evidenced in publicly voiced anxieties about the participation of *hijras* and those who behave in ways marked as *hijra*-like in Queer Pride events.[20] It also includes the "murder" of those parts of themselves that found solace, companionship, and family among *hijra* groups, since their connections to *hijras* must be covered up.

What might be lost for those trans women who do not acknowledge their connections to *hijras*? Recall Akrithi, whose story appeared in Chapter 2. She is the person who rose "up" from sex work to being an office worker at an NGO, and she then climbed the employment ladder within her organization. By the time my fieldwork ended, Akrithi was among the most well-known trans women in south India. She appeared regularly in news and print media, where she often related her process of self-affirming her identity. Given how often I had heard her story, I was surprised when Akrithi mentioned to me one afternoon that *hijras* were among the first GNC people she interacted with when she self-affirmed her identity as a teenager. This information was surprising to me because I had never heard her mention that *hijras* had been a part of her self-affirmation process. Akrithi explained that when she met *hijras* for the first time, she felt a strong affinity with them. She recounted,

> When I saw them [*hijras*], I was 16 years old [and I was walking] at Cubbon Park Circle. I was so happy to go and meet them.... I was so happy after seeing them. I went to them, I spoke to them, I took their flowers [that they gave me] and put them in my hair.... I never felt scared

seeing *hijras*.... I wanted to be like them. I felt that [*pause*] they are my family. That thought came to my mind because ... [in my own family,] there was lots of rejection, no acceptance, there was kind of torture, violence, [I was placed under] house arrest.... I thought, you know, "this is the community where I want to live." They have the same feelings, same attitude, [they are wearing the] same clothing [that I want to wear], [*pause*] yeah, everything.

While many people had been taught to fear *hijras*, Akrithi experienced joy and acceptance upon seeing them. In fact, she thought of these *hijras* as "family" and emphasized her feelings of belonging and community. She further explained that she had been getting off a bus when she saw two *hijras*, and the sight of them made her so happy that she started crying inexplicably. She tearfully approached the *hijras* and told them, "I want to be like you." They responded to her in a kind manner and took her to meet the person who would later become her *guru*.

Akrithi frequently "comes out" in media and at public events, sharing her story of confusion, familial abuse, and ultimately self-acceptance. It is telling that her initial interactions with *hijras* did not appear in any (public) narrative of her experiences that I had heard or read about. Like many other trans women I spoke to, Akrithi de-emphasized her connection to *hijras*, which I read as a "murder" of that part of herself who sought and found warmth, kindness, and feelings of "family" with them as a young GNC person. Because this part of herself could bring into question the notion of clear boundaries between trans women and *hijras*, it must be glossed over, hidden, and even "murdered."[21]

I read this distancing of trans women from their connections to *hijras* as a "murderous" form of inclusion.[22] In this process, trans women do not often acknowledge the forms of belonging and support that *hijra* groups have provided to people who do not identify as *hijras*. This unfortunately negates the possibility for political solidarity between trans women and *hijras* that might enable them to collectively advocate against their marginalization. The kind of identity work trans women engage in as they put forth their case to be included in the category of (ideal) womanhood leads to "deadly outcomes"[23] not only for *hijras* but also for trans women themselves, whose ability to act is ultimately circumscribed through their efforts to differentiate themselves from *hijras*.

If Not Inclusion, Then What?

The kinds of demands for inclusion that some trans women engage in are increasingly coming under scrutiny because they can perpetuate exclusion for other groups (like *hijras*). What, then, are the other options for groups wanting to resist their marginalization? One answer lies in the perspectives of A. Revathi and Living Smile Vidya, two GNC people in south India who are publicly active in social justice struggles. Both are authors[24] and activists[25] who encourage nuanced conversations about the intersectional nature of gender hierarchies, transphobia, and caste oppression as they interrogate the politics of inclusion described in this book.

Revathi identifies herself as both a transgender woman and as a *hijra*, a double identification that not many GNC people claim publicly. Although she now lives alone, as a young GNC person, Revathi joined a *hijra* group and became a *chela*. As someone who lived outside of *hijra* communities and received opportunities through her activism and her writing, Revathi could have simply identified herself as a trans woman and eschewed any mention of her connections with *hijras*. But when discussing her identity, instead of exclusively emphasizing her identity as a trans woman, Revathi regularly highlights her connections with *hijras*. Indeed, she acknowledges the connections between the societal stigmatization of *hijras* and the overall status of GNC people: "Whatever affects the *hijra* community, also affects me personally."[26] Because she witnessed firsthand the kinds of violence and discrimination *hijras* are regularly subjected to, she found it "impossible for me to look the other way or keep quiet" in the face of such injustice.[27] Like Revathi, Vidya also identifies herself as both a *thirunangai* (a Tamil word meaning *hijra*) and as a transgender woman. Vidya also became a *chela* in a *hijra* group as a young GNC person and now lives apart from *hijra* groups. And she too seeks to raise awareness of *hijras'* life experiences, particularly the stigma and discrimination they face.

Both Vidya and Revathi emphasize the intersections of caste oppression and transphobia. Vidya is especially attuned to issues of caste injustice, as her family came from "the lowest of the Dalits" and regularly experienced practices of untouchability.[28] As a child, when Vidya would visit friends in other Dalit neighborhoods, she had to be careful to avoid walking near the neighborhoods where high-caste people lived "because they would yell [at you] if you walk[ed] near their property."[29] As an adult from a Dalit background, she endured significant hardships in order to earn a master's degree. Revathi's autobiography reveals that she is from a dominant-caste background. Yet her writing is partly inspired by Bama, a well-known contemporary Dalit Tamil writer and activist, whose reflections on "the multiple forms of oppression" she experienced as a Dalit woman informed her own writing about the injustices faced by *hijras* and other GNC people.[30] In fact, the insights about caste and gendered oppression in Vidya's autobiography inspired Revathi to write her own.

In their written and performance work, Vidya and Revathi challenge unacknowledged inequalities that result from systems reinforcing the societal dominance of privileged groups. Drawing parallels among structured forms of oppression, they point to the simultaneity of oppressions for people like Vidya, who experience both caste oppression and transphobia. For example, the issue of employment for GNC people and Dalits is a topic that both Vidya and Revathi focus on. As Vidya explains, Dalits have "been made to feel less human by [higher] castes, in a way similar to how society treats [GNC people]."[31] Part of the reason is due to their reduced ability to obtain respectable employment. Vidya makes the connection between transphobic attitudes and Brahmanical caste practices explicit: "Transphobia is a type of Brahminism. It gives us no other option but to do 'dirty' jobs like sex work and begging and then calls us 'dirty,' just like the caste system did with Dalits."[32]

Like many trans women I spoke with, Revathi points out that the connection between GNC people (particularly *hijras*) and sex work opens them up to discrimination. "Society is still negative about transgender people because we are involved in sex work. Like they screw up their noses at Dalits and Adivasis ... out of a sense of aversion and disgust, similarly they have the same feelings for trans people across caste." Yet instead of suggesting *hijras* and other GNC people eschew these stigmatizing jobs to pursue middle-class employment, Revathi places the responsibility for alleviating the discrimination trans women experience directly on the government. "Why can't the government decriminalize sex work? Then, maybe, the stigma would be considerably less."[33]

Vidya similarly emphasizes that GNC people face reduced access to employment. "When [feminine-presenting GNC people] first realize that they are trans women, they immediately think they will have to beg, because they see [*hijras* working] only in one place—begging on the street."[34] As a result, the idea that GNC people are limited to soliciting money (and sex work) "becomes fixed" as the only option in people's minds, similar to how one's place in the caste hierarchy[35] is tied to one's occupation.[36] As Vidya explains, "Dalits are socially conditioned to internalize that they are meant to do only some jobs," which makes it hard to imagine engaging in other work, especially jobs that require education.[37] In her own experience, "one major fear of mine when I transitioned was that I knew [at the time] there were only two options of begging and sex work" for GNC people.[38] Facing constrained employment opportunities as a GNC person, "I felt this was again like a caste occupation where *hijras* become a caste with only these two options available to us."[39]

But Vidya also calls attention to the casteism that is sometimes present among groups of *hijras* and to the transphobia she faced among Dalits. Even among *hijras*, Vidya observes, "[s]ome castes are very proud ... always proudly asserting their caste. I have seen some ... *hijras* say things like, 'I might be a transgender like you, but I am a Thevar [that is, a dominant caste] in the village.'"[40] Vidya has also been told by other Dalit *hijras* and GNC people to make sure not to reveal her caste background by discussing practices associated with Dalits, such as eating beef, "so that no one ... figures out I am Dalit."[41] However, Vidya "never hide[s] from other Dalits the fact that I am also Dalit" any more than she would "hide from other [*hijras*] that I am also one of them."[42]

In Vidya's experience, many Dalits are openly transphobic. When she witnesses Dalits expressing transphobic attitudes, Vidya intervenes by pointing out their similar experiences in oppressive systems of power.

> I ask them why they don't understand [GNC people's] pain when they have had similar experiences individually and historically. When they ask me, "Why do transgenders beg and not work? You will get more respect if you just work like other people," I say, "Why don't Dalits become bankers, doctors, engineers? Why are they still stuck in the same jobs after all these years? It is because we Dalits are not capable? Or because we are lazy and don't want those jobs? Actually, it is because of lack of opportunity and discrimination. The same goes for transgenders.... And begging itself is very hard work.[43]

By making these connections, Vidya encourages Dalits to rethink their transphobia and GNC people to question their caste discrimination. When she is asked to give a talk about transgender issues, "I always talk about working together" with other oppressed groups, emphasizing an intersectional approach to understanding and trying to change systems of domination.[44]

In their writing and their activism, Revathi and Vidya highlight the plight of other oppressed GNC groups, particularly masculine-presenting GNC people and transgender men. According to Revathi, for *hijras* and other feminine-presenting GNC people, "[t]here is no denying the support and solace" that *hijra* communities provide[45]—a point Vidya makes as well.[46] Vidya also notes how the social expectation that *hijras* solicit money offers them an income. "[U]nfortunately, there is nothing like this for trans men," Revathi observes.[47] Vidya concurs: masculine-presenting GNC people "can't ask for money in public and do not have this traditional community" to help them survive.[48] Without these options to earn an income and a recognized community support system, masculine-presenting GNC people often struggle to access social and financial support. In order to raise awareness about differences among GNC people, Revathi explains, "I always talk about trans men in all public discussions."[49]

Through endorsing an intersectional, coalitional feminist politics, the work of Revathi and Vidya can be read as a counternarrative to "new" trans womanhood. By emphasizing their identification as both *hijras* and trans women, Vidya and Revathi reject the notion that trans women should seek inclusion as middle-class, respectable women. This would require that they engage in "murderous" tactics of inclusion[50] that construct *hijras* as legitimately excluded from respectable womanhood. Instead, Revathi and Vidya interrogate the hierarchies upon which these systems of oppression are based, drawing connections between oppressed groups to advocate for a coalitional politics of resistance. They challenge their own oppression in ways that do not risk re-marginalizing other groups while encouraging collective action and solidarity, offering an intriguing alternative to the politics of inclusion (and assimilation) endorsed by the trans women in this book.

However, even well-known trans women like Revathi and Vidya cannot control how they are identified by others, pointing to the challenges facing trans women who use intersectional politics to challenge the discourse of "new" trans womanhood. For example, in an article in *The Hindu* newspaper (aimed at educating readers about the differences between trans women and *hijras*),[51] Revathi is lauded for how different she appears from *hijras*. Upon meeting her, the reporter writes that Revathi "belies the image of a *hijra*" and describes her as displaying "no makeup, no gaudy dressing and no exaggerated mannerisms."[52] Dressed in "a simple cotton green *kurta* and a handbag slung over her shoulder, Revathi is your regular working woman one encounters on a local train."[53] When contrasted with the "gaudy dressing" and "exaggerated mannerisms" associated with *hijras*, Revathi's depiction as a "regular" woman who dresses modestly in "simple" attire positions her as respectable and aligns her with "new" trans womanhood. Ironically, the reporter probably thought they were complementing Revathi by characterizing her in this way, illustrating the power of discourses that uphold "new" trans women through favorably contrasting them with *hijras*.

Notes

1. Aizura and Stryker 2013: 3
2. Reddy 2005; see also Cohen 1995; Nanda 1990.
3. A marker of the kind of stigmatization that *hijras* are subjected to is in the form of the *thikri*, a manner of loud clapping that is strongly associated with *hijras*. As Reddy (2005) points out, "[m]ore than any other gesture or movement, this loud clapping of hands is indelibly associated with *hijras*" (Reddy 2005: 137; see also Dutta 2012a). This manner of clapping is often performed publicly by *hijras* to mark themselves or others as *hijras*, and it is also performed within *hijra* groups to signify *hijra* identity (Reddy 2005: 138). Among non-*hijras*, this kind of clapping is often used in a "parodic" (and frequently derogatory) way to make fun of *hijra* identification and behaviors (Reddy 2005: 137). Within sexual minority and GNC communities, invoking the *thikri* is increasingly a way that the (non-*hijra*) person invoking it can mark (and mock) *hijra* behavior, usually in order to distance themselves from it.
4. This dynamic is similar to Dutta's finding that working-class, feminine-identified *kothis* in West Bengal voice disagreement with public behavior deemed "excessive or aggressively campy"; their disapproval is "especially evident during Pride meetings where there have been repeated complaints against [such] disruptive practices" (Dutta 2012a: 129).
5. The series was first published on the online news platform *The Better Indian*, where it was later taken down due to complaints that it expressed anti-*hijra* sentiments (D. M. Sengupta 2016: 3). Subsequently, the series was published on the popular website *Buzzfeed* and *The Logical Indian*. The widespread attention it received throughout India suggests that some trans women's desires to clarify their distinctness from *hijras* are salient (and contentious) issues beyond my field site in Bangalore.

6. M. Das 2016: 2.

7. D. M. Sengupta 2017: 1.

8. D. M. Sengupta 2017: 1.

9. Haritaworn, Kuntsman, and Posocco 2013: 446; see also Lamble 2013; Spade 2015; Brandzel 2016.

10. Brandzel 2016: 4.

11. Haritaworn, Kuntsman, and Posocco 2013: 446; see also Brandzel 2016; Spade 2015

12. Puar 2007.

13. Puar 2007.

14. Brandzel 2016: 15.

15. Haritaworn 2010: 74.

16. Haritaworn 2010: 74.

17. Haritaworn 2010: 74.

18. Lamble 2013: 246; see also Haritaworn 2015, 2010.

19. Haritaworn, Kuntsman, and Posocco 2013.

20. See also Dutta 2012a; Dutta and Roy 2014.

21. Haritaworn, Kuntsman, and Posocco 2013.

22. Haritaworn, Kuntsman, and Posocco 2013.

23. Haritaworn, Kuntsman, and Posocco 2013.

24. Revathi's first book, *Our Lives, Our Words*, published in 2004, is a collection of *hijra* life narratives. Her other two books, *The Truth about Me: A Hijra Life Story* (2010) and *A Life in Trans Activism* (2016), are autobiographical. Vidya became the first transgender person to write her autobiography, *I am Vidya: A Transgender's Journey*, published in 2007.

25. Revathi has been involved in gender and sexual rights activism (from within and outside of the NGO sphere) for several decades. Vidya is known as an actor, director, writer, and activist for transgender and Dalits' rights issues.

26. Revathi 2016: 78.

27. Revathi 2016: 79.

28. Roundtable India 2013: 1.

29. Roundtable India 2013: 2.

30. Revathi 2016: 82.

31. Roundtable India 2013: 5.

32. Roundtable India 2013: 5.

33. Revathi 2016: 72.

34. Roundtable India 2013: 4.

35. The specifics of how a trans woman's place in caste interacts with their class aspirations falls outside the scope of this research. Even within marginalized caste groups, there are caste hierarchies that shape people's aspirations and outcomes in ways that are relevant for thinking about class aspirations. It is possible that caste mediates the degree to which feminine-presenting GNC people understand "new" trans womanhood as being available to them. The pre- and post-colonial history of caste, its grounding in gender hierarchies, and its complex contemporary realities in urban and rural India make this a salient topic for future research (see Bayly 1999; Chakravarti 2003; Dirks 2001; Fuller and Narasimhan 2014; Gupta 2016; Jodhka 2015; Moody 2015; Viswanath 2014).
36. Roundtable India 2013: 4.
37. Roundtable India 2013: 4.
38. Roundtable India 2013: 4.
39. Roundtable India 2013: 4.
40. Roundtable India 2013: 4.
41. Roundtable India 2013: 4.
42. Roundtable India 2013: 5.
43. Roundtable India 2013: 5.
44. Roundtable India 2013: 5.
45. Revathi 2016: 130.
46. Roundtable India 2013: 3.
47. Revathi 2016: 130.
48. Roundtable India 2013: 3.
49. Revathi 2016: 131.
50. Haritaworn, Kuntsman, and Posocco 2013.
51. Mount 2020.
52. Mary 2014: 1.
53. Mary 2014: 1.

Acknowledgments

This book is a true labor of love—a journey of heart and mind that has spanned many years. It is a testament to the collective spirit and generosity of the countless people who have contributed to this endeavor.

At the heart of this research are the participants who graciously invited me into their lives, sharing their experiences with patience and openness. Though confidentiality precludes me from naming them, their contributions are the foundation of this work, and for that, I am deeply thankful.

As a graduate student, my research interests and perspectives were shaped by the knowledge I gained from the Women's and Gender Studies and Sociology Departments at Syracuse University, as well as the memorable Democratizing Knowledge lecture series. Special thanks to Jyoti Puri, whose intellectual imprint on my work is sharp, and to Gretchen Purser for her invaluable guidance. I also want to thank my friends: Jinhee Park, Jessica ("GB") Green-Barnes, Ellen Royse, Dolly Haddad, Emy Matheson, Anya Stanger, and Tre Wentling, whose friendship and support were my anchor during this time. I am grateful to Caleb Simmons and Nikki Aaron for their camaraderie and support in Mysore; their friendship was a beacon during those formative days.

My journey has been brightened by the presence of former colleagues whom I am fortunate to call friends: Zhibek Kadyrsizova, Paula Doumani Dupoy, Kyung-min Baek, Edwin Sayes, Elliott Bowen, Gwen McEvoy, Lorna Bracewell, Nic Miller, Lauren Bates, and Jen Saracino. A special note of appreciation to the Proctor Library staff at Flagler College, particularly Jessie Rutland and Maria Dintino, for their unwavering research support.

The camaraderie and insights I have gained from my writing groups have been invaluable. Ilana Horwitz and Landon Schnabel have been the best "peer-plus" book and proposal writing mentors I could have imagined, often believing in this project more than I did. The Sociologists for Women in Society's Friday Morning Writing Group and the Women Faculty Writing Group at Texas Tech University provided a sense of community and encouragement that I particularly cherished during the challenges of the Pandemic.

I want to extend a heartfelt thanks to my editorial team at Cambridge University Press, including Anwesha Rana, Qudsiya Ahmed, and Aniruddha De. And a special mention to D. Olson Pook, whose editorial assistance has made this book more readable and polished. I am very indebted to Vaibhav Saria for their keen eye and thoughtful feedback.

I am grateful for the financial support of the American Institute for Indian Studies, the Maxwell School at Syracuse University, the Syracuse University Sociology Department, and Nazarbayev University. Texas Tech University and Flagler College also provided financial contributions that were crucial in bringing this project to fruition.

My family in the United States, Leslie Mount, Michael Mount, Katherine Mount Schramm, Sven Schramm, Andrew Mount, LeighAnn Leitgeb Mount, Ian Mount, and Mariana Cerecero Mount, have been a constant source of support. More recently, George Mount, Oliver Schramm, Bennett Mount, Charlotte Schramm, and Charles Mount bring joy and laughter to everyone.

My family in India, Veena Bansal, Ravi Bansal, Anupam Singh, Anand Bansal, Manvi Arora, and Reyaansh Bansal, have offered warmth, support, and acceptance from day one. Whether it is sharing a comforting cup of *chai* or indulging in sweet treats, their genuine care and hospitality have brightened my life immeasurably.

But my greatest debt goes to Payal Bansal, whose influence on my life and work is profound. Meeting her has been the most cherished stroke of luck on this research journey. And a special thanks to Vihaan, whose presence enriches my life in ways I can hardly put into words.

This research has truly been a collaborative effort. From the bottom of my heart, thank you.

Bibliography

Abdelrahman, M. (2007). "NGOs and the Dynamics of the Egyptian Labour Market." *Development in Practice* 17 (1): 78–84.

Acharya, M. (2017). "Meet India's First Transgender Judge Joyita Mondal." *SBS Hindi*, October 16. https://www.sbs.com.au/language/hindi/en/article/meet-indias-first-transgender-judge-joyita-mondal/p6ct0rimu. Accessed April 15, 2024.

Ahmad, M. (2002). "Who Cares? The Personal and Professional Problems of NGO Fieldworkers in Bangladesh." *Development in Practice* 12 (2): 177–191.

Aizura, A. (2018). *Mobile Subjects: Transnational Imaginaries of Gender Reassignment*. Durham, NC: Duke University Press.

Aizura, A., and S. Stryker (2013). "Introduction: Transgender Studies 2.0." *The Transgender Studies Reader* 2, edited by Susan Stryker and Aren Aizura. New York: Routledge.

Almeida, R. (2021). "Meet 7 of India's Transgender Icons, Thriving Despite Social Taboo." *Homegrown*, June 8. https://homegrown.co.in/homegrown-creators/meet-7-of-indias-transgender-icons-thriving-despite-social-taboo. Accessed April 15, 2024.

Aranha, J. (2018). "How a Homeless Graduate Became Andhra Govt's First Transgender Employee." *The Better India*, January 8. https://www.thebetter india.com/126932/transgender-graduate-andhra-govt/. Accessed April 15, 2024.

Bannerjee-Guha, S. (2009). "Neoliberalizing the 'Urban': New Geographies of Power and Injustice in Indian Cities." *Economic and Political Weekly* 44 (22): 95–107.

Bano, M. (2012). *Breakdown in Pakistan: How Aid Is Eroding Institutions for Collective Action*. Palo Alto, CA: Stanford Economics and Finance.

Bansal, R. (2020). "India Has Social Schemes for Poor in Crises Like Covid. But It Needs a 'Who to Pay' Database." *The Print*, April 23. https://theprint.in/opinion/india-needs-a-who-to-pay-database-covid-crisis/406783/. Accessed February 10, 2021.

Bayly, S. (1999). *Caste, Society and Politics in India from the Eighteenth Century to the Modern Age*. Cambridge, UK: Cambridge University Press.

Beliappa, J. (2013). *Gender, Class and Reflexive Modernity in India*. London: Palgrave Macmillan UK.

Berry, K. (2008). "Good Women, Bad Women and the Dynamics of Oppression and Resistance in Kangra, India." *Humboldt Journal of Social Relations* 31 (1/2): 4–38.

Bhatt, A., M. Murty, and P. Ramamurthy (2010). "Hegemonic Developments: The New Indian Middle Class, Gendered Subalterns, and Diasporic Returnees in the Event of Neoliberalism." *Signs: Journal of Women in Culture and Society* 36 (1): 127–152.

Boellstorff, T. (2011). "But Do Not Identify as Gay: A Proleptic Genealogy of the MSM Category." *Cultural Anthropology* 26 (2): 287–312.

Boyce, P. (2007). "'Conceiving Kothis': Men Who have Sex with Men in India and the Cultural Subject of HIV Prevention." *Medical Anthropology* 26 (2): 175–203.

Brandzel, A. (2016). *Against Citizenship: The Violence of the Normative*. Urbana-Champagne, IL: University of Illinois Press.

Chakravarti, U. (2003). *Gendering Caste: Through a Feminist Lens*. New Delhi: Stree.

Christy, R. (2011). "Video Volunteers: Empowering Community Voices." 24 March. https://www.videovolunteers.org/radio-jockey-transgender-empowered/. Accessed April 16, 2024.

Cohen, L. (1995). "The Pleasures of Castration: The Postoperative Status of Hijras, Jankhas, and Academics." In *Sexual Nature/Sexual Culture*, edited by P. a. S. P. Abramson, 276–304. Chicago, IL: University of Chicago Press.

——— (2005). "The Kothi Wars: AIDS Cosmopolitanism and the Morality of Classification." In *Sex in Development: Science, Sexuality, and Morality in Global Perspective*, edited by Vincanne Adams and Stacy Leigh Pigg, 269–303. Durham, NC: Duke University Press.

Cohn, D'Vera (2011). "India Census Offers Three Gender Options." Pew Research Center, February 7. https://www.pewresearch.org/social-trends/2011/02/07/

india-census-offers-three-gender-options/#:~:text=India's%202011%20
national%20census%2C%20which,by%20that%20nation's%20highest%20
court. Accessed April 15, 2024.

Conklin, G. (1976). "The Household in Urban India." *Journal of Marriage and Family* 38 (4): 771–779.

Conley, D. (2015). *You May Ask Yourself: An Introduction to Thinking Like a Sociologist.* New York: W.W. Norton.

D'Cruz, P. and S. Bharat. (2001). "Beyond Joint and Nuclear: The Indian Family Revisited." *Journal of Comparative Family Studies* 32 (2): 167–194.

Dalit Camera (2016). "Grace Banu: India's First Transgender Engineering Student & Activist." https://www.youtube.com/watch?v=1WAVhQQKfTo. Accessed April 15, 2024.

Das, M. (2016). "As Awesome As It Can Get: A Website By and For Transgenders." *The News Minute*, July 12. https://www.thenewsminute.com/article/awesome -it-can-get-indian-website-and-transgenders-46350. Accessed April 13, 2024.

Das, V. (2019). "Dating Applications, Intimacy, and Cosmopolitan Desire in India." In *Global Digital Cultures: Perspectives from South Asia*, edited by Aswin Punathambekar and Sriram Mohan, 125–141. Ann Arbor, MI: University of Michigan.

Dave, N. (2012). *Queer Activism in India: A Story in the Anthropology of Ethics.* Durham, NC: Duke University Press.

David, E. (2015). "Purple-Collar Labor: Transgender Workers and Queer Value at Global Call Centers in the Philippines." *Gender and Society* 29 (2): 169–194.

Deswal, V. (2019). "Need to Revisit the Concept of 'Age of Consent.'" *Times of India*, November 25. https://timesofindia.indiatimes.com/blogs/legally-speaking/need-to-revisit-the-concept-of-age-of-consent/. Accessed April 13, 2014.

Dickey, S. (2012). "The Pleasures and Anxieties of Being in the Middle: Emerging Middle-Class Identities in Urban South India." *Modern Asian Studies* 46 (3): 559–599.

——— (2016). *Living Class in Urban India.* Rutgers, NY: Rutgers University Press.

Dirks, N. B. (2001). *Castes of Mind: Colonialism and the Making of Modern India.* Princeton, NJ: Princeton University Press.

Duggan, L. (2002). "The New Homonormativity: The Sexual Politics of Neoliberalism." In *Materializing Democracy: Toward a Revitalized Cultural Politics*, edited by Russ Castronovo and Dana D. Nelson, 175–194. Durham, NC: Duke University Press.

Dutta, A. (2012a). "Claiming Citizenship, Contesting Civility: The Institutional LGBT Movement and the Regulation of Gender/Sexual Dissidence in West Bengal, India." *Jindal Global Law Review* 4 (1): 110–141.

—— (2012b). "An Epistemology of Collusion: Hijras, Kothis and the Historical (Dis)continuity of Gender/Sexual Identities in Eastern India." *Gender and History* 24 (3): 825–849.

—— (2013). "Legible Identities and Legitimate Citizens: The Globalization of Transgender and Subjects of HIV/AIDS Prevention in Eastern India." *International Feminist Journal of Politics* 15 (4): 494–514.

—— (2014). "Contradictory Tendencies: The Supreme Court's NALSA Judgment on Transgender Recognition and Rights." *Journal of Indian Law and Society* 5 (Monsoon): 225–236.

—— (2016). "Gatekeeping Transgender." *RAIOT: Challenging the Consensus,* October 4. https://raiot.in/gatekeeping-transgender/. Accessed April 13, 2024.

Dutta, A. and R. Roy (2014). "Decolonizing Transgender in India: Some Reflections." *TSQ: Transgender Studies Quarterly* 1 (3): 320–337.

Fernandes, L. (2015). "India's Middle Classes and the Post-Liberalization State: A Theoretical Perspective". In *The Trajectory of India's Middle Class: Economy, Ethics and Etiquette,* edited by L. Lobo and J. Shah, 82–94. Cambridge, UK: Cambridge Scholars Publication.

Fernandes, L. and P. Heller. (2006). "Hegemonic Aspirations: New Middle Class Politics and India's Democracy in Comparative Perspective." *Critical Asian Studies* 38 (4): 495–522.

Films Media Group (2009). *Emerging Superpower: Booming Bangalore.* Superpower India. https://films.com/id/21031/Emerging_Superpower_ Booming_Bangalore.htm. Accessed April 12, 2024.

Fuller, C. J., and Haripriya Narasimhan (2014). *Tamil Brahmins: The Making of a Middle-class Caste.* Chicago: University of Chicago Press.

Ganguly-Scrase, R. and T. J. Scrase (2008). *Globalisation and the Middle Classes in India: The Social and Cultural Impact of Neoliberal Reforms.* New York: Routledge.

Ghosh, A. (2005). "Public–Private or a Private Public?" *Economic and Political Weekly* 40 (47).

Ghosh, S. (2021). "7 Years After SC Judgment, Third Genders Say They Feel Like Second Class Citizens." *India Today,* June 17.

Gupta, C. (2016). *The Gender of Caste: Representing Dalits in Print.* Seattle: University of Washington Press.

Hall, K. (2005). "Intertextual Sexuality: Parodies of Class, Identity, and Desire in Liminal Delhi." *Journal of Linguistic Anthropology* 15 (1): 125–144.

Haritaworn, J. (2010). "Queer Injuries: The Racial Politics of 'Homophobic Hate Crime' in Germany." *Social Justice* 37 (1): 69–89.

—— (2015). *Queer Lovers and Hateful Others: Regenerating Violent Times and Places*. London, UK: Pluto Press.

Haritaworn, J., A. Kuntsman, and S. Posocco (2013). "Murderous Inclusions." *International Feminist Journal of Politics* 15 (4): 445–452.

Hegarty, B. (2017). "The Value of Transgender: *Waria* Affective Labor for Transnational Media Markets in Indonesia." *Transgender Studies Quarterly* 4 (1): 78–95.

Higginbotham, E. (1994). *Righteous Discontent: The Women's Movement in the Black Baptist Church, 1880–1920*. Cambridge, MA: Harvard University Press.

Hinchy, J. (2014). "Obscenity, Moral Contagion and Masculinity: *Hijras* in Public Space in Colonial North India." *Asian Studies Review* 38 (2): 274–294.

—— (2019). *Governing Gender and Sexuality in Colonial India: The Hijra, c. 1850–1900*. Cambridge, UK: Cambridge University Press.

Hindustan Times. (2015). "Indian Joint Families Breaking Down as Seniors Opt for Retirement Homes." April 3.

Hines, S. (2006). "Intimate Transitions: Transgender Practices of Parterning and Parenting." *Sociology* 40 (2): 353–371.

Homans, P. (1979). *Jung in Context: Modernity and the Making of a Psychology*. Chicago, IL: University of Chicago Press.

ILGA (The International Lesbian, Gay, Bisexual, Trans and Intersex Association) (2012). "Radio Gives Voice to India's Transgender Community." September 10. https://globalpressjournal.com/asia/india/radio-gives-voice-to-india-s-transgender-community/. Accessed April 13, 2024.

India Today (2017). "India's First Transgender Police Officer Appointed in Tamil Nadu." April 5.

—— (2018). "Eight Indian Transgender People Who Were the Firsts in their Fields." July 4.

Irving, D. (2008). "Normalized Transgressions: Legitimizing the Transsexual Body as Productive." *Radical History Review* 8 (100): 38–59.

Iyengar, R. (2019). "Toxic Air and Gridlock: India's Tech Cities Are Choking on Their Success." CNN video. https://www.facebook.com/cnn/videos/toxic-air-and-gridlock-indias-tech-cities-are-choking-on-their-success/28857425 24789779/. Accessed April 12, 2024.

Jarrin, A. (2016). "Untranslatable Subjects: Travesti Access to Public Health Care in Brazil." *TSQ: Transgender Studies Quarterly* 3 (3/4): 357–375.

Jodhka, S. (2015). *Caste in Contemporary India*. New Delhi: Routledge.

Kabeer, N. (1999). "Resources, Agency, Achievements: Reflections on the Measure of Women's Empowerment." *Development and Change* 30 (3): 435–464.

Kathuria, C. (2018). "Transgender Women Who Are Trailblazers in Their Fields." *Shethepeople*, July 7. https://www.shethepeople.tv/news/transgender-women-trailblazers-fields/. Accessed April 16, 2024.

Khatri, A. A. (1972). "The Indian Family: An Empirically Derived Analysis of Shifts in Size and Types." *Journal of Marriage and Family* 34 (4): 725–734.

Keshava, S. R. (2006). "Urbanization and Solid Waste Management in Bangalore: Growth, Options and Challenges." In *Environmental Issues of Development*, edited by Ganesh Kawadia and Kanhaiya Ahuja, 225–241. New Delhi: The Associated Publishers.

Khubchandani, K. (2020). *Ishtyle: Accenting Gay Indian Nightlife*. Ann Arbor, MI: University of Michigan Press.

Knight, K. (2019). "India's Transgender Rights Law Isn't Worth Celebrating." *The Advocate*, December 5. https://www.hrw.org/news/2019/12/05/indias-transgender-rights-law-isnt-worth-celebrating#:~:text=India's%20parliament%20passed%20a%20bill,one%20was%20introduced%20in%202016. Accessed April 16, 2024.

Kunzel, R. (2014). "The Flourishing of Transgender Studies." *TSQ: Transgender Studies Quarterly* 1 (1/2): 285–297.

Lamble, S. (2013). "Queer Necropolitics and the Expanding Carceral State: Interrogating Sexual Investments in Punishment." *Law and Critique* 24 (3): 229–253.

Lamont, M. (1992). *Money, Morals and Manners: The Culture of the French and the American Upper-Middle Class*. Chicago, IL: University of Chicago Press.

Lampe, N. M., S. K. Carter, and J. E. Sumerau (2019). "Continuity and Change in Gender Frames: The Case of Transgender Reproduction." *Gender and Society* 33 (6): 865–887.

Liddle, J., and R. Joshi (1986). *Daughters of Independence: Gender, Caste and Class in India*. Delhi: Kali for Women.

Liechty, M. (2003). *Suitably Modern: Making Middle-class Culture in a New Consumer Society*. Princeton, NJ: Princeton University Press.

Long, S. (2014). "Buggery and Beggary, and Ferguson." *A Paper Bird* (blog). November 28. https://scottlong1980.wordpress.com/2014/11/28/buggery-and-beggary/. Accessed April 13, 2024.

Lukose, R. (2009). *Liberalization's Children: Gender, Youth and Consumer Citizenship in Globalizing India*. Durham, NC: Duke University Press.

Mankekar, P. (1999). *Screening Culture, Viewing Politics: An Ethnography of Television, Womanhood, and Nation in Postcolonial India*. Durham, NC: Duke University Press.

Mary, S. B. V. (2014). "Transcending Gender Barrier." *The Hindu*, November 3. https://www.thehindu.com/features/metroplus/society/transcending-gender -barrier/article6560631.ece. Accessed May 3, 2024.

Massey, D. (1994). *Space, Place and Gender*. Minneapolis, MN: University of Minnesota Press.

Mathew, P. (2017). "Meet Tharika Banu, TN Transgender Woman who Fought for and won a Medical Seat." *The News Minute*, December 8. https://www. thenewsminute.com/tamil-nadu/meet-tharika-banu-tn-transgender-woman-who-fought-and-won-medical-seat-72872#:~:text=Tharika%20and %20her%20mother%20Grace's,was%20not%20an%20easy%20one.&text =She%20left%20home%20unable%20to,journey%20to%20becoming%20a %20doctor. Accessed April 16, 2024.

Meadow, T. (2018). *Trans Kids: Being Gendered in the Twenty-First Century*. Berkeley, CA: University of California Press.

Menon, G. (dir.) (2012). *Chittegalu Haradali* (Let the Butterflies Fly): 74 minutes. https://www.imdb.com/title/tt30137976/. Accessed April 16, 2024.

Misra, J. (2006). "Empowerment of Women in India." *The Indian Journal of Political Science* 67 (4): 867–878.

Mitra, I. (2012). "A Joint Family Is More Than Living Together." *Times of India*, New Delhi, July 5. https://timesofindia.indiatimes.com/life-style/ relationships/love-sex/a-joint-family-is-more-than-living-together/ articleshow/12673451.cms. Accessed April 16, 2024.

Mount, L. (2020). "'I am Not a Hijra': Class, Respectability and the Emergence of the 'New' Transgender Woman in India." *Gender and Society* 34 (4): 620–647.

Munshi, S. (1998). "Wife/Mother/Daughter-in-law: Multiple Avatars of Homemaker in 1990s Indian Advertising." *Media, Culture and Society* 20 (4): 573–591.

Moody, M. (2015). *We Were Adivasis: Aspiration in an Indian Scheduled Tribe*. South Asia Across the Disciplines. Chicago: University of Chicago Press.

Nair, J. (2005). *The Promise of the Metropolis: Bangalore's Twentieth Century*. Oxford, UK: Oxford University Press.

Nanda, S. (1990). *Neither Man Nor Woman: The Hijras of India*. Boston, MA: Cengage Learning.

Narrain, A., and G. Bhan (2006). *Because I Have a Voice: Queer Politics in India*. New Delhi: Yoda Press.

Narrain, S. (2013). "Policing Hijras." https://www.academia.edu/20351522/Policing _Hijras. Accessed April 13, 2024.

Nelson, D. (2011). "Indian Families Abandon Communal Living." *UK Telegraph*, February 6. https://www.telegraph.co.uk/news/worldnews/asia/india/8306917/ Indian-families-abandon-communal-living.html. Accessed April 16, 2024.

Netting, N. (2010). "Marital Ideoscapes in 21st Century India: Creative Combinations of Love and Responsibility." *Journal of Family Issues* 31 (6): 707–726.

Newbigin, E., L. Renault, and R. De (2009). "Personal Law, Identity Politics and Civil Society in Colonial South Asia." *Indian Economic and Social History Review* 46 (1): 1–4.

Nikore, M. (2019). "Where Are India's Working Women?" *Times of India*, October 14. https://timesofindia.indiatimes.com/blogs/irrational-economics/where-are -indias-working-women. Accessed April 12, 2024.

Nolen, S. (2009). "A Transgender Star Sparkles in India's TV Firmament." *The Globe and Mail*, London, July 22. https://www.theglobeandmail.com/news/ world/a-transgender-star-sparkles-in-indias-tv-firmament/article1200401/. Accessed April 16, 2024.

Oza, R. (2006). *The Making of Neoliberal India: Nationalism, Gender and the Paradoxes of Globalization*. New York: Routledge.

People's Union for Civil Liberties–Karnataka (PUCL-K) (2004). "Human Rights Violations Against the Transgender Community." https://www.scribd.com/ document/167055309/PUCL-K-Human-Rights-Violations-Against-the- Transgender-community. Accessed April 12, 2024.

Pfeffer, C. (2012). "Normative Resistance and Inventive Pragmatism: Negotiating Structure and Agency in Transgender Families." *Gender and Society* 26 (4): 574–602.

—— (2017). *Queering Families: The Postmodern Partnerships of Cisgender Women and Transgender Men*. New York, NY: Oxford University Press.

Prasad, R. (2007). "India's Shrinking Families." *The Guardian*, April 13. https:// www.theguardian.com/lifeandstyle/2007/apr/14/familyandrelationships. family2. Accessed April 16, 2024.

Prasad, S. (2015). "City's Worst Kept Secret Throws Up 264 Skeletons." *Bangalore Mirror*, August 1. https://bangaloremirror.indiatimes.com/bangalore/others/ skeletons-central-relief-committee/articleshow/48301323.cms. Accessed April 13, 2024.

Puri, J. (1999). *Woman, Body, Desire in Post-Colonial India: Narratives of Gender and Sexuality*. New York: Routledge.

———. 2010. "Transgendering Development: Reframing Hijras and Development." In *Development, Sexual Rights, and Global Governance*, edited by Amy Lind, 39–53. New York: Routledge.

——— (2015). "Sexualizing the State: Sodomy, Civil Liberties and the Indian Penal Code." In *Contesting Nation: Gendered Violence in South Asia*, edited by Angana Chatterji and Lubna Nazir Chaudhry, 100–141. Delhi: Zubaan.

Qureshi, I. (2014). "India's First Transgender News Anchor." BBC World News, September 29.

Radhakrishnan, S. (2008). "Examining the 'Global' Indian Middle Class: Gender and Culture in the Silicon Valley/Bangalore Circuit." *Journal of Intercultural Studies* 29 (1): 7–20.

Rahilly, E. (2015). "The Gender Binary Meets the Gender-Variant Child." *Gender and Society* 29 (3): 338–361.

——— (2020). *Trans-Affirmative Parenting: Raising Kids across the Gender Spectrum*. New York: NYU Press.

Rajan, R. S. (1999). *Signposts: Gender Issues in Post-Independence India*. New Delhi: Kali for Women.

Ramachandra, T. V., and B. H. Aithal (2016). "Bangalore: Unlivable City." *Current Science* 110 (12). https://ces.iisc.ac.in/?q=node/411. Accessed April 12, 2024.

Ramanathan, U. (2008). "Ostensible Poverty, Beggary and the Law." *Economic and Political Weekly* 43 (44): 35–44.

Ramaswamy, S. (2004). *The Lost Land of Lemuria: Fabulous Geographies, Catastrophic Histories*. Berkeley, CA: University of California Press.

Ramu, G. N. (1972). "Geographic Mobility, Kinship and the Family in South India." *Journal of Marriage and Family* 34 (1): 147–152.

Reddy, G. (2005). *With Respect to Sex: Negotiating Hijra Identity in South India*. Chicago: University of Chicago Press.

Reuters (2015). "Protesters Give a Goodbye Kill to Liberal Bengaluru." February 25. https://www.reuters.com/article/idUS208193218820150219/. Accessed April 12, 2024.

Revathi, A. (2010). *The Truth about Me: A Hijra Life Story*. Translated by V. Geetha. New Delhi: Penguin Books India.

——— (2016). *A Life in Trans Activism*. New Delhi: Zubaan.

Romani, S. (2016). "Being NGO Girls: Gender, Subjectivities, and Everyday Life in Kolkata." *Gender, Place and Culture* 23 (3): 365–380.

Roundtable India (2013). "(Trans)gender and Caste Lived Experience—
Transphobia as a Form of Brahminism: An Interview with Living Smile
Vidya." January 26. https://www.roundtableindia.co.in/transgender-and-caste
-lived-experience-transphobia-as-a-form-of-brahminism-an-interview-of
-living-smile-vidya/. Accessed May 3, 2024.

Roy, S. (2022). *Changing the Subject: Feminist and Queer Politics in Neoliberal
India*. Durham, NC: Duke University Press.

Rubin, M., N. Denson, S. Kilpatrick, K. E. Matthews, T. Stehlik, and D. Zyngier
(2014). "'I Am Working Class': Subjective Self-definition as a Missing
Measure of Social Class and Socioeconomic Status in Higher Education
Research." *Educational Researcher* 43: 196–200

Ruiz, J. (2008). "The Violence of Assimilation: An Interview with Mattilda aka
Matt Bernstein Sycamore." *Radical History Review* 8 (100): 237–247.

Salaria, S. (2017). "Babli Is First Transgender to Become a Legal Assistant at
Delhi High Court." *Times of India*, December 2. https://timesofindia.
indiatimes.com/city/noida/babli-is-first-transgender-to-become-a-legal-
assistant-at-delhi-high-court/articleshow/61886819.cms. Accessed April
16, 2024.

Samuels, G. and F. Ross-Sheriff (2008). "Identity, Oppression, and Power:
Feminisms and Intersectionality Theory." *Affilia: Journal of Women and
Social Work* 23 (1): 5–9.

Sanger, T. (2010). *Trans People's Partnerships: Towards an Ethics of Intimacy*. New
York, NY: Palgrave MacMillan.

Saria, V. (2019). "Begging for Change: Hijras, Law and Nationalism." *Contributions
to Indian Sociology* 53 (1): 133–157.

——— (2021). *Hijras, Lovers, Brothers: Surviving Sex and Poverty in Rural India*.
New York, NY: Fordham University Press.

Schilt, K. (2011). *Just One of the Guys? Transgender Men and the Persistence of
Gender Inequality*. Chicago, IL: University of Chicago Press.

Semmalar, G. I. (2014). "Unpacking Solidarities of the Oppressed: Notes on Trans
Struggles in India." *Women's Studies Quarterly* 42 (3/4): 286–291.

Sengupta, D. M. (2017). "I Am Not a *Hijra*: A Damaging, Offensive Transgender
India Photo Campaign." *Catch News*. http://www.catchnews.com/gender-
and-sex/i-am-not-a-hijra-a-damaging-offensive-transgender-india-photo-
cam-paign-1471618717.html. Accessed April 14, 2024.

Sengupta, J. (2016). "Rising Inequality and Urban Exclusion." Observer Research
Foundation, February 16. https://www.orfonline.org/research/rising-in
equality-and-urban-exclusion/. Accessed April 13, 2024.

Serano, J. (2014). "A Personal History of the "T" Word (and Some More General Reflections on Language and Activism)." *Whipping Girl Blog*. https://juliaserano.blogspot.com/2014/04/a-personal-history-of-t-word-and-some.html#activistlanguage. Accessed April 10, 2023.

——(2015). "Regarding Trans and Transgenderism." *Whipping Girl Blog*. https://juliaserano.blogspot.com/2015/08/regarding-trans-and-transgenderism.html. Accessed April 10, 2023.

Shah, S. (2014). "Queering Critiques of Neoliberalism in India: Urbanism and Inequality in the Era of Transnational 'LGBTQ' Rights." *Antipode* 47 (3): 1–17.

Shaw, A. (2012). "Metropolitan City Growth and Management in Post-liberalized India." *Eurasian Geography and Economics* 53 (1): 44–62.

Singh, S. and M. Bhandari (2012). "Money Management and Control in the Indian Joint Family across Generations." *Sociological Review* 60 (1): 46–67.

Skeggs, B. (2004). *Class, Self, Culture*. London: Routledge.

Snow, D. (2001). "Collective Identity and Expressive Forms." UC Irvine: Center for the Study of Democracy. https://escholarship.org/uc/item/2zn1t7bj. Accessed April 16, 2024.

Sooryamurthy, R. (2012). "The Indian Family: Needs for a Revisit." *Journal of Comparative Family Studies* 43 (1): 1–9.

Spade, D. (2015). *Normal Life: Administrative Violence, Critical Trans Politics, and the Limits of Law*. Durham, NC: Duke University Press.

Steinmetz, K. (2014). "The Transgender Tipping Point." *Time Magazine*, May 29. https://time.com/135480/transgender-tipping-point/. Accessed April 10, 2024.

Stryker, S. (2008). "Transgender History, Homonormativity and Disciplinarity." *Radical History Review* 100 (Winter): 144–157.

Stryker, S., and A. Aizura (eds.) (2013). *The Transgender Studies Reader 2*. New York: Routledge.

Taber, J. (2019). "Mom, Dad, or Somewhere in Between: Role-relational Ambiguity and Children of Transgender Parents." *Journal of Marriage and Family* 81 (2): 506–519.

Thapar, S. (1993). "Women as Activists; Women as Symbols: A Study of the Indian Nationalism Movement." *Feminist Review* 44 (Summer): 81–96.

The Hindu (2015). "India Gets Its First Transgender College Principal." May 27. https://timesofindia.indiatimes.com/india/india-gets-its-first-transgender-college-principal/articleshow/47436427.cms. Accessed April 16, 2024.

Times of India (2017). "India's First Transgender Cop Inspires 27 Others to Join Police Force." May 22. https://timesofindia.indiatimes.com/videos/

news/indias-first-transgender-cop-inspires-27-others-to-join-police-force/ videoshow/58787637.cms. Accessed April 16, 2024.

Uberoi, P. (1993). *Family, Kinship and Marriage in India*. Delhi: Oxford University Press.

UCA News (Union of Catholic Asian News) (2010). "26 Beggars Die in Karnataka State Home." August 23. https://www.ucanews.com/story-archive/?post_name=/2010/08/23/26-beggars-die-in-karnataka-state-home&post_id=53154. Accessed April 13, 2024.

———. 2013. "India's First Transgender Pastor Finds Fulfilment." July 23. https://www.ucanews.com/news/indias-first-transgender-pastor-finds-fulfilment/68824#:~:text=Ten%20years%20ago%2C%20Bharathi%2C%20 then,minister%20to%20her%20fellow%20transgenders. Accessed April 15, 2024.

UNAIDS (1999). "Peer Education and HIV/AIDS: Concepts, Uses and Challenges." *UNAIDS Best Practice Collection*. Geneva, Switzerland.

Upadhya, C. (2016). *Reengineering India: Work, Capital and Class in an Offshore Economy*. Oxford: Oxford University Press.

Vaid, D. (2014). "Caste in Contemporary India: Flexibility and Persistence." *Annual Review of Sociology* 40 (1): 391–410.

Valentine, D. (2007). *Imagining Transgender: An Ethnography of a Category*. Durham, NC: Duke Unversity Press.

Vidya, Living Smile (2007). *I Am Vidya: A Transgender's Journey*. New Delhi: Rupa.

Vijayalakshmi, S., and K. Raj (2020). "Economic Estimation of Health and Productivity Impacts of Traffic Congestion: A Case of Bengaluru City." Working paper 485, The Institution for Social and Economic Change, Bangalore.

Vijaykumar, G. (2013). "Gender, Class and Flexible Aspirations at the Edge of India's Knowledge Economy." *Gender and Society* 27 (6): 777–798.

——— (2021). *At Risk: Indian Sexual Politics and the Global AIDS Crisis*. Palo Alto, CA: Stanford University Press.

Viswanath, R. (2014). *The Pariah Problem: Caste, Religion, and the Social in Modern India*. New York: Columbia University Press.

Waldrop, A. (2012). "Kitty-Parties and Middle-class Femininity in New Delhi." In *Being Middle-class in India: A Way of Life*, edited by H. Donner, 162–183. New York: Routledge.

Walkerdine, V. (2003). "Reclassifying Upward Mobility: Femininity and the Neoliberal Subject." *Gender and Education* 15 (3): 237–248.

Warner, M. (1999). *The Trouble with Normal: Sex, Politics and the Ethics of Queer Life*. Cambridge, MA: Harvard University Press.

Watson, T. J. (2008). "Managing Identity: Identity Work, Personal Predicaments and Structural Circumstances." *Organization* 15 (1): 121–143.

Weston, K. (1991). *Families We Choose: Lesbians, Gays, Kinship*. New York: Columbia University Press.

Yadav, A. (2021). "How Effective Are Social Security and Welfare in India?" *The Hindu*, February 10. https://www.thehindu.com/news/national/how-effective -are-social-security-and-welfare-in-india/article6823320.ece. Accessed April 13, 2024.

Yasmeen, B. S. A. (2010). "Beggar's Death Probe Yet to Reach CID." *The Hindu*, December 28. https://www.thehindu.com/news/cities/bangalore/Beggars -death-probe-yet-to-reach-CID/article15611779.ece. Accessed April 13, 2024.

Interviews

Akrithi, June 27, 2011, NGO office, Bangalore.

———, November 21, 2013, NGO office, Bangalore.

Andavar, November 25, 2012, public park, Bangalore.

Deepa, 19 February, 2014, NGO office, Bangalore.

Girish, March 28, 2014, Girish's house, Bangalore.

Johan, January 30, 2014, Johan's house, Bangalore.

Kanika, February 24, 2014, NGO office, Bangalore.

Malika, August 2, 2011, Malika's *hammam*, Bangalore.

Manisha, December 5, 2013, Manisha's friend's house, Bangalore.

Manjunath, August 5, 2011, NGO office, Bangalore.

Manvi, October 17, 2013, Manvi's house, Bangalore.

Mariyamma, October 11, 2013, NGO office, Bangalore.

Mohan, August 4, 2011, NGO office, Bangalore.

Monika, October 22, 2013, NGO office, Bangalore.

Neelima, September 19, 2013, NGO office, Bangalore.

Nisha, November 21, 2013, Nisha's workplace, Bangalore.

Pari, 18 February, 2014, NGO office, Bangalore.

Ramarajan, December 5, 2016, NGO office, Bangalore.

Rani, April 9, 2014, Rani's friend's house, Bangalore.

Rishabh, May 7, 2011, Rishabh's house, Bangalore.

Saira, January 14, 2014, Saira's house, Bangalore.

Sanya, October 15, 2013, Sanya's house, Bangalore.

Shanthi, February 13, 2014, coffee shop, Bangalore.

Suma, October 30, 2013, Suma's house, Bangalore.

———, September 25, 2013, Suma's house, Bangalore.

Sunitha, January 14, 2014, Sunitha's house, Bangalore.

———, November 28, 2013, NGO office, Bangalore.

Uma, November 27, 2012, Uma's house, Bangalore.

Utham, September 28, 2012, NGO office, Bangalore.

Vandana, February 5, 2014, Vandana's *hammam*, Bangalore.

Vasudha, September 11, 2013, Vasudha's house, Bangalore.

Vidyamma, February 7, 2014, Vidyamma's house, Bangalore.

Violet, September 17, 2013, NGO office, Bangalore.

Index

age factor, for GNC people seeking
    employment, 68–70
Akrithi (trans woman), story of,
    52–54, 60
    shifting class–gender identities,
        59–60
anglophone, 61
anti-"beggary" laws, 62
anti-discrimination laws and policies,
    11
aspirational city, 39–43
aspirations, 40, 61, 115, 156
    consumer, 34
    gender and class, intersectionality
        of, 32, 39, 70
    of GNC people, 14, 46
    middle-class, 4–6, 22, 38, 43, 54,
        57–59
    for social mobility, 22, 41
    trans women, 4–6, 39
        identity work, 5
        middle-class womanhood, 7
        newly emerging, 5
        social class, 57–58
    for upward mobility, 39

authority
    bonds of familial, 104
    of *chelas*, 110–111
    of *gurus*, 101–105, 108–115, 119
    loss of, 120–123
    to make financial decisions, 105
    middle-class cisgender women's
        relationship to, 104
    and new women, 104
    patriarchal, 130
    political, 54
    relationships within *hijra* families,
        23
        hierarchy in, 104–106
    social, 54
aversion and disgust, sense of, 163

backward immigrants, 159
badhai, *hijras* livelihood through,
    74n65
balance of power, 92, 129, 143–144
Bangalore, city of, 39–43, 78
    bodies of water, 41
    connections between gender and
        class aspirations in, 39

economic mobility of the middle
   classes, 41
as "Garden City" of India, 39, 41
general society in, 84
as a "global city", 40
IT industry in, 39–40
   economic growth due to, 41
levels of urban growth, 41
loss of green spaces, 41
market-driven and *laissez-faire*
   policies, 40
moral policing, 42
opportunities for the new woman,
   39
rights of GNC people in, 42
sexual rights NGOs, 42–43
shrinking *hammam*s and shifting
   geographies of wealth in, 81–82
trans women's aspirations in, 39
urban sprawl of, 41
water availability, 41
working-class neighborhoods, 41
Bangalore trans women activists, 68
beggary syndicate, 83
begging, 57, 67, 163
   anti-"beggary" laws, 62
   Karnataka State Prohibition of
      Beggary Act (1975), 62–63
   rehabilitation of beggars, 63
Bharatiya Janata Party (BJP), 42
birth families, 75, 90, 108, 127, 140–142
   degree of acceptance from, 96
   gay and lesbian people relationship
      with their, 140
   GNC people living with their, 85,
      92, 138
   GNC people running away from, 79,
      83, 115

*hijra*s returning to their, 137
*hijra*s severing of ties with, 86
problems faced by GNC people
   when forced out of, 78
support system for GNC people, 85
and stigma associated with GNC
   child, 58
blood ties, notion of, 140
bonded labour, 82–83
Brahminism, 163
British colonial administration, 112,
   131
British colonial laws, governing
   property and inheritance, 131
British Empire, 33, 149n45
business process outsourcing, 40

caste–class nexus, 6–8, 168n35
caste hierarchies, 7, 36, 164, 168n35
caste identities, 6–7
caste inequalities, 36
caste oppression, 162–163
*chela*s, 67, 75, 88, 95, 107. *See also guru–
      chela* relationships
   authority, 109–111
   complains at the police station
      against their *guru*, 113
   decision-making process, 94
   disidentification with *hijra*s, 77, 79,
      91, 105, 115–119
   dispute with the *guru*, 110
   engaging in sex work and soliciting
      money, 117
   financial autonomy, 109–111
   as forced labourer, 83
   gender affirmation surgery, 87
   impacts of shifting authority on
      expected behavior of, 113–114

information-centered shopping, 95
"new" *chelas*, 109–111
"new" womanhood, 92–96
nonresidential, 114
obligation of, 128
physical and financial abuse by their
    gurus, 112
standard of living among, 110
choice of livelihood
    of cisgender women, 55
    for GNC people, 68, 77, 93
    for *hijras*, 95
    importance of, 92–96
chosen families, concept of, 129,
    139–141, 146
cisgender women, in India, 20, 32, 77,
    129
    ability to engage in paid
        employment, 55
    ability to make empowered
        consumption, 96
    employment of, 54
        white-collar, 56
    "empowerment through
        employment" for GNC people,
        55–57
    history of employment for, 55
    joint family, 130
    middle-class, 12, 29, 39, 47
    postcolonial history of, 54
    sexual modesty, 130
    womanhood of, 6
civil society organization, 152
class aspirations, 47, 70, 168n35
    in Bangalore, 86
    of feminine-presenting GNC
        people, 38
    intersectionality of gender and, 32

of social class, 57–58
trans women and middle-class
    aspirations, 4–6, 7, 13, 22, 43,
    54
class hierarchies, 15–16
class identification, 44
class identities, 6, 44, 59, 60–61
class mobility, 46, 60
"common" women, 12, 33
communal living, 76, 78, 81, 91–92
community building, 42
community people, 56, 113
companionship, notion of, 144
crime against transgender persons, 83
criminal tribe, classification of *hijras*
    as, 73n48, 112
cross-gender identification, 18

dai ma (midwives), gender affirmation
    surgery performed by, 87
Dalits, 162–163
    transphobic attitudes, 164
dangerous Others, 160
"demobilized constituency" of gays, 18
dominant-caste identities, 6
dominant castes, 34, 36, 72n22, 81,
    163–164
    cis women, 7
    employment opportunities, 56
    English-medium education, 33
    ideals of womanhood, 8
    middle-class identities, 6
    white-collar work, 7
dominant-caste women, 33

economic liberalization, 27n86, 92–93,
    150
    benefits and values of, 35

and ideals of globalization, 34
impact on
    hijra communities, 96
    rates of growth in the service
        sector, 35
    women's upward mobility, 37
and middle-class aspiring groups,
    43
social changes connected to, 131
women empowerment and, 12
egalitarianism, ideal of, 145
emancipated woman, portrayal in TV
    shows, 104
employment
    age factor for GNC people seeking,
        68–70
    discrimination faced by *hijra*s,
        61–65
    "mainstream" jobs, 67
    media coverage of trans women's
        employment opportunities,
        65–68
    middle-class occupations, 66
    office employment, 65
    opportunities as a GNC person,
        164
    and sex work, 69
    stigmatized forms of, 61
    work-from-home job, 69
empowerment, concept of, 12, 47,
    55–58, 70, 93

FabIndia clothing, 59–60, 72n22
family acceptance, of GNC people,
    85–86
family's honor, 36, 130
feminization surgeries, 45
financial insecurity, 80

financial security, among
    working-class people, 67
forced labour, 82–83

gender affirmation surgery, 44, 79
    access to, 87–91
    chelas' surgeries, 87
    in licensed clinics, 99n50
    performed by *dai ma* (midwives),
        87
    by "quack" surgeons, 88
    in Tamil Nadu, 99n48
gender and class aspirations, 14
    complexities of, 43–46
    in context of trans women's identity
        work, 5
    for employment, 22
    generational differences in, 54
    intersectionality of, 32, 39
    among middle-class in India, 4
    middle-class womanhood and, 7
    for newly emerging trans women, 5
    in social hierarchies, 6
gender-based discrimination, 42
    in employment, 34
    prohibition against, 33
gender identities, 26n43, 70, 156–157,
    158
    anglophone, 61
    anti-discrimination laws and
        policies regarding, 11
    class–gender identities, 59–60
    connection with office employment,
        54
    and employment opportunities, 57
    of GNC people in India, 2, 4–5, 9–11,
        18
    new forms of, 150

gender nonconforming (GNC) people, 24n1, 110, 129, 135, 153, 156
   access to kinship relationships, 129
   association with stigmatized employment, 58
   codification of state recognition of, 82
   consumption decisions, 93
   decision-making processes, 93
   discrimination and abuse of, 69
   economic and social opportunities, 4
   employment opportunities as, 164
   empowerment through employment for, 55–57
   family acceptance of, 85–86
   family relationships of, 140
   gender affirmation surgery, 79
   in the Global South, 61
   identity in India, 2
   intelligibility and acceptance in urban India, 16
   legal recognition of, 11
   living in *hijra* families, 57
   male-assigned groups, 5
   media representations of, 94
   new housing opportunities for, 83–86
   public awareness of, 11
   public perception of, 56
   risk for HIV transmission, 5
   stigmatization of, 71
   travesti in Brazil, 61
   waria in Indonesia, 61
   working-class, 6, 37, 45
gender rights activism, 10
general society, 84, 108, 112
global capitalism, 18
global cultural economy, 41
global economy, 34–35
globalization, ideals of, 34
global labor markets, 61
Global North, 150, 159
Global South, GNC groups in, 61
"good" gays, 18–19, 159
grey rupee, rise of, 133
guru(s), 75, 83, 94–95, 107
   behavioral changes among, 119–120
   claim to authority, 114
   dispute with the *chela*, 110
   loss of authority over their *chela*s, 120–123
   monetary expectations, 108
   policing of *chela*s' earnings, 109
   use of violence to control *chela*s, 112
   value of being kind and gentle, 119–120
*gurubhai*s, 91
guru–chela relationships, 75–81, 89, 123, 127
   authority and hierarchy in, 104–106
   balance of power in, 92, 144
   changes in, 103, 124
   changing costs–benefits calculus in, 106–109
   consequences of *guru*s' authority on, 103
   in context of "new" womanhood, 92–93
   crime against transgender persons, 83
   devaluation of *guru*s' contributions in, 109
   dynamics of, 22, 79, 96, 109, 110, 113, 121, 123

financial support and obligations,
128
hierarchical nature of, 109
impacts of outside scrutiny,
111–113
key features of, 101–102
"liberal" *gurus*, 119
middle-class cisgender,
heterosexual couple
relationships, 129, 141–145
as middle-class husband is to
middle-class wife, 141–145
nonresidential, 92, 95, 116, 137
perceived resemblance to joint
families, 141–145
power dynamics between, 110, 114,
119
reciprocal exchanges of material
support, 79, 105
residential, 103, 109, 129, 137
rise of nonresidential, 91–92
in terms of family resemblance,
141–145
traditional, 120
vulnerability of, 121
willingness of a *chela* to continue,
121

hammams, 93, 98n15, 101
ability of *hijras* to live together in, 3,
13, 76, 83
communal houses, 78
effects on real estate prices, 81
sex work in, 67, 85, 91
shifting geographies of wealth,
81–82
state-sponsored displacement of, 81
in working-class neighborhoods, 81

heteronormativity, concept of, 17–18,
27n86
heterosexual couple, 131–132
living along with patrilineal
generations under one roof,
131
living outside of joint families, 132
heterosexuality, 17, 140
hierarchies, 136, 143
bargaining power, 146
caste, 7
class, 15–16, 34, 36, 39, 153
gender, 39
in *guru–chela* relationships, 109, 123
in *hijra* relationships, 104–106
social, 6, 13, 15–16, 21–23, 151
hijra(s), 2–3, 29–30, 43, 46, 54, 58, 64
as perceived agents of sexual
contagion, 73n48
alleged "anti-social" activities, 82
aspects of coercion, placation, and
humor, 62
connection with backwardness,
poverty, and stigma, 61
difference from trans women, 2–4,
10, 13–16, 19–21, 30, 70, 115
disidentifying with, 158–161
disreputability of, 160
employment discrimination faced
by, 61
engaged in sex work, 3, 64
family relationships (*see hijra*
families)
guru–chela relationships (*see*
guru–chela relationships)
income-generating activities, 96
from jobs, 155
occupations associated with, 57

through soliciting money and sex
work, 73n30
jobs of, 155
kinship systems, 5
limited employment options,
61–65
livelihood through *badhai*, 74n65
lives of, 54
marginalization and exclusion, 38
occupations associated with, 57
overlapping identities with trans
women, 13–16
past, 8–10
present, 8–10
societal perceptions about, 4
societal recognition and respect for,
10–11
relationships in the context of
criminalization, 82–83
relationships with their
surrounding communities, 81
representation in media, 112
respect for their supposed
asexuality, 72n30
rural-based, 85, 86
soliciting money and sex work, 54
stereotypes of, 155
stigmatization of, 14–15, 154–156,
158
as third gender, 26n43
on trains requesting money, 62
as transgender people, 10
trans women and, 3–4
urban-based, 86
vulnerable to state violence and
incarceration, 62
hijra families, 5, 90, 126, 128
changes in, 96

as collective poverty management
systems, 80
communal living, 78
as resistant institutions, 78–80
criminalizing of, 83
and desire for freedom and
independence from joint
family, 128–130
financial insecurity, 80
impact of social change on, 129
implications of Transgender
Persons (Protection of Rights)
Bill on, 82
narratives of freedom and
constraint in, 135–139
relation with their neighbors, 81
residential *hijra* relationships,
139–141
social and financial support, 78
state-sponsored displacement of, 81
state surveillance of, 83
hijra households, 84, 96
concept of, 98n22
hijra-trans woman divide, 115
Hindu joint family. *See* joint family
Hindu nationalism, rise of, 42
HIV/AIDS pandemic, 1, 56
risk for male-assigned GNC
groups, 5
homonormativity, concept of, 17–18,
159
housing opportunities, for GNC
people, 83–86

"I am Not a *Hijra*" photo project, 15,
23, 115–116, 154–158
"ideal" trans, 16–19
"ideal" woman, 6, 22

identity, 12, 21, 30, 42, 54, 136
  class, 59, 60–61
  gender, 18, 26n43, 57, 60, 150–151, 157
  of GNC people, 2, 8, 31–32
  of *hijra* group, 4–5
  kothi, 60
  of liberalized women, 36
  of "new" trans women, 46
  of "new" womanhood, 16
  social, 49n20
  of trans women, 3, 13, 20, 59, 70, 124,
    161
  in urban areas of India, 14
identity work, 6, 46, 54, 151, 161
  by sexual rights NGOs, 5
  by trans women, 5, 16, 31–32, 39, 146,
    151, 156
inclusion, politics of, 16–17, 24, 162
  gay people, 18
  into the category of "ideal" women,
    22
  of LGBTQ+, 159
  perils of, 24
  and social change for marginalized
    groups, 16
  trans women disidentifying with
    hijras, 158–161
Indian family
  adoptive families, 147n19
  birth families, 138, 140
  chosen families, 140
  contemporary family forms, 147n19
  dual earner families, 147n19
  joint family, 128–131, 147n19
  nuclear family setups, 131–132,
    147n19
  residential *hijra* relationships,
    139–141

single parent families, 147n19
  traditional, 131–132
inequality
  class, 86
  in *guru–chela* relationship, 116
  marginalized groups, 16
  trans women, 15, 23, 156
International Lesbian and Gay
    Association (ILGA), 73n52
International Lesbian, Gay,
    Bisexual, Trans and Intersex
    Association. *See* International
    Lesbian and Gay Association
    (ILGA)

joint family, 128–131
  and *hijra* residential relationships,
    136
  perspectives of
    family members without access
      to resources, 133–135
    young and (wealthy) old,
      132–133
  rhetoric of freedom from, 132–133
  supposed decline of, 131, 145

Kanika, story of, 69
Karnataka State Prohibition of
    Beggary Act (1975), 62–63, 82
kothi identity, 60

legal gender recognition, process of,
    26n51
LGBTQ+ community, 10, 17, 159
  depoliticized gay culture, 18
  global activism, 26n43
  "good" lesbians and gays, 17–19
  "wrong body" story, 18–19

liberal individualism, demands of, 19

linguistic nationalism, 42

marginalized castes, 7, 16

Mariyamma, story of, 75

marriages

  age of consent to, 149n45

  arranged, 144

  love, 144

media representations, of GNC people, 94, 112

men who have sex with men (MSM), 4

middle-class aspirations

  and gender identities, 54, 115

  of GNC people, 38, 46, 54

  intersectionality of gender and class, 32

  of "new" womanhood, 156

  normative, 61

  trans women and, 4–6, 13, 22

    complexities of class in lives of, 43–46

    office employment and womanhood, 57–59

    for upward mobility, 39

    in urban India, 14

    of working-class families, 86

middle-class consumption decisions, in India, 95

middle-class households, 35

middle-class identities, 6

middle-class marriage, 144

moral boundaries (tied to class and caste), 6–7

moral policing, 42

mother–daughter relationship, 80

multinational company (MNC), 54, 56, 66, 69

naani guru, 97n1

NALSA Judgment (Supreme Court of India), 11

nationalist movement, modernization of, 33

Neelima, story of, 101–103, 112–113

"new" Indian woman

  domestic role in the patriarchal household, 36

  ideology of, 104

  policing "new" women in joint families, 129–131

  relationship with men, 36

  social change, class, and respectability, 32–34

"new" liberalized woman, 34–37

  criteria of respectability, 36

  economic and social benefits of their employment, 36

  employment opportunities, 36

  middle-class status, 36

  in urban middle-class families, 36

"new" transgender woman, 46, 68, 166

  versus hijra "others", 11–13

  opportunity and symbolic class projects, 37–39

    ability to access, 38

    constrained by the resources, 37

    media coverage of, 38

    variation in income levels, 37

  rise of, 23

new womanhood, notions of, 13, 15–16, 21, 31–32, 38, 92–96

nongovernmental organization (NGO), 1, 3, 5

non-hijra identities, 5

non-hijra kinship formations, 78

non-*hijra* sexual minorities, 153
nuclear family, 128, 131–132, 148

occupations associated with *hijras*,
    57, 64
office employment, 52, 103, 115, 143, 158
    associated with middle-class
        womanhood, 54
    connection with transgender
        identities, 54
    and contemporary womanhood,
        57–59
    for feminine-presenting GNC
        people, 38, 54, 55–59, 70
    in NGOs and MNCs, 54
    for trans women, 11–12, 43, 47, 55
        ability to control their income, 57
    women's independence and
        empowerment through, 58
opportunity, 46–47, 164
    to become less dependent on *gurus*,
        129
    cis women access to, 12
    for constructions of "new"
        middle-class (cis)
        womanhood, 6
    economic, 145
    for GNC people, 15–16, 57, 145
    about liberalization, 37
    for "new" Indian women, 12
    for NGO employment, 56
    for trans women
        identity work, 31–32
        narratives of "new" womanhood,
         31
        perception of opportunity, 68–70
        to position themselves as
        empowered, 13

symbolic class projects, 37–39
working-class women lack of, 37

paam padti, 76, 97n2, 114
"pay-as-you-go" social security
    systems, 106–107
perceived "anti-social" activities, by
    hijras, 82
politics of respectability, notion of,
    16, 47
power of conformity, 16–19
privatization of industry, 35
public participation, of women in
    India, 12, 33

"quack" surgeons, 88
Queer Pride Week, 151, 153, 160

reciprocity in *hijra* relationships,
    principle of, 82
Reddy, Gayatri, 26n43, 106, 110,
    166n3
regional nationalism, 42
rent rates, for GNC people, 84
respectability, 3, 39, 151, 157
    associated with
        middle-class womanhood, 15
        status of women in the family,
         50n54
    criteria of, 34, 36
    demand for, 39
    gendered form of, 57, 130
    in Global South countries, 61
    of GNC people, 71
    of *hijras*, 124
    middle-class cis women, 7, 12, 36, 55,
        115, 124, 163
    and moral virtue, 130

of "new" Indian women, 32–34, 36
notions of, 11
of the occupation, 34
politics of, 16, 47
trans women pursuit of, 15, 38, 160
women's empowerment and, 47
Revathi, A., 125n16, 162–163, 165–166, 167n25
Romani, Sarhar, 72n22
romantic love, cultural idealization of, 145
Roy, Srila, 72n22
rural-based *hijras*, 25n32, 85–86

salwar kameez (women's clothing), 2
Saria, Vaibhav, 86, 170
self-validation, sense of, 54
sense of belonging, 106
sexual abuse, 65
in working-class jobs, 69
sexual health programs, 10, 59
sexual minorities
activism, 26, 42
male-assigned, 4
rights of, 56
working-class, 59
sexual minority rights, 21, 26n47
activism for, 26
sexual modesty, for cisgender women, 130
sexual rights
activism, 19, 42, 92, 120, 167n25
advocacy, 42
sexual rights NGOs, 1, 3, 5, 19, 56, 138
in Bangalore, 42–43
sex work, 52–53, 55, 57–58, 67, 69, 76, 163
earning money through, 122

fear and violence associated with, 64
in *hammams*, 91
hijras engaged in, 3, 64
for livelihood, 88
risks associated with, 65
street-based, 64
sex workers, 57–58
abuse of, 65
social changes, 11, 76, 124, 158
among feminine-presenting GNC people, 4
to claim transgender identities, 9
connection with economic liberalization, 131, 150
impact on
hijra relationships, 15, 23, 122, 141, 146
lives of GNC people, 15, 26n43, 96, 103, 116
"new" trans women, 32
transgender's sexual and gender identity, 4
for marginalized people, 16
office employment, 71
social hierarchies, 6, 154
of "good" gays, 159
of GNC person, 153
of *hijras*, 23
of trans women, 13, 15, 151, 156–157
of "new" transgender women, 21
social justice, 18, 27, 27n86, 53, 162
social "outcasts", 9
social safety net, 78, 145
soliciting money, 58, 62, 79
criminalization of, 82
state surveillance, of *hijras*, 82–83, 112
strategic life choices, 55

street-based work, 62
  sex work, 64

technological growth, 35
"traditional" Indian woman, 35
  portrayal of, 35–36
transgender healthcare worker, 2
transgender identities, 61, 157
  relation with office employment, 54
Transgender India, 154–155, 158
Transgender Persons' (Protections
  of Rights) Act (2019), 11, 82,
  98n29
transgender rights and activism in
  Asia, 53
  conference on, 68
transgender selfhood, 18–19
transgender women, 2–3, 124. *See also*
  "new" transgender woman
  access to office employment, 55
  aspirations in context of Bangalore,
  39–43
  and class–caste nexus, 6–8
  class identity, 60–61
  complexities of class in lives of,
  43–46
  crime against, 83
  demand for respectability, 15, 39
  desires for respectable employment,
  58
  difference from *hijras*, 70
  emergence of, 9, 157
  employment options, 55
  and *hijras*, 3–4
  identity struggles among, 13
  media accounts of newfound
  opportunities of, 65–68
  media coverage of, 38

middle-class aspiration in India,
  4–6, 43–46
  office employment and
  contemporary womanhood,
  57–59
  moral boundaries of, 6–7
  newfound employment
  opportunities, 66
  opportunities for "dignified"
  employment, 57
  overlapping identities with *hijras*,
  13–16
  perception of employment
  opportunity, 68–70
  portrayal of, 66
  recognition and respect of, 10–11
  respectable embodiment, 57
  social class aspirations, 57–58
  as transgender icons, 66
  working-class, 157
transphobia, 48n2, 162–164
trans woman–*hijra* distinction, 2–3,
  13–14, 39, 124
trans woman identity, 3–4, 20, 151
travesti in Brazil, 61

untouchability, practices of, 162
urban *hijra* groups, 86
urbanization, process of, 41
urban middle-class femininity, 54
urban planning, 40

Vidya, Living Smile, 162

waria, 61
Weston, Kath, 140
  notion of "chosen families", 141
white-collar employment, 56

"white-collar" work, 7
womanhood
    cisgender, 6, 29
    concept of, 151
    dominant-caste, 8
    middle-class, 7, 24, 38, 46, 60, 115
    notion of, 30
        ideal womanhood, 32
        new womanhood, 13, 15, 38
    office employment and, 57–59
    patriarchal constructions of, 16
    representations in India, 25n29,
        48n4
    trans women's desire for the
        respectability associated
        with, 15
women's empowerment and
    respectability, 47
    for middle-class women, 58
    symbol of, 93

women's role, in patriarchal
    household, 36
women's status
    in globalizing society, 36
    in India, 32
working-class people, 44, 46
    activism for sexual minorities, 42
    educational background of, 67
    hijras as, 155
    middle-class, 86
    transgender, 14, 59
    in urban areas, 7
working-class trans women, 20, 58–59,
    153, 157
working-class woman, 12, 32, 39, 47,
    155
world class cities, 40
"wrong body" story, 18–19

Yellamma, goddess, 81